D0043973

Bloom's Literary Guide

DUBLIN

LONDON

NEW YORK

PARIS

ROME

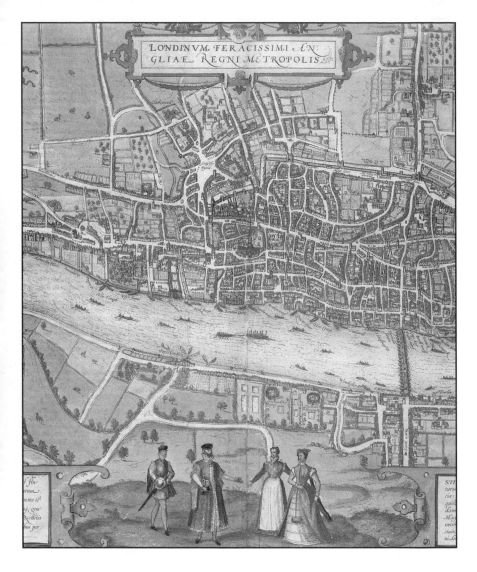

Civitates Orbis Terrarum–1572. This map of London by Georg Braun and Franz Hogenberg shows an overview of London rather than an accurate representation of the city today.

Bloom's Literary Guide to

LONDON

Donna Dailey and John Tomedi

Introduction by
Harold Bloom

☑Checkmark Books®
An imprint of Infobase Publishing
OCM 82133592

Bloom's Literary Guide to London

Copyright © 2007 by Infobase Publishing
Introduction copyright © 2007 by Harold Bloom

Checkmark Books
An imprint of Infobase Publishing
132 West 31st Street
New York NY 10001

Library of Congress Cataloging-in-Publication Data

Dailey, Donna.
　London / Donna Dailey and John Tomedi ; edited by Harold Bloom.
　　p. cm. — (Bloom's literary guide)
　Includes bibliographical references.
　ISBN 0-7910-9377-8 (pbk.)
　1. Literary landmarks—England—London—Guidebooks. 2. Authors,
English—Homes and haunts—England—London—Guidebooks. 3. Eng-
lish literature—England—London—History and criticism. 4. London
(England)—Intellectual life—Guidebooks. 5. London (England)—In liter-
ature—Guidebooks. 6. London (England)—Guidebooks. I. Tomedi, John.
II. Bloom, Harold. III. Title. IV. Series.
　PR110.L6D34 2007
　820.9'9421—dc22　　　　　　　　　　　　　　　　　2007018928

Checkmark Books are available at special discounts when purchased
in bulk quantities for businesses, associations, institutions, or sales
promotions. Please call our Special Sales Department in New York at
(212) 967-8800 or (800) 322-8755.

You can find Facts On File on the World Wide Web at
http://www.factsonfile.com

Series and cover design by Takeshi Takahashi

Printed in the United States of America

Bang EJB 10 9 8 7 6 5 4 3 2 1

This book is printed on acid-free paper.

TABLE OF CONTENTS ⬤

CITIES OF THE MIND
    HAROLD BLOOM   vii

INTRODUCTION
    HAROLD BLOOM   xiii

CHAPTER ONE
London Today   1

CHAPTER TWO
After the Conquest   8

CHAPTER THREE
Elizabethan London   15

CHAPTER FOUR
London and the Restoration   29

CHAPTER FIVE
Georgian and Regency London   50

CHAPTER SIX
Victorian London   70

CHAPTER SEVEN
London at the Turn of the Twentieth Century   92

CHAPTER EIGHT
London between the Wars   108

CHAPTER NINE
The London of Gravity's Rainbow   140

CHAPTER TEN
The Millennial City   161

PLACES OF INTEREST   175
CHRONOLOGY   208
BIBLIOGRAPHY   213
FURTHER READING   217
INDEX   219
CONTRIBUTORS   231

HAROLD **BLOOM**

○

Cities of the Mind

It could be argued that the ancestral city for the Western literary imagination is neither Athens nor Jerusalem, but ancient Alexandria, where Hellenism and Hebraism fused and were harvested. All Western writers of authentic aesthetic eminence are Alexandrians, whether they know it or not. Proust and Joyce, Flaubert and Goethe, Shakespeare and Dante rather uneasily share in that eclectic heritage. From the mid third century before the Common Era through the mid third century after, Alexandria was the city of the spirit and mind and where Plato and Moses did not reconcile (which would be impossible) but abrasively stimulated a new kind of sensibility that we have learned to call Modernism, now twenty-six centuries old. The first Modernist was the poet Callimachus, who said that a long poem was a long evil, and together with his colleagues were approvingly named as *neoteroi* (modernists) by Aristarchus, the earliest literary critic to attempt making a secular canon. Dr. Samuel Johnson, Boileau, Sainte-Beuve, Lessing, Coleridge, I.A. Richards, Empson, and Kenneth Burke are descendants of Aristarchus.

F.E. Peters, in his lucid *The Harvest of Hellenism*, summarizes

the achievement of Hellenistic Alexandria by an impressive cat-
alog: "Gnosticism, the university, the catechetical school, pastoral poetry, monasticism, the romance, grammar, lexicography,
city planning, theology, canon law, heresy and scholasticism". I
don't know why Peters omitted neo-Platonism, inaugurated by
Plotinius, and I myself already have added literary criticism, and
further would list the library. Alexandria has now exiled its
Greeks, Jews, and mostly everyone else not an Arab, and so it is
no longer the city of the mind, and of the poetic tradition that
went the long span from Callimachus to Cavafy. Yet we cannot
arrive at a true appreciation of literary places unless we begin
with Alexandria. I recommend the novelist E.M. Forster's guide
to the city, which deeply ponders its cultural significance.

We are all Alexandrians, as even Dante was, since he
depended upon Hellenistic Neo-Platonic interpretations of
Homer, whose poetry he had never read. Vergil, Dante's guide,
was Hellenistic in culture, and followed Theocritus in pastoral
and Alexandrian imitations of Homer in epic. But though our
literary culture remains Alexandrian (consider all our ongoing
myths of Modernism), we follow St. Augustine in seeing
Jerusalem as the City of God, of King David and his martyred
descendant Jesus of Nazareth. Our universities, inescapably
Alexandrian in their pragmatic eclecticism, nevertheless continue to exalt the Athens of Socrates, Plato, and Aristotle as the
city of cognition and of (supposed) democracy. The actual Peri-
clean Athens was a slave-owning oligarchy and plutocracy,
which still prevails in much of the world, be it Saudia Arabia or
many of the Americas. Literary Athens, in its Golden Age, built
on Homer and produced the only Western drama that can chal-
lenge Shakespeare: Aeschylus, Euripides, Sophocles, and the
divine Aristophanes (I follow Heinrich Heine who observed
that: "There is a God and his name is Aristophanes").

Athens now slumbers except for Olympic games and
tourism, while Jerusalem is all too lively as the center of Israeli-
Arab contention. Alas, their literary glories have waned, but so
have those of Rome, where Vergil and even the Florentine

Dante are little read or emulated. Cities of the mind are still represented by Paris and London, both perhaps at this moment in cognitive decline. The international language is now American English, and New York City is therefore the literary place-of-places. That, of necessity, has mixed consequences, but those sharpen my renewed comparison to ancient Alexandria, which mingled inventiveness with high decadence, at the end of an age. Alexandria was consciously belated and so are we, despite our paradoxical ecstasy of the new.

2

Is a literary place, by pragmatic definition, a city? Pastoral, like all other literary forms, was an urban invention. The Hebrew Bible, redacted in Babylonian exile, has as its core in Genesis, Exodus, and Numbers, the Yahwist's narrative composed at Solomon's highly sophisticated court in Jerusalem. We cannot locate the inception of what became *Iliad* and *Odyssey*, but the Greece they taught centered at Athens and Thebes. Florence exiled Dante and Cavalcanti, yet shared all further vernacular literary development with Rome and Milan. If Montaigne tended to isolate himself from embattled Paris, he knew his readers remained there. Elizabethan-Jacobean literature is virtually all fixated upon London, and centers upon Shakespeare's Globe Theater. If the American Renaissance emanates out of the Concord of Emerson, Thoreau, Hawthorne, it is equally at home in the New York City of Whitman, Melville, and the burgeoning James family. Though Faulkner kept, as much as he could, to Oxford, Mississippi, and Wallace Stevens to Hartford, if I had to nominate the ultimate classic of the United States in the twentieth century, unhesitatingly I would choose the poetry of Hart Crane, Whitman's legitimate heir as the bard of New York City. Kenneth Burke, whenever I saw him from 1975 on, would assure me again that Whitman's "Crossing Brooklyn Ferry" and Hart Crane's *The Bridge* were the two greatest American poems.

Our best living novelists—Philip Roth, Pynchon, DeLillo—

have become inseparable from the ethos of New York City. Only the elusive Cormac McCarthy, seer of *Blood Meridian*, keeps far away from the city-of-cities, which has displaced London and Paris as the world's imaginative capital.

3

However solitary a major writer is by vocation, he or she tends to find a closest friend in a contemporary literary artist. Perhaps rivals attract: Shakespeare and Ben Jonson, Byron and Shelley, Hawthorne and Melville, Hemingway and Scott Fitzgerald, Eliot and Pound, Hart Crane and Allen Tate are just a few pairings, to stay within Anglo-American tradition. Yet the tendency is everywhere: Goethe and Schiller, Wordsworth and Coleridge, Swift and Pope, Tolstoy and Chekhov, Henry James and Edith Wharton, and many more, too numerous to list. The locales waver: Hemingway and Fitzgerald in Paris, Byron and Shelley in Italian exile together, Eliot and Pound in London. There are giant exceptions: Cervantes, Milton, Victor Hugo, Emily Dickinson, Joyce and Beckett (though only after their early association).

Cities are the essential requisite for literary relationships, including those dominated by a father-figure, the London assemblage of the Sons of Ben Jonson: Carew, Lovelace, Herrick, Suckling, Randoph and many more, or Dr. Samuel Johnson and his club of Boswell, Goldsmith, Burke, among others, or Mallarmé and his disciples, including Valéry, who was to surpass his master. Modernist London always calls up Bloomsbury, with Virginia Woolf as its luminous figure, the ornament of a group that in its own idiosyncratic mode saw E.M. Forster as its patriarch.

Even in the age of the computer screen, proximity is essential for literary fellowship. But so far I have considered the city as literary place only in regard to writers. As subject, indeed as *the given* of literature, the city is a larger matter. The movement from garden to city as literary focus is powerfully clear in the Hebrew Bible, when Yahweh moves his abode from Mount

Sinai to Mount Zion, and thus to Solomon's Temple. As the mountain of the Covenant, Sinai stands at the origin, but surprisingly Ezekiel (28:13 following) locates "Eden, the garden of God" as a plateau on Zion, both cosmological mountain and paradise. When Yahweh takes up residence in the Temple, his Eden is close by, yet nevertheless the transition from garden to city has been accomplished. This is the Holy City, but to the literary imagination all the great cities are sacred: Paris, London, Dublin, Petersburg, Rome, and New York are also sanctified, whatever suffering and inequity transpire in them.

4

In the United States the national capital, Washington D.C., is scarcely a city of the mind, not only when contrasted to New York City, but also to Boston, Chicago, San Francisco. Paris, London, and Rome are at once capitals and literary centers, but Washington D.C. has harbored few major American writers and has provided subjects only for political novelists, like Henry Adams and Gore Vidal. The Great American Novel perpetually remains to be written, despite such earlier splendors as *The Scarlet Letter*, *Moby-Dick*, *Huckleberry Finn*, and *The Portrait of a Lady*, and a handful of later masterpieces from *As I Lay Dying* and *The Sound and the Fury*, *The Sun Also Rises* and *The Great Gatsby*, on to *Gravity's Rainbow*, *Sabbath's Theater*, *Underworld*, and *Blood Meridian*. I rather doubt that it will take Washington, D.C. as subject, or be composed by an inhabitant thereof.

The industrialization of the great cities in the nineteenth century gave us the novels of Victor Hugo, Dickens, Zola which produced a realism totally phantasmagoric, now probably no longer available to us. Computer urbanism does not seem likely to stimulate imaginative literature. Visual overdetermination overwhelms the inward eye and abandons us to narrative or the formal splendors of poetry and drama. There is something hauntingly elegiac about fresh evocations of literary places, here and now in the early years of the Twenty-first century.

Introduction

Of all Shakespeare's thirty-eight plays only one, *The Merry Wives of Windsor,* is set in his contemporary England. I like it least of the plays, partly because of the victimage, by sadistic practical jokes, of an impostor merely called Sir John Falstaff, who has nothing in common with the immortal Falstaff of the *Henry IV* plays. In a sense though, nearly everything Shakespeare wrote is set either in London or the Warwickshire countryside. The greatest of all literary creators never had visited the Continent, and perhaps had not wandered very far north of his native Stratford. The dramas are set in Italy or France or Scotland, or in Greece, but substantially they could just as well occupy only the small world Shakespeare knew, London and Stratford and what lies between.

Shakespeare's world was London, centered upon the Globe Theater. All his cities are London, all his pastoral landscapes are not far from where he grew up. His geography was visionary, his history frequently legendary, his temporality fanciful. The Roman tragedies are not less English for being Plutarchan. Hamlet lives and dies at the Danish court in Elsinore and is an undergraduate at Wittenberg, yet the wandering players are

Shakespeare's own company, and the Prince of Denmark clearly was a truant who spent his time at the Globe.

This undersong subtly inhabits many of the major plays. The decadent court of James I is ironically refigured in the Egyptian court of *Antony and Cleopatra*, far more vividly rendered than the court of *Henry VIII*. Bottom, Peter Quince and their fellow "mechanicals" of *A Midsummer Night's Dream* are English rustics, scarcely Athenians. Since all the world's a stage, it follows directly that the Globe's stage is all the world. Shylock and Iago are Londoners, not Venetians, and the bawdy Vienna of *Measure for Measure* is the London scene of whorehouses that Shakespeare knew all too well. We never will know the identity of the Dark Lady of the Sonnets, but I am imaginatively persuaded by Anthony Burgess's *Nothing Like the Sun*, which reveals her to be Lucy Negro, London's leading East Indian sex worker. I break ranks with Shakespeare scholars by finding in *Twelfth Night's* Malvolio an ironic portrait of Ben Jonson, and in *King Lear's* Edmund a final Shakespearean vision of another great rival, Christopher Marlowe.

There has been an immense cavalcade of London poets, dramatists, and novelists since Shakespeare, but even the greatest among them are gloriously in his shadow. London's prophet was William Blake, the English Ezekiel, who struggled to "correct" John Milton, yet Milton also is Shakespeare-haunted. So is London's novelist, Charles Dickens, and so indeed is London's literary critic, Dr. Samuel Johnson. After Shakespeare and Geoffrey Chaucer, Dickens must be accounted the strongest and most influential of all London writers. From *The Pickwick Papers* on through *David Copperfield* to his masterpiece, *Bleak House*, and on to the end in the unfinished *Mystery of Edwin Drood*, Dickens recreates London even as Shakespeare reinvented the world. Kafka's visionary Prague is the grandchild of Dickens's phantasmagoric London, just as the Dublin of Joyce's *Ulysses* is unable to avoid re-minting the fusion of symbolism and naturalism in *Bleak House*. So rich is

London's literary heritage that any brief characterization of it will be tainted by arbitrariness, but to view it as the fused grandeur of Shakespeare and Dickens is at least an authentic starting-point.

CHAPTER ONE

London Today

The landscape of London has changed immensely since Dr. Samuel Johnson—writer, lexicographer, and man about town— made this observation in the mid-eighteenth century. But his words still hold true in spirit, for London today offers a wealth of experiences: historical sites, theatre, music and entertainment, fine food, and outstanding museums and galleries containing everything from classical art to popular culture.

With a population of over seven million in the metropolitan area, London is Europe's largest city. Many visitors come here looking for merry old England and end up discovering the world. While the capital is the repository of British history and culture, it is also a diverse city with a dynamic mix of residents and visitors from all around the globe. In different parts of the city a typical Londoner is as likely to wear a sari or a chador as a business suit. The ethnic mix embraces 37 different groups, each with more than 10,000 people. Some of the best-selling and most highly acclaimed contemporary British novels have been written by young London writers who came from the Caribbean, Pakistani, and Indian communities.

CLASS AND CULTURE

The old British obsession with class, explored by authors from Jane Austen to Evelyn Waugh, is now largely confined to the musings of journalists in newspaper columns. And London is a veritable Babel of accents: some talk 'posh,' others Cockney, and others mockney—a somewhat snide label for those affecting a *de rigueur* working class accent. Being fashionable in London today is about attitude and not origins.

Most Londoners embrace the variety that different races and cultures bring to the city, and are as happy to have a curry or kebab after an evening at the pub as fish and chips. London has long since outgrown its reputation as a culinary wasteland. Celebrity British chefs have inundated popular culture; there's usually a chef peering out of bookshop windows from the cover of his latest bestseller.

Eating out has become the great London pastime. There is a fantastic range of restaurants serving every kind of cuisine and every budget. But nothing can outshine that great British institution, the pub. It is still the heart and soul of London social life. One can seek out the old-fashioned pubs that have retained their original character. Some noteworthy pubs date back to the 17th century and were frequented by writers from Charles Dickens to Oscar Wilde—pubs such as the Anchor, the George Inn, and Dr Johnson's local, Ye Olde Cheshire Cheese.

THE LAYOUT OF LONDON

Running through the heart of the city is the river Thames, the most venerable of London landmarks. The Romans established the first settlement, Londinium, along its banks in AD 43, and by the 13th century the city had become the capital of the kingdom and a major trading port.

The remains of Roman London have disappeared beneath today's financial district, known simply as the City or the

Square Mile. It is the biggest business center in Europe, where bankers and stockbrokers constitute the country's commercial hub. Though few people actually live here today, for centuries the City *was* London, teeming with residents from all walks of life. St. Paul's Cathedral, rebuilt by Sir Christopher Wren after the Great Fire of 1666 destroyed medieval London, is the great monument to the City's bygone age.

Unlike other cities, London has two distinct centers. This unique arrangement developed when Edward the Confessor became king in 1042 and moved his court upstream to build the new palace and abbey of Westminster. Since that time, the center of government and royalty at Westminster and the center of financial and commercial activity in the City have remained separate.

THE LANDMARKS OF LONDON

Several of London's top attractions lie along the Thames between these two axes. One of the best introductions to the city is to take a riverboat cruise from Tower Bridge to Westminster Pier. At the eastern end is the massive Tower of London, whose construction was begun by William the Conqueror in the 11th century and which remains one of the few medieval buildings in the city. For much of its history it was a place of terror, where enemies of the Crown were imprisoned, tortured, and often beheaded. Today's jovial guardians, the red-and-black-coated Beefeaters, regale visitors with tales of the Tower on free, guided tours. The Crown Jewels, the priceless regalia used at coronations of the British monarchy, are also housed within these formidable walls.

Opposite the Tower are some of the wharves of the old City port, now converted into fashionable apartments, restaurants, and a shopping gallery. The nondescript outline of London Bridge surprises many visitors, who confuse it with the more flamboyant Tower Bridge. Historically, however, London Bridge outshines its more noticeable Victorian neighbor. It was the only bridge across the Thames until 1750, and in Shakespeare's day it was lined with houses and shops. Near the bridge's northern end, hidden by modern buildings, is the Monument to the Great Fire, which started nearby.

Just beyond Southwark Bridge, the remains of Shakespeare's original Globe Theatre were discovered, and in 1997 a faithful replica reopened near the spot. The Bard's plays are performed here in season, just as they were in his day: in the open air.

Farther along the south shore is the Tate Modern, which opened in 2000 in the former Bankside Power Station. This enormous edifice makes a superb exhibition space for an international collection of modern art. It also gave the original Tate Gallery at Millbank room to breathe in its reincarnation as Tate Britain, which houses the world's largest collection of British art spanning five centuries. Opposite the Tate Modern, the Millennium Bridge is the latest crossing to span the Thames. This pedestrian-only walkway affords an impressive view from the river to the dome of St. Paul's Cathedral.

At the head of the Victoria Embankment are a cluster of buildings that have been associated with the legal profession for over 500 years: Temple and the Inns of Court. The young Charles Dickens toiled here as a clerk before finding his muse as a writer.

Farther ahead across the river is London's premier arts complex, the South Bank Center. The minimalist, concrete-block architecture seems dated now, but it houses some of the country's finest institutions: the Royal Festival Hall, the National Theatre, the Hayward Gallery and the National Film Theatre.

Next comes the city's newest and most exciting attraction, the London Eye. When it was built for the millennium, many feared this giant Ferris wheel would blot the landscape and spoil the stately view of Westminster. But a ride in this amazing structure soon silenced its critics. As the wheel rotates slowly above the river, its glass capsules provide a view over London that is simply stunning. It affords a new perspective on the cityscape and its buildings.

London's most famous symbol, Big Ben, is plainly in sight from the Eye. The great bell in its handsome clock tower looms over the Houses of Parliament, and is heard round the world on daily broadcasts of the BBC.

The Houses of Parliament stand on the site of the old Westminster Palace, most of which was destroyed by fire in 1834. Behind the ornate facade the laws of Britain are debated and decided between the two houses. The House of Commons consists of Members of Parliament (MPs) elected from the different political parties. The party with the most MPs becomes the government in power, with its leader as Prime Minister. Titled Peers make up the House of Lords; some have hereditary titles, others have titles bestowed by the monarch for service to their country.

Magnificent Westminster Abbey is as much a national monument as it is a place of worship. Kings and queens are crowned and buried here, and many of the country's great literary figures have been commemorated in Poet's Corner. Its superb medieval architecture encloses lavish monuments, simple tombs, and many national treasures.

Buckingham Palace, home of the Queen, stands between Westminster and Hyde Park. Visitors flock here each day to watch the Changing of the Guard.

In central London it is easy—and often quicker—to walk between many places of interest. The former covered vegetable market at Covent Garden is now a lively shopping area. Street performers entertain crowds in the piazza, just as they did in Dr. Johnson's day. Covent Garden and nearby Leicester Square are at the heart of the West End Theatre District, where more than 30 venues, many of them with ornate Victorian decor, carry on London's great theatre tradition.

Charing Cross Road leads back toward the river and the monumental Trafalgar Square, with its proud lions, fountains, and statue of Admiral Nelson perched atop his soaring column. Facing the square is the National Gallery, with masterpieces from the 13th through 19th centuries, and the adjacent National Portrait Gallery.

The neon-lit Piccadilly Circus is the anchor of London's main shopping district. Three major shopping thoroughfares—Piccadilly, Regent Street, and Oxford Street—enclose some of the most expensive real estate in the city between here and Hyde Park.

In essence, London is a collection of villages that were knitted together as the city sprawled. It's hard to fathom that in Jane Austen's day, the now-central Bloomsbury was an airy village well outside the city. For a time it was synonymous with the publishing world, and is home to one of the country's greatest treasures, the British Museum. Its outstanding collections span the globe from prehistoric times through ancient civilizations to the present day.

Kensington is home to several museums, including the Victoria and Albert Museum. Overflowing with exquisite jewelry, porcelain, ceramics, textiles, silver, metalwork, and other furnishings, it is one of the most comprehensive collections of decorative arts in the world. The museum features British and European crafts, and its galleries of Indian and Chinese art are particularly strong. Many visitors make a pilgrimage to nearby Kensington Palace, former home of the much-loved Princess Diana.

One of the best features of London is the amount of parkland within the confines of its bustling, urban environment. Kensington Gardens adjoins Hyde Park, creating a vast swath of green in central London. Regent's Park, at the top of Baker Street just beyond the fictional address of Sherlock Holmes, forms a bolt-hole to the north of the center. Countless smaller parks and leafy squares are dotted throughout the city.

Almost anyplace of interest to visitors in London is accessible by public transport. The London Underground, better known as the Tube, is generally the quickest way across the city, and there is a comprehensive network of buses. The red double-decker buses so familiar from films and postcards can often provide good sightseeing from the upper deck.

BEYOND THE CITY CENTER

Greater London has much to offer visitors who are willing to explore outside the city center. Many former villages retain much of their old atmosphere and character. Places like Hampstead and Chelsea have long been magnets for writers and artists. The East End, particularly around Brick Lane and Spitalfields Market, is teeming with life in the way the City must have been in Dr. Johnson's day. South of the river, Southwark is no longer the downtrodden pocket of poverty described in Dickens's novels, but the latest area of London to be dusted off and spruced up.

Slightly farther out, the Thames leads to two other historic highlights. To the east, the village of Greenwich grew up around a former palace and naval base of Henry VIII. It has several stately buildings and museums, including the Royal Observatory, which stands on the meridian that divides the earth's eastern and western hemispheres. Greenwich Mean Time, and (thus) the world's time zone system, is measured from here.

West of London, Henry's palace at Hampton Court is a glorious landmark of Tudor architecture with later additions by Sir Christopher Wren. Surrounded by beautiful gardens, it makes a fine day trip just beyond the city.

Over the centuries, hundreds of poets, playwrights, and authors have made London their home. Many have loved it, some have loathed it, but all have been inspired by this vibrant, pulsating, ever-changing city and its unforgettable cast of characters. London has given rise to such literary figures as Fagin and Scrooge, Peter Pan and Sherlock Holmes, Henry Higgins and Eliza Dolittle. Their modern-day equivalents are there for the finding.

CHAPTER TWO

After the Conquest

For the first thousand years of its existence, London was a fairly unremarkable place. After its Roman founders withdrew in the early 5th century, the old walled city was all but abandoned for the next 200 years. It emerged from the Dark Ages under the rule of the Anglo-Saxons, who controlled most of the south of England from their base in Wessex, in the town of Winchester.

When the Saxons embraced Christianity in the 7th century, missionaries from Rome founded a cathedral dedicated to St. Paul in London, and later an early abbey at Westminster. But Canterbury, in Kent, became the country's religious seat.

In the 9th century, the country was repeatedly besieged by Viking invaders and the Saxon kings re-occupied the city for both strategic and commercial purposes. By then, London had regained the prosperity it knew in Roman times. Its great tidal river, the Thames, enabled trade with merchants from France, Italy, and elsewhere on the Continent. England's raw materials found a ready market at London's ports. The wool trade, which provided the foundation of the country's wealth for many centuries, was established during this time. The Venerable Bede, a Christian historian, recorded that London was "the mart of many nations resorting to it by land and sea."

Though next to nothing of Saxon London remains, it was an important time in the city's development, when its central parishes, wards, and street patterns were established. The more familiar sights of today's London took shape in the 11th century, when the pious King Edward, known as "the Confessor," acceded to the throne and built his great Westminster Abbey. It was finished just 10 days before his death in 1065.

The first king crowned in the Abbey was William of Normandy (the Conqueror), who settled the dispute over Edward's successor by invading England and killing his rival, Harold, in battle at Hastings. To protect himself from disgruntled citizens as much as from marauding warriors, he built the White Tower at the eastern end of the old Roman wall. This formed the core of what was to become the massive fortress known as the Tower of London.

From Anglo-Saxon times onward, monasteries were the main centers of learning. Latin was the literary language of the day, and most works of the time were religious or administrative in nature. However, the monks also recorded many of the bardic songs, fables, and heroic tales that made up the oral tradition of the time. The most famous of these is the epic poem *Beowulf,* which is set in Denmark and tells the story of a warrior's quest for glory through battles with monsters and dragons.

With the Norman Conquest, French became the language of the court and the aristocracy, while Anglo-Saxon remained the language of the countryside. Over time, the blending of these Germanic- and Romance-based languages from the north and south of Europe enriched and expanded both spoken and written English. Though not exactly a literary work, William's *Domesday Book,* an account of the population, landholdings, and other details of the kingdom that he commissioned at the outset of his rule, is an invaluable historical record of the time.

For the next four centuries, London continued to flourish and it remained the seat of royal power, government, and commerce. English gradually supplanted French as the language of court and of literature, and in the second half of the 14th century a series of mystery play cycles became popular in the countryside. Written in the common tongue, they were performed

The Anglo-Saxon tradition

By the time London opened its gates to the Conqueror and the French influence began, England had already forged one of the world's strongest literary traditions. The earliest material was oral—epic and/or elegiac works in verse performed by itinerant poets among the Germanic courts of Europe, whose languages were still quite similar. Most of this, like the peasant tradition, was not preserved, but fragments do survive in later texts. The surge in Latin literacy that began with Bede and Alcuin at Jarrow lasted until the Norse invasions of the eighth and ninth centuries, when the monasteries were destroyed and their culture forgotten. Recovery began in 871 with Alfred the Great, a true visionary, who enlisted scholars to translate great works from Latin into the vernacular Old English.

The Old English works that survive are somber, fatalistic, and rich in metaphor. Some are explicitly religious, like the Dream of the Rood; some are secular, celebrating battles, heroes, emotional experience, or common life; and some balance precariously between the two. Secular characters and episodes span the Germanic traditions and seem quite long-lived; King Lear, Cymbeline, King Arthur, Macbeth, and Hamlet all can be traced to this time. The newly arrived Normans sometimes felt they were civilizing the English—but the English cultural heritage was among the richest of the time.

by members of trade guilds who traveled to towns such as York, Chester, and Coventry, using carts as their stage.

GEOFFREY CHAUCER

The end of the 14th century also saw the blossoming of English literature in the works of Geoffrey Chaucer (1343–1400), who has been called the "Father of English poetry". His masterpiece, *The Canterbury Tales*, presents a lively description of contemporary life through his depiction of a group of 14th-century pilgrims on their way to Canterbury to the shrine of St. Thomas à Becket.

Chaucer was a Londoner, born in 1342 or 1343 in the Vintry, the area of the city where the wine merchants traded. Their guildhall still stands today. Nearby is the church of St. Michael Paternoster Royal, whose name denotes its medieval connections with La Reole, a wine-making center near Bordeaux.

Employed by the Crown, Chaucer's career as a soldier, spy, diplomat, customs official, and Member of Parliament took him to France, Italy, and Flanders. He later supervised work at Westminster as a building project manager. His position, as well as his apartments in the gatehouse of Aldgate overlooking one of the main entrances to the city, allowed him to meet and observe people from all walks of life and represent them to great effect in his stories.

Although he was fluent in French, Latin, and Italian, Chaucer earned his place in literary history by writing in the London dialect of the day. The main difficulty in reading his text in its original form lies in the great number of words that have become obsolete or have undergone a change in meaning. There is a gap of around 200 years between the works of Chaucer and Shakespeare, whose language, though archaic, is much more understandable and still widely read. Yet *The Canterbury Tales* endure, and Chaucer's characters and their stories are regularly transposed into modern tales for stage and screen.

The Arthurian legends were also given literary birth around this time. Circa 1370, an anonymous poet described Arthur's court and brought its tales of chivalry and adventure to life in *Sir Gawain and the Green Knight*. A century later, Sir Thomas Malory wrote his famous work, *Le Morte d'Arthur* (The Death of Arthur) in 1469. These stories remain well loved today.

THE TUDOR DYNASTY

The ascension of Henry VII to the throne ushered in the Tudor dynasty in 1485, the same year that William Caxton published Malory's story to great acclaim. Caxton had set up England's first printing press near Westminster Abbey a decade earlier. He printed more than 90 books, including the *Canterbury Tales*, and became a major importer of books from Europe. Upon Caxton's death, his assistant Wynkyn de Worde took over his press and moved the business to Fleet Street. The area remained London's printing center until the 1990s.

Literacy rates rose swiftly in Tudor times. Although Henry VIII banned the import of foreign books in an effort to suppress unorthodox ideas, this only served to stimulate the domestic industry. Within a century of Caxton's first enterprise, London had some 50 printing presses in operation. Alongside Greek translations, contemporary plays, and religious bestsellers such as Foxe's *Book of Martyrs*, they churned out thousands of low-cost, lowbrow pamphlets, ballads, almanacs, and lurid "penny-dreadfuls." The Company of Stationers was given a royal charter to oversee (and censor) the city's publishing and book-selling industry, and their Stationers' Hall still remains near St. Paul's churchyard.

Thanks to his six wives, Henry VIII is undoubtedly England's most famous king. Until his reign, the Church held enormous wealth and power. By the 12th century, approximately 100 parish churches had been built within London's walls. Over a dozen abbeys and priories flourished within or just outside its boundaries, each holding large tracts of land. But in 1532, Henry broke with the Roman Catholic Church over its refusal to grant him a divorce from his first wife, Catherine of Aragon, who had failed to produce a son and heir. He declared himself the head of the Church of England, and proceeded to strip the religious houses of their lands and wealth in the Dissolution of the Monasteries.

The scene in London was particularly tumultuous. Churches lost their altars, statues, paintings, and relics. The great episcopal houses and palaces were plundered and given to favored courtiers. Many were razed or converted to other uses. Church gardens and lands were seized and sold off cheaply to developers. Yet while the Protestant Reformation destroyed many of London's medieval treasures, it also paved the way for the city's expansion.

Tudor times were prosperous times for the city. Trade continued to grow, and London dominated the market in the manufacture of finished cloth, now the country's main export. New industries also sprang up, such as glassmaking and silk-weaving. Although there were social gaps between rich and poor, there was enough work for the populace. Plagues and fires were a greater threat to Londoners than starvation. Four large food markets stretched along the city's east-west thoroughfare, one of which—Leadenhall Market—still operates today.

The city's craftsmen and merchants grouped themselves into guilds, or livery companies, to regulate their respective trades. The twelve largest guilds, which included the Mercers, the Grocers, and the Drapers, became dominant in local politics, with most of the city's aldermen elected from their ranks. They built grand halls in which to meet and conduct their affairs, and many of these still exist (though the buildings themselves date from later times).

The greatest symbol of London's success was the Royal Exchange. It was built by the merchant and financier Thomas Gresham, and opened by Queen Elizabeth in 1570. It gave local businessmen a commercial exchange where they could meet to fix prices and trade their commodities, allowing London to rival the great European trading centers, such as Antwerp's bourse. Although Gresham's building was destroyed in the Great Fire, its Victorian replacement remains one of the city's grander facades.

At the beginning of the 16th century, London was still small compared to other European cities. Its population was barely 50,000. But during the Tudor era migrants flocked to the city from the countryside and abroad in the hopes of bettering their fortunes. Despite repeated outbreaks of plague that killed thousands, the city's population mushroomed. London doubled in size between 1550 and 1600, to around 200,000 inhabitants. Fifty years later the population doubled again, making London the largest city in the world.

CHAPTER THREE

Elizabethan London

Picture London in 1558, when Henry VIII's daughter Elizabeth ascended to the throne. The city proper was surrounded by its medieval walls, which ran from the Tower in the east, north to Moor Fields, and down to Blackfriars in the west. Seven gates gave entry to the city, and most of their names survive in the names of streets and tube stations today: Aldgate, Bishopsgate, Moorgate, and Ludgate, for example. Most people still lived within the walls, but the city was now spreading beyond and south of the river to accommodate the growing population.

London was dense, noisy, and overcrowded, its streets thronged with pedestrians, carts, and coaches. Residents, craftsmen, merchants, and manufacturers lived and worked together inside the walls. There was little separation between workshops, stores, and homes. Street names such as Bread Street, Fish Street, and Ironmongers Lane survive to this day and indicate the trades once plied there. The wooden buildings were tightly packed together, with the spires of the numerous parish churches poking out above the thatched roofs. There were dozens of taverns and alehouses.

WILLIAM SHAKESPEARE

Into this bustling scene, sometime around 1587, walked the greatest English playwright in history, William Shakespeare. Coming from Stratford, where he was born in 1564, he entered the city through the western Newgate. Little is known of his early years in the city. It is thought that he conducted a business while maintaining a wife and three children back home. In the 1590s he lodged in the parish of Bishopsgate. By 1591 he had written his first play, *The Comedy of Errors.*

Shakespeare and his contemporaries—playwrights Christopher Marlowe, Ben Jonson, and others—were leading figures in what has been called the English Renaissance. The arts flourished during Elizabeth's reign. There was a keen interest among the nobility in classical culture, and the Queen herself was educated in Latin and Greek. Poetry, painting, and music flourished under rich patrons. But literature and drama commanded the cultural scene.

London was now under the strict thumb of the Puritans, who hated the theater. They considered it a corrupting influence and thought it led to immoral pursuits. They would not allow playhouses to be built within the city walls. Despite Puritan disapproval, theater flourished. In the late 16th and early 17th centuries, eleven theaters opened outside the walls in the suburbs and "liberties," which were beyond the regulation of the city fathers. Acting companies were formed under court patronage, giving stability to traveling players.

The core of a company was made up of eight to ten players. Shakespeare's plays have major speaking roles for that number. There were no women actors and the female romantic leads were often played by boys. A company would generally perform a different play every afternoon of the week, and actors might have to learn up to 30 parts.

The earliest plays in the city were performed on temporary stages in the courtyards of inns. James Burbage built the first playhouse, simply called The Theatre, in Shoreditch, north of Bishopsgate, in 1576. It could hold an audience of around one

thousand. It was such a success that another, The Curtain, opened nearby the following year. In 1594, Shakespeare joined Burbage's company, the Lord Chamberlain's Men, which later became the most popular in the city. Burbage's son Richard was the leading actor, and he was the first to play Shakespeare's famous characters.

Another theater entrepreneur, Philip Henslowe, had built The Rose in 1587. It lay south of the river in Southwark, just west of London Bridge. This area, called Bankside, was the red-light district of its day. Londoners came here for all the pleasures they were not allowed in the city. It was full of brothels (called "stews"), alehouses, cock-fighting dens, and bull- and bear-baiting arenas. The cruel sport of bear-baiting was very popular in the 16th and 17th centuries. Even Queen Elizabeth enjoyed it. Bears were tethered to a stake and subjected to vicious attacks by pit-bull mastiffs, while people bet on which animal would win.

The Rose was an immediate success. Its company, the Admiral's Men, was led by the actor Edward Alleyn, who later founded Dulwich College. Christopher Marlowe's *Tambourlaine the Great* and *Dr. Faustus* debuted here, and Ben Jonson later became its resident playwright. Two of Shakespeare's plays, *Richard VI part I* and *Titus Andronicus*, are said to have been first performed at The Rose.

When the lease for The Theatre ran out in 1598, James Burbage's sons, Richard and Cuthbert, dismantled the playhouse and moved the timbers over the river to Bankside. Shakespeare and four other players in the company bought shares in their new enterprise, and a year later the Globe Theatre opened across from the Rose, just 50 yards away. The Globe soon became the most popular theater of its day. It was bigger than The Rose, and by 1606 it had put its rival out of business.

Many of Shakespeare's greatest works, including *Hamlet*, *Macbeth*, and *Othello*, were first performed at the Globe. He affectionately called it the "wooden O." As a shareholder in the company, Shakespeare would have been closely involved in all

aspects of the theater, and most likely acted in many of its productions. It is thought that he moved to Southwark for a while and possibly lived in the house known to have adjoined the Globe. When Queen Elizabeth died in 1603, the new king, James I, became the company's patron and the troupe was renamed the King's Men.

Thomas Dekker: A Playwright's Frustrations

Among the most active voices of Shakespeare's time was Thomas Dekker, a London-based playwright and pamphleteer who ruthlessly satirized city life. Among his pamphlets are *The Wonderful Year*, an account of the plague of 1603; and numerous rants against urban vice, such as *The Seven Deadly Sins of London* and *News from Hell* (both 1606). Dekker's "How a Gallant Should Behave Himself in a Playhouse" (The Gull's Hornbook, 1609) expresses a playwright's frustration with a privileged playgoer:

> ... By sitting on the stage you have a signed patent to engross the whole commodity of censure; may lawfully presume to be a girder; and stand at the helm to steer the passage of scenes; yet no man shall once offer to hinder you from obtaining the title of an insolent, overweening coxcomb....
>
> It shall crown you with rich commendation to laugh aloud in the midst of the most serious and saddest scene of the terriblest tragedy; and to let that clapper, your tongue, be tossed so high that all the house may ring of it.... [A]ll the eyes in the galleries will leave walking after the players and only follow you; the simplest dolt in the house snatches up your name, and when he meets you in the streets, or that you fall into his hands in the middle of a watch, his word shall be taken for you; he'll cry "He's such a gallant," and you pass.

Shakespeare's last play was *Henry VIII.* During a performance of it in June 1613, a cannon was fired and a stray spark caught fire on the theater's thatched roof. The Globe burned to the ground. Amazingly, though it was filled with 3,000 spectators, no one was injured. One man's breeches reportedly caught fire, but they were quickly put out with bottled ale. Luckily, all of the Globe's props, costumes, and manuscripts were also rescued. Half of Shakespeare's plays had not yet been published, and it is sobering to think that they might have been lost forever.

The Globe was quickly rebuilt and reopened in 1614, this time with a tiled roof. It continued to be profitable long after Shakespeare's death. But in 1642 the Puritans finally had their way, and London's theaters were closed by an order of Parliament. The Globe was demolished around 1644.

Between 1591 and 1612, Shakespeare wrote 38 plays. He also wrote more than 150 sonnets. The tragedies are among his most famous works, but he also developed new dramatic forms with his romantic comedies and historical dramas. His work helped establish play writing and acting as viable professions. He is said to have retired a wealthy man to Stratford, where he continued to write until his death in 1616, at the age of 52.

Shakespeare became the most famous playwright of all time. But in fact more than 400 plays from the Elizabethan period have survived in print, though most of them are long forgotten. Shakespeare's life remains in many ways a mystery. None of his personal papers survive, and because of his poor country background some scholars question whether he was the true author of his works. Although he was educated at Stratford Grammar School, he married at the age of 18 and therefore could not attend university, which only took single men. Where did he acquire the breadth of knowledge about foreign countries, classical literature, and court life so evident in his plays?

The likely answer is that Shakespeare received his higher education from his chosen city. London's trade links with Europe and the East and West Indies brought many foreign travelers to the city. Their stories, manners, clothes, books, and possessions all served to teach the young playwright about other cultures and inspire his works. In 1497, John Cabot's discovery of New-foundland had given England its first territory in the New World, and during Elizabethan times there was a great obsession with exploration and travel. In a river inlet near Southwark Cathedral is a replica of the *Golden Hinde*, the ship in which Sir Francis Drake circumnavigated the world.

Shakespeare's characters often make references to well-known London places and events. "My lord, when shall we go to Cheapside ..." (Shakespeare, *Henry VI* part 2 IV:8) refers to what was then the city's main shopping district, a street that still exists today.

Theaters were closed during outbreaks of plague, which caused more than 100,000 deaths between 1564 and 1625. "Suspecting that we were both in a house where infectious pesti-lence did reign, Sealed up the doors and would not let us forth." (Shakespeare, *Romeo and Juliet* V:2)

The Thames looked much different in Shakespeare's day. It was wider and shallower than it is now, with the pylons of London Bridge and the refuse dumped into the river by the res-idents and industries impeding its flow. In a hard winter, it could freeze over completely. In those years, Frost Fairs were held on the ice, with dancing, archery, and stalls selling food and drink. Queen Elizabeth attended one in 1564.

Stairs and landings lined the banks of the river on both sides. Watermen ferried passengers across for a penny, and the air echoed with their cries of "eastward, ho!" or "westward, ho!" to tell people which way they were going. Shakespeare would probably have crossed by boat to the theater each day.

The only bridge spanning the river was London Bridge. It had 19 arches, only three of which could admit large boats. It provided the only access to the city from the south, and its defensive gates were firmly closed at night. More daunting to new arrivals were the wooden spikes protruding from the bridge, which displayed the severed heads of traitors executed in the Tower of London.

London Bridge was lined with shops and houses. It had its

own street market and even a church. A wooden bridge had stood here since Roman times, and the stone bridge of Shakespeare's day was built in 1176 and not replaced until 1831.

SOUTHWARK

Far from being a mere den of vice, Southwark was a booming commercial area of the city. Farmers from the surrounding counties brought their produce here to market, and it was a stopping off place for travelers at this southern gateway to the city. Borough High Street, then known as "Long Southwark," was lined with inns. One of these, the Tabard Inn (now gone), was where Chaucer's pilgrims gathered before setting off for Canterbury.

Two others were well known to Shakespeare. The original George Inn, where he drank with friends, burned down in a fire, but its replacement, built in 1677, is a splendid example of the old-style coaching inns of the day. Shakespeare's plays are sometimes performed in the yard in summer.

The parallel White Hart Yard is all that is left of the White Hart Inn, another of Shakespeare's watering holes. In *Henry VI* part 2, he refers to it in Jack Cade's speech: "Hath my sword therefore broke through London gates, that you should leave me at the White Hart in Southwark!" (*Henry VI part 2* IV:8)

Though Southwark attracted prostitutes, highwaymen, and others who operated outside the law, it was also home to the rich and respectable. Sir John Fastolf built a grand mansion surrounded by a wall and moat in the 1450s. Shakespeare borrowed his name for his character, Falstaff. Also here was the palace of the Bishops of Winchester. The pious bishops profited from the area's vices by collecting rent from the playhouses and stews. Thus, the prostitutes gained their nickname, "Winchester Geese."

Jail scenes were often featured in Shakespeare's plays. No fewer than five jails were located in Southwark. One of these, the Clink, belonged to the bishops' estate. Its horrors are recalled in the Clink Prison Museum, situated on its former site.

By the Victorian era, Southwark had sunk into poverty and remained a rough area until the late 20th century. Today it is greatly gentrified and a thriving part of the city, and Shakespeare's Globe is once again at the heart of Bankside's popularity.

REBIRTH OF THE GLOBE

In 1949, American actor Sam Wanamaker came to London to make a film. He went looking for the cradle of English theater, but to his surprise the only remnant of Shakespeare's Globe was a plaque on the side of an old brewery in Southwark that stood near its former site. In 1970, he set in motion what became a life-long project: to rebuild an authentic replica of the Globe.

The project faced years of opposition, both political and financial. Some felt the project was too highbrow for a rundown area. The theater received no government funding, and money had to be raised from private sources at every step, from buying the land to constructing the building. Sadly, Wanamaker died before he saw his dream realized. But in 1997, the Globe opened to spectacular acclaim, and remains one of contemporary London's finest achievements.

The new Shakespeare's Globe is situated along the Thames, very near the original site. The polygonal timbered building is a striking sight, a rare specimen of Tudor-style architecture in the city. In the 1580s and 1590s, all theaters would have looked like this. Every detail has been re-created, as closely as possible, to the way it was in Shakespeare's day. No architectural plans for Elizabethan theaters have survived, but much was learned about their structure and appearance from excavations of the nearby Rose Theatre.

Today, buying a ticket to a play at Shakespeare's Globe is like taking a walk back in time. The Globe is a 20-sided building, made of oak timbers and lime-cast walls. It is held together by 12,000 oak pegs, rather than nail or screws, just like the original. It also has the only thatched roof allowed in London since the Great Fire of 1666, though concealed sprinklers were installed to satisfy the fire laws.

Plays are performed in the open air, just as they were in the Bard's day. The performances run May through September, when the weather is at its best. There is no theatrical lighting. Plays begin at 2:00 PM to take advantage of the natural light.

At the foot of the stage is the open yard, where the "groundlings," as Shakespeare called them, could stand and see the play for a penny. Surrounding the yard are the tiered balcony seats where the gentility sat, for two or three pennies. The best seats, at six pennies, were in the Lords' Gallery above the stage itself. It was considered better to be seen than to have a good view. However, in those days plays were written for the ear, not the eye. Thus Hamlet says "We'll hear a play" (Shakespeare, *Hamlet* II:2).

The most striking thing about the Globe is the stage itself, bursting with color and paintwork. In Elizabethan times it was described as "entering a jewel box." The overhang, called the Shadow, is supported by the Pillars of Hercules—made of two huge oak trees painted to look like marble columns, complete with gold capitals. The ceiling is painted with a sun, moon, and stars and, since the Elizabethans had strong beliefs in the metaphysical, with the signs of the zodiac. A device called the *deus ex machina*, which means "the god out of the machine" lowers heavenly characters onto the stage, while a trap door gives access to Hell. Above the stage in the center is the Minstrel's Gallery, which also serves as Juliet's balcony in *Romeo and Juliet*. All sound effects and music for the plays are performed live, exactly as they were in Shakespeare's time, and the musicians literally have center stage.

One thing that won't be authentic, however, is the smell. Hygiene was rudimentary in Elizabethan times. People rarely bathed, and their outer garments, made of wool or leather, were never washed but simply hung out to air. A theatre performance was no sedate affair, but more like a pop concert. The audience brought food, wine, and ale into the theater. They chewed garlic and, with no public toilets, relieved themselves in the arena. The smell from the yard wafted up into the balconies, where the upper class patrons dubbed the groundlings "the penny stinkards." The actors often struggled to be heard above the babble of the crowd. Shakespeare's contemporary, the journalist and playwright Thomas Dekker, wrote "The audience is a great beast which the actor must tame into silence."

Despite its imperfections, the Elizabethan era was the golden age of democratic theater. Everyone from the highest to the lowest, the richest to the poorest, attended the plays. It all ended in 1644, when the theatres were pulled down, and it has never happened since.

A performance costs rather more than a penny today, though at the time of writing entry for the groundlings was still a bargain at £5. The original Globe packed one thousand people into the yard and another two thousand in the seats, but today's fire laws "allow" considerably more breathing space.

Visitors who come outside the season can still see the Globe Theatre on guided tours, which also take place in the mornings before performances. Beneath the theater and open year-round is the Globe Exhibition, which presents a fascinating look at Shakespeare's life and times and examines all aspects of the theater, from music to acting to costumes. The Globe also operates as an educational charity, giving workshops and readings, and generating resources worldwide.

SITES AROUND THE GLOBE

Tours of the nearby Rose Theatre are also available from the Globe. Its foundations were discovered in 1989 during the building of a new office block on the site. Excavations began, but exposure to air caused the ancient oak timbers to decay. The site has now been submerged in water to stop the deterioration (oak swells in water and this helps preserve it).

Inside the gloomy basement there is not much to see, but the shape of the inner and outer walls are outlined in red lights, visible from an overlooking platform. It is moving to hear the story of The Rose while looking at the actual site, without the distractions of modern London intruding on the imagination. Coins, jewelry, and many other artifacts were found here, and though it still holds many secrets, we know more about The Rose than any other theater. Readings are occasionally performed here.

Remnants of Shakespeare's times can still be seen around Bankside and elsewhere in the city. To commemorate his birthday (thought to be April 23) each year, the Globe stages two guided walks, called "Sweet Love Remember'd," that takes in the Bard's old haunts.

A few yards from the Globe at the corner of the cobbled street named Bear Gardens, an ancient stone seat has been set into the concrete wall of a modern building. This is the Ferryman's Seat, once used by the watermen as they waited for their customers.

Bear Gardens runs south from the river. Its name recalls the old bear-baiting arena that once stood here, visited by Queen Elizabeth. It was later replaced by the Hope Theatre, which doubled as a stage and bear-baiting ring. Ben Jonson's play *Bartholomew Fair* was first performed here. Farther along, at 2 Bear Gardens, a plaque commemorates the last of the bear-baiting rings, the Davies Amphitheatre, which operated from 1662 to 1682. References to bear-baiting appear in several of Shakespeare's plays. "They have tied me to a stake; I cannot fly, But bear-like I must fight the course." (Shakespeare, *Macbeth* part V VII:1)

Parallel to Bear Gardens is Rose Alley. In Elizabethan times, it was an open sewer that ran to the Thames. Thus, to the audience, the line from Romeo and Juliet, "that which we call a rose by any other name would smell as sweet (*Romeo and Juliet* II:2)" was also an inside joke.

Just beyond, an unmarked black door on the left is the entrance to The Rose. Farther along Park Street (called Maiden Lane in Shakespeare's time) is the site of the original Globe. The few parts of its foundation that remain are hidden beneath the courtyard of the surrounding apartments, but they are outlined in colored cobblestones. Signboards mark this historic spot.

Back on the Thames Path, near London Bridge, the Anchor Pub was built in 1775 on the site of a 15th-century inn patronized by Shakespeare. Behind the pub, along the cobbled alleyway of Pickford's Wharf, are the ruined walls of the Great Hall of Winchester Palace. The fine rose window, carved in stone, gives an idea of its former glory.

Shakespeare probably worshipped at Southwark Cathedral, then known as St. Mary Over-the Water. The church dates back to the 7th century. Many of Shakespeare's fellow actors are listed on its register. Shakespeare's younger brother Edmund was buried here in 1607. A memorial to the Bard himself was put up in 1912, which features his statue and a carved frieze of Bankside, set below a stained-glass window depicting scenes from his plays.

Shakespeare sites on the north side of the Thames are a little more obscure. Just north of Blackfriars tube station, a small lane called Playhouse Yard is the only clue to another theater that the Burbages once built here on the grounds of the former monastery. Shakespeare had shares in this theater, too, and the company began playing here in 1608. Blackfriars was then a desirable residential area. In 1613, Shakespeare bought an apartment in the former gatehouse in nearby Ireland Yard. It passed to his daughter Susannah after his death.

Farther north in Shoreditch, a plaque marks the site of London's first playhouse, The Theatre, on Curtain Road. In Great St. Helen's Church, off Bishopsgate, there is a stained glass window of Shakespeare. It is thought that this was his parish church. Bishopsgate becomes Gracechurch Street, where Leadenhall Market still stands. In Elizabethan times, several of the inns along this street were used for traveling players, including the Cross Keys, used by Shakespeare's company in 1594.

Smithfield Market has been a meat and livestock market since at least the 12th century, and it is mentioned in Ben Jonson's *Bartholomew Fair*. Opposite is St. Bartholomew's Hospital, the only one of the city's medieval hospitals still standing on its original site, and St. Bartholomew-the-Great church, which still has its original Norman arches. Nearby in Ely Place, St. Etheldreda is London's oldest Catholic church.

In Shakespeare's day it was renowned for the fine strawberries grown in its garden, and these are praised in *Richard III.* The church holds a Strawberrie Fayre each June.

Acting companies were often invited to entertain at court or noblemen's houses. Shakespeare's *King Lear* had its debut at court in 1606. His company also staged performances at the Inns of Court, the prestigious law colleges where the sons of merchants and landowners went to study. Middle Temple Hall, with its double hammerbeam roof and exquisitely carved oak screen, provided a splendid backdrop for the premiere of *Twelfth Night* in 1602, attended by distinguished guests—including Queen Elizabeth.

Middle Temple Hall is one of London's few surviving buildings from the Elizabethan age, and its beautiful interior is an awesome monument to the times. Visitors can request permission to see it when it is not in use.

Shakespeare's plays—including his earliest work, the *Comedy of Errors*—were also performed at Gray's Inn in 1594. One of its members, the Earl of Southampton, became the young playwright's patron. An appointment is required to see the interior with its beautifully carved wooden screen. More accessible is the magnificent Staple Inn, nearby on Chancery Lane. Built in 1586, it is the only Elizabethan half-timbered building left in central London. Wool was once weighed and taxed here.

INIGO JONES

A further glimpse into Shakespeare's times can be seen in the works of his contemporary, Inigo Jones (1573–1652), England's first classical architect. In his early career he designed scenery and costumes for court "masques," written by Ben Jonson, which became popular under Elizabeth's successor, James I. Instead of professional actors, members of the court, including women, performed in these private evening entertainments. Inspired by the Italian Renaissance, Jones created elaborate stages for these performances, with lighting effects, music, and dancing adding to the spectacle.

After further travels in Italy in 1613–14, Jones returned to England and was appointed King's Surveyor. The classical Palladian style of his buildings was considered revolutionary at the time. Three of his finest royal works survive: Banqueting House, which was originally part of Whitehall Palace; Queen's House at Greenwich, now an art gallery; and Queen's Chapel at St. James Palace, which is closed to the public. Jones also designed the Italian-style arcaded piazza at Covent Garden, and the adjoining St. Paul's Church.

In 1616, the king asked Jones to draw up plans for a new covered playhouse. Though it was never built at the time, the plans were discovered in the archives at Oxford in the 1960s. They have been used to build a new indoor playhouse, the Inigo Jones Theatre, at Shakespeare's Globe.

CHAPTER FOUR

London and the Restoration

The greatest piece of writing to emerge in the 17th century was not a novel or a play, but a man's diary. Samuel Pepys was a Londoner born and bred, and he lived through one of the most turbulent periods of English history. He grew up during the turmoil of the bloody Civil War, skipping school to watch the execution of the king. His diary, which he kept as a young man from 1660 to 1669, recorded a decade that brought sweeping changes to the city with the restoration of the monarchy, the horrors of the Great Plague, and the destruction of medieval London in the Great Fire.

Religious discord dominated politics throughout most of the century. When Queen Elizabeth died without an heir in 1603, she was succeeded by James I, ruler of Scotland (as James VI) and son of Elizabeth's half-sister, Mary Queen of Scots. He ushered in the Stuart dynasty.

James was an intelligent and experienced monarch, but he was not accustomed to the English system of government, which was influenced by both Parliament and the Church. A moderate Protestant, he tried to mediate between the opposing factions of the Puritans and the Catholics, both of whom sought his support. The Puritan movement was made up of Protestant sects who disliked the established Church of England. When they asserted too much independence, James vowed to make them conform. Many fled to Holland, determined to form their own communities. In 1620, a group of Puritan exiles set sail from Plymouth in the *Mayflower*, and founded the New England colonies in America.

Although James initially allowed greater freedom for Catholics to worship, he later re-enacted old penalties for failing to attend Church of England services. In 1605, a group of Catholic conspirators hatched the Gunpowder Plot, aiming to kill the king and the government by blowing up the Houses of Parliament. The plot was discovered and Guy Fawkes was caught in the cellars with explosives. The narrow escape is commemorated each year on November 5 with bonfires and fireworks.

Tensions between the king and Parliament, and between Church and Crown, ebbed and flowed throughout the reigns of James and his son Charles I, who succeeded his father to the throne in 1625. London became a breeding ground for evangelical Puritans—both official clergymen and street preachers such as Praisegod Barebones, a leather-seller who set up a congregation in Fleet Street near Pepys's boyhood home. Religious fervor was easily stirred up, particularly against "popery." Charles was criticized for his French Catholic queen, Henrietta Maria, and her large foreign entourage.

Under the Stuarts, the court at Westminster doubled in size from the time of Elizabeth's reign. More and more of the aristocracy came to London for politics, business, and pleasure, followed by a growing train of lawyers, doctors, teachers, musicians, jewelers, art dealers, tailors, craftsmen, and servants to cater to their needs. London property development took its first major steps westward.

KING CHARLES

Charles had kingly tastes, and sought to give Westminster a more stately air. Whitehall Palace had been the main royal residence in London since Henry VIII's time, and Charles planned to remodel it in a grand Italianate style, to the designs of Royal Surveyor and architect Inigo Jones. The plans never materialized, and the rambling palace, which had some two thousand rooms and stretched for half a mile along the Thames, burned down in 1698 in a fire started by a careless laundrywoman. But Whitehall remains synonymous with British government, and this street that once ran through the palace complex is now lined with the main government offices and ministries.

The only part of Whitehall Palace that survived the fire is the magnificent Banqueting House, completed in 1622. Jones's masterpiece was the first Renaissance building in England, and its elegant, classical lines stood in stark contrast to the Tudors' pedestrian wooden dining hall. The beautiful ceiling paintings by Rubens are allegorical tributes to the Stuart dynasty, depicting the union of England and Scotland and the virtues of James I. Commissioned by Charles, they were intended to glorify the Stuarts' reign. But they also represented the sort of royal arrogance that angered Oliver Cromwell and his Commonwealth supporters.

From its opening, Banqueting House was the focus of state events and court entertainment (it is still occasionally used for state ceremonies). Lavish masques were performed here until 1634, when Charles forbade them to prevent damage to the ceiling paintings by candle smoke. Charles' court came to symbolize extravagance and love of luxury. Meanwhile, financial crisis and ill-fated royal schemes severely tried the loyalty of the city's merchant class.

SAMUEL PEPYS

Amidst London's brewing discontent, Samuel Pepys was born on February 23, 1633, above his father's tailor's shop in Salisbury Court. It was reached by a narrow lane off Fleet Street, a mixture of large and small houses that had once been part of a bishop's estate, with gardens running down to the Thames. Pepys was christened at St. Bride's parish church, which stood behind the house.

Pepys was the fifth child in the family, although two older sisters had died before he was born. Altogether he had ten siblings, but only three—his younger brothers Tom and John and a sister Paulina, called Pall—reached adulthood.

John Pepys's main customers were lawyers who worked in the nearby Temple and Inns of Court, still the focus of legal London today. One was a neighbour, Bulstrode Whitelocke, who lived in a large house in Salisbury Court. The young lawyer was also a budding composer, and some of the first music Samuel would have heard were the rehearsals for a court masque that Whitelocke was preparing to perform for King Charles at Candlemas (observed on February 2).

The Pepys were not of great social rank, and no one would have guessed that another baby, born later that same year, would one day become one of Samuel Pepys's close associates: James, Duke of York, the second son of the king. Another great literary figure of the era, the poet John Milton, was Pepys's neighbor and lodged with another tailor in St. Bride's churchyard when Samuel was six. He too was a Londoner, born in Bread Street, Cheapside.

The Pepys boys were often sent to board in Kingsland and Hackney during the summers. Today these are some of the most densely populated urban areas of east London, but in those days they were rural hamlets offering open fields and fresh air. Pepys recalled boyhood trips with his family to the King's Head, then a rural pub in Islington, where they had cakes and ale. Now in one of London's trendiest districts, the King's Head on Upper Street is the city's oldest pub theater.

CIVIL WAR

The first decade of Pepys's life was marked by the growing tide of political unrest on the streets of London, including rioting, propaganda, religious attacks, and executions of hated political figures. Many complicated issues contributed to the impending Civil War, but foremost among these were religious zeal and fear that the king would implement absolute rule. Puritans allied with the political enemies of the king as they attempted to curb his power. The king refused to accept any limitations on his authority by Parliament, and Parliament refused to accept the king's supremacy.

In January 1642, King Charles tried to arrest five rebel Members of Parliament and pursued them into the City, where he was mobbed by an angry crowd. He left London soon after, and Parliament began to raise its own army, supported by fighting bands of citizens. The royalist mayor was imprisoned in the Tower and a Puritan was appointed in his place. London became what John Milton called "the mansion house of liberty."

Meanwhile, the king was gathering his own forces. The Civil War officially began when he raised his standard at Nottingham in August 1642. It split the country in every respect, as people sided with the king or Parliament according to social rank, profession, religion, or region of the country they lived in.

London stood firmly on the side of Parliament. Although the king tried to reclaim the city early in the war, in November 1642 he was turned back, greatly outnumbered, at Turnham Green. Fearing another attack, Londoners built barricades and surrounded the city with ramparts, ditches, and two dozen forts and batteries. About 20,000 volunteers joined in, including women and children. But the royalist forces never returned.

Though Pepys's own prospects at birth were limited, he had wealthier and well-connected relatives who took an interest in the clever, inquisitive boy. A year after the war broke out he was sent to Brampton, 60 miles northeast of London, to attend the nearby Huntingdon grammar school where his cousin, Edward Montagu, eight years his senior, had studied. Montagu was now a lieutenant, fighting for the Parliamentarians in Oliver

Cromwell's army. Cromwell too was an alumnus of Huntingdon School.

Three years later, Pepys was back home in London and a pupil at St. Paul's School, beside the cathedral. Strongly Puritan in its teachings, St. Paul's had an excellent reputation. John Milton was also educated there. Riots and political divisions continued to wrack the city as the war raged on.

By January 1649, the king's army had been defeated and the Parliamentarians were in power. Charles was sentenced to death. Ironically, the spot chosen for his execution was Banqueting

Milton and the Freedom of the Press

The Civil War brought a tightening of governmental control over the publishing industry—but "the freedom of the press" found an early advocate in John Milton.

The Stationers' Company, the guild of London's publishers, had been strengthening its hold on the industry since the time of the Tudors; by the Civil War it demanded prior registration for almost every item printed. It was under pressure from the Stationers that Parliament passed the Licensing Order of 1643, reinstating a level of censorship not seen since the Star Chamber's demise in 1641. Milton wrote a powerful pamphlet in response, stressing the importance of diverse ideas, even bad ones, and of freedom of thought from institutional control. He argued that accountability should come after publication, not before it—for "how can a man teach with authority, which is the life of teaching, whenas all he teaches, all he delivers, is but under the tuition, under the correction of his patriarchal licenser, to blot or alter what precisely accords not with the hidebound humour which he calls his judgment?"

The pamphlet had no effect on Parliament, however, perhaps because Milton had already courted controversy with pamphlets on divorce. But Areopagitica remains an eloquent and vital work, often called the first modern argument for a free press.

House. Pepys, who was fiercely republican at this stage and had no sympathy for the king, slipped away to join the crowd that gathered outside.

Charles wore several shirts to prevent himself from shivering in the cold, lest it be mistaken for fear. He walked through the room for the last time beneath his beloved paintings, and stepped out through a tall window onto the scaffold. His last word, before he was beheaded, was "remember!" When the axe fell, a bystander reported "a dismal universal groan amongst the thousands of people who were in sight of it, as if it were with one consent ..."

The king is remembered on the last Sunday of each January, by a branch of the Civil War Society who parade in royalist uniforms to lay a wreath at his statue. A bust above the entrance to Banqueting House commemorates the execution.

An equestrian statue of Charles I, cast in 1633, also survives. It was seized during the Commonwealth and given to a local brazier, John Rivett, who was instructed to melt it down. Instead, Rivett hid the statue and made a handsome profit by selling bronze mementos allegedly made from the remains. After the Restoration, he sold the statue back to the city, and it was placed in sight of Banqueting House, on the spot where those who had signed the king's death warrant were themselves executed in 1660.

Today, the statue stands south of Trafalgar Square, at the top of Whitehall. It is from this spot that all distances are measured in London. It was the site of the original Charing Cross, one of twelve crosses erected by Edward I in 1290 to mark the funeral procession of his wife, Eleanor, from Nottingham to Westminster Abbey. The old stone cross was torn down during the Civil War, one of the many acts of destruction against royal and religious landmarks. A replica was put up outside Charing Cross station in Victorian times.

After the king's execution, a republic was declared. This was the period known as the Commonwealth. In 1653, Cromwell was declared Lord Protector, and moved into Whitehall the following year.

Pepys continued his education at Magdalene College, Cambridge, receiving a BA in 1654. He then began work as a clerk and general assistant to his cousin Edward Montagu, who had risen swiftly and was now at Whitehall as part of Cromwell's Council of State.

The next year, Pepys married his wife, Elizabeth, who was barely 15 years old, at St. Margaret's Church, Westminster. John Milton had also married here, and so would Winston Churchill.

The white stone church, which stands in the shadow of Westminster Abbey, dates to the late 15th century, but was rebuilt following bomb damage in World War II. Its highlight is the stained-glass east window depicting the marriage of Catherine of Aragon to Prince Arthur in 1501. The prince died five months later, and Catherine married his brother, the future Henry VIII. Other windows commemorate Milton and William Caxton, England's first printer, who is buried here. In a niche above the church's doorway is a bust of Charles I. It looks across to a statue of his old nemesis, Oliver Cromwell, at the end of Whitehall.

When Cromwell died in 1658 his son Richard became his successor. By this time, however, Londoners had grown tired of Puritan rule. They resented the forced religious observance, and the banning of Christmas celebrations, dancing, theater, and Sunday sports. Political tensions were rising and many feared anarchy and a return to civil war. Desperate for peace and stability, Montagu and other prominent statesmen quietly switched allegiances and extended an olive branch to Charles II, who awaited his chance in exile in Holland.

Music, art, and poetry flourished in the final years of the Protectorate. John Milton, who had been a prominent supporter of the Commonwealth and served Cromwell's council as chief secretary, was now blind. Living in the City near Cripplegate, he began to write his great epic poem, *Paradise Lost*, which he dictated to his daughters. He died in 1674 and was buried at St. Giles, Cripplegate.

THE DIARY OF SAMUEL PEPYS

On January 1, 1660, Pepys began his diary. He was 26 years old. His reasons for writing it are unknown, although he was a keen observer of everything around him and seemed to have a sense of destiny, even if he had not yet begun to fulfill it. But Pepys's diary is more than a mere chronicle of the times. Today it is considered one of the world's great literary works. Written in a clear, exuberant style, it presents a fascinating picture of daily life in Restoration London. His sharp eyewitness accounts give illuminating insights on the key people and events of the period.

Pepys was by no means the only diarist of his day. His friend, John Evelyn, also kept a journal that is an intelligent and thoughtful historical portrait. Others kept journals of their official work and travels, or for spiritual purposes. What makes Pepys's diary so outstanding is that, unlike the others, he also records the intimate details of his personal life, thus presenting us with a character, warts and all, as likeable and engaging as any of Dickens's creations.

Remarkably, Pepys's original diary survives intact. It was written in six notebooks that Pepys purchased from John Cade's stationer's shop, called the Globe, near the Royal Exchange. Pepys carefully prepared the pages, lining left and top margins with red ink. He wrote in a small, neat hand, using a quill pen and black or brown ink, with ornate capitals letters for the months. Fountain pens had been used on the Continent since the early 1600s, but the first use in England was recorded in Pepys's diary on August 5, 1663, when he was given a silver pen "to carry inke in."

Pepys wrote his diary in shorthand. A great womanizer, he was keen to conceal his infidelities from his wife, though he unashamedly recorded his extra-marital dalliances in detail. He used a shorthand system created by Thomas Shelton, much in use in recording legal proceedings of the day, in which words are replaced by symbols and contractions. He also peppered his accounts with Latin and Spanish words. His shorthand was not deciphered until 1825, after which the diaries were first published in edited form.

Pepys describes his day-to-day experiences in fine detail: what he ate, where he drank, friends he met and their conversation, places he walked, and music, books and theater he enjoyed. Intimate accounts of his turbulent marriage are also provided. He gossips, snipes at his enemies, praises his friends, admires his betters, and admits jealousy, greed, cheating, lust and pleasure—a full and honest range of human emotions. He ends each day's entry with the memorable phrase "and so to bed."

Work and ambition are two of the great themes of the diary. Pepys had a mere £25 to his name when he began writing the diary. Through hard work and his outstanding abilities, he eventually became a wealthy man, with a salary of £500, a "mighty handsome" home, a gilded coach, and £10,000 in savings. In 1668, Pepys records buying a second-hand coach in Covent Garden. The building on Long Acre Street that now houses St. Martin's School of Art was a former carriage manufacturer, possibly the very place where Pepys watched his coach being painted yellow.

At the opening of the diary, Pepys was living in his "poor little house" in Axe Yard, a cul-de-sac in Westminster, which existed near where the Cenotaph now stands. He remained a valued aide to Montagu, but had secured a second job as a clerk to George Downing, for whom one of the most famous addresses in Britain is named. No. 10 Downing Street has long been the residence of the nation's prime ministers.

Both Montagu and Downing were waiting for the right moment to declare their support for Charles II. When it came, in March of that year, Pepys was asked to accompany Montagu on the ship that sailed to Holland to bring back the exiled Charles. When they returned, Charles was met by cheering crowds in London, and was crowned in April 1661.

The Restoration reinstated not only the monarchy, but also the House of Lords and the Church of England, both of which had been abolished under the Puritans. Whatever his faults, Charles II was the right ruler to preside over the restoration of normalcy to London. He was cultured, sociable, and accessible, often seen in Whitehall and St. James Park. Pepys's diary describes informal briefings with the king in the park. Known as the "Merrie Monarch," he indulged in many pleasures and surrounded himself with clever courtiers and beautiful women.

Charles II was an eager patron of writers and artists, and he supported many city improvements. He licensed two theatres, including the King's Theatre in Drury Lane. In 1662, he granted a charter to the Royal Society of London for Improving Natural Knowledge, set up by Christopher Wren, Robert Boyle, and other scientists to gain knowledge through observation and experiment. It was one of the first public scientific societies in Europe, with members drawn from a wide social circle. Pepys joined in 1665 and later became its president. Today, the Royal Society occupies an enviable address, at 6 Carlton House Terrace in St. James.

Perhaps Charles's finest legacy for Londoners today is St. James Park, one of the prettiest green spots in the inner city. He had Henry VIII's old deer park landscaped in the French style, and added an aviary on what is now Bird Cage Walk. Charles opened the park to the public, and used to stroll through the grounds with his mistresses. The Russian ambassador gave him a pair of pelicans as a present, establishing the park as a wildfowl sanctuary. About 30 species reside around its tree-lined lake, including black swans. There is a grand view of Buckingham Palace from the bridge over the lake.

The most famous of Charles's many mistresses was Nell Gwyn, England's first great comedy actress. When he reinstated the charters to theater companies that the puritans had closed down, he insisted that they hire actresses, rather than boys, to play the female roles, as was done on the French stage. Nell's house was on nearby Pall Mall, a street named after another French custom popularized by Charles: the game of *paglio a maglio*, which means "ball and mallet." Similar to croquet, it was played here and on The Mall.

Like so many Londoners today, Charles liked to escape the city on weekends. The King's Road in Chelsea was named for his preferred route out of London to his country palaces at Hampton Court and Windsor.

Montagu was rewarded for his role in bringing Charles II back to the throne with a new title, the Earl of Sandwich. He in turn rewarded Pepys for his loyalty by securing him a new job as Clerk of the Acts for the Navy Board, the office responsible for building and repairing ships and managing the dockyards. Along with a salary of £350, it gave him the opportunity to increase his wealth through the many gratuities and gifts that came with the position, as well as to increase his social standing. It also came with a house in Seething Lane, across the courtyard from his office, where most of the diary was written.

The new mood of London suited Pepys's gregarious personality. Taverns and alehouses were the focal points of social life, and the diary describes his meals, drink, companions, and liaisons at taverns all around the city. He also describes evenings at the theater, musical performances, and even the first *Punch and Judy* show in England, given by an Italian puppeteer, which he saw in the piazza at Covent Garden in May 1662. It is commemorated each May with a Punch and Judy Festival, held in the gardens of the adjoining St. Paul's Church. Coffee houses were also popular, much as they are in London today. Pepys reports the "very witty and pleasant discourse" at Will's, formerly on the corner of Bow and Russell streets on the opposite side of the piazza, in 1668.

Most of the taverns Pepys's mentions are long gone, but one, Ye Olde Cock Tavern on Fleet Street, still stands. Pepys writes of an assignation with an actress there, and how his angry wife threatened him with red-hot tongs upon his return home. The tall, narrow building looks interesting from the outside, but modern renovations to the interior have taken away its historic charm.

Pepys enlightens us on the fashions and social customs of the day, from wigs and artificial teeth made of whalebone and ivory to the mourning rings given out to favored friends at funerals. He enjoyed shopping and dressed stylishly out of pride and ambition, writing on October 21, 1664, "I find I must go handsomely, whatever it cost me." On January 22, 1660, he mentions a new fashion: "This day I began to put buckles to my shoes, which I had bought yesterday of Mr. Wotton."

THE GREAT PLAGUE

The most memorable passages in Pepys's diary deal with two of London's greatest tragedies, which occurred within a year of each other. The first was the Great Plague of 1665. The plague was a regular occurrence in the city. Since 1563, when London lost around one-fifth of its population, there had been severe outbreaks in every decade. The plague claimed thirty thousand lives in 1603, the year James I took the throne, while Charles I's ascension in 1625 saw forty thousand deaths.

When the plague broke out early in 1665 it initially caused no great alarm. It began in the slum area of St. Giles, noted for epidemics, and for the first five months the number of deaths was not unusual. The disease, carried by fleas on rats, was known as "the poor's plague" because wealthier residents escaped sickness by leaving the city during an outbreak, while the poor, living in overcrowded, unsanitary conditions and unable to get away, were a perfect target.

A heat wave in early June brought a rapid spread of the infection. Pepys described June 7 as "the hottest day that ever I felt in my life," and recorded seeing red crosses on houses in Drury Lane that day. Plague was believed to be contagious, though no one knew how it spread. When someone was stricken, their house was locked up for forty days and marked with a red cross.

By July, people were fleeing the city in droves, including doctors, lawyers, king, and court. Pepys sent his wife and mother to the country, but he himself stayed in the city until the end of August, recording the horrors around him. As panic spread, crazed victims were seen running naked in the street, foaming at the mouth. Dead-carts were piled high with corpses, church-yards overflowed, and the air reeked of decay. In desperation, the lord mayor ordered all dogs and cats to be killed, in case they spread pestilence, and huge bonfires were lit to cleanse the air. Pepys described the terror all Londoners felt:

> To see a person sick of the sores, carried close to me by Gracechurch Street in a hackney-coach.... To hear that poor Payne hath buried a child and is dying himself ... and that one of my own watermen, that carried me daily, fell sick as soon as he had landed me on Friday morning last ... is now dead of the plague ... doth put me into great apprehensions of melancholy, and with good reason.

The plague peaked in September, with twelve thousand deaths recorded in one week. It then abated with the onset of cooler weather. Those who crept back to the city in October found an eerie stillness. On October 16, Pepys wrote:

> Lord, how empty the streets are and melancholy, so many poor sick people in the streets, full of sores: and so many sad stories overheard as I walk, everybody talking of this dead, and that man sick, and so many in this place, and so many in that.

Over 68,500 plague deaths were recorded, but modern histo-rians estimate a more accurate number to be between 80,000 and 100,000. The economy collapsed as many of the shop-keepers who survived went bankrupt, and others became unem-ployed. The king did not return to London until February 1666, and another 2,000 people died that year. It was November before a public thanksgiving was celebrated for the end of the plague. Londoners did not know that it was indeed the end, for the plague never again returned to England. It was not the end of London's sorrows.

THE GREAT FIRE

In 1666, Pepys recorded the destruction of the medieval city in the Great Fire. In the early hours of September 2, a fire broke out in Farynor's bakery in Pudding Lane. A strong wind carried the sparks, and soon the whole neighborhood was in flames. The mayor was called out, but dismissed the danger and went back to bed. Pepys was woken by his servant Jane, who had risen early to cook and noticed the fire. He too was unconcerned.

By morning, 300 houses had burned down and London Bridge was on fire. Efforts to fight the fire with buckets of water and primitive hoses did little good, especially when it reached the warehouses full of oil, tallow, and other flammable materials. Pepys found a boatman to take him to Whitehall to inform the king, and as he passed under the bridge he observed people along the riverbank throwing their goods into flat-bottomed boats or into the water itself. He noted that many put off leaving their homes until the last possible moment, and that the pigeons behaved in the same way, hovering about their roosts until their wings were burned.

Charles sent Pepys back with a message to pull down houses to create a fire break and contain the flames. But the mayor "cried like a fainting woman" and delayed, worried about the cost of rebuilding.

Pepys recorded his experiences almost hour by hour, and his account of the fire is the most famous section of the diary. He described its progress, measures taken to fight it, and the general scene as Londoners tried to move their families and goods to safety.

On that first day, he walked through the city and then took to the river with his wife and friends. "With one's face in the wind you were almost burned with a shower of fire drops," he wrote. They retreated to an alehouse on Bankside, where they watched London burning up the hill, "a most horrid malicious bloody flame, not like the fine flame of an ordinary fire ... it made me weep to see it."

Returning home, Pepys began to salvage his goods and set out early the next morning for Bethnal Green, where his friend Sir William Rider had agreed to store his most valued possessions—including his diary—at his mansion. Tuesday's activities provide readers today with a bit of comic relief. Pepys and his navy colleague and neighbor, Sir William Penn (father of the founder of Pennsylvania), dug a pit in the garden to bury their wine, " ... and I my parmazan [*sic*] cheese as well ..."

On Wednesday, when the flames reached the bottom of Seething Lane, Pepys evacuated his wife and returned, expecting the worst. But the wind had dropped and his house was still standing. He climbed the steeple of All Hallows Church "and there saw the saddest sight of desolation that I ever saw."

Gradually, the fire burned itself out. It had raged for four days and devastated the old medieval city. Nearly 400 acres—about four-fifths of the city within the walls—and 63 acres beyond lay in ruins. St. Paul's Cathedral was destroyed, along with 86 other churches, 13,200 houses, and 44 livery halls. Pepys's father's house in Salisbury Court, St. Bride's, much of Fleet Street, and his school at St. Paul's were all gone.

More than 100,000 people were homeless and camping out in Moorfields and Highbury Fields. Remarkably, only eight people were killed. It might have been even worse, had King Charles not stepped in and supervised the fire-fighting efforts himself, ordering streets in the fire's path to be blown up, thus stopping its further spread.

"London was," wrote John Evelyn, "but is no more."

Within a few days, plans for rebuilding London were submitted to the king. The architect Christopher Wren and others envisioned a magnificent new city, with wide thoroughfares, open spaces, grand vistas, and stately squares surrounding a new St. Paul's Cathedral and the Royal Exchange. But the city needed to rebuild as soon as possible. The cost of reconstruction was enormous, and to negotiate property rights for a new capital would prove a legal nightmare. Homeowners naturally wanted to rebuild on their own sites.

In the end, London's ancient street plan was retained, though many of the narrow winding roads were widened. New building regulations required houses to be built of brick or stone and flat-fronted (rather than the medieval overhangs). The first raised sidewalks for pedestrians were installed. The Fleet River was dredged and made into a canal, and new quays were built along the Thames. The greatest landmarks from the post-Fire reconstruction are the churches designed by Wren, which rose over the years on the sites of their medieval predecessors, including his splendid new St. Paul's Cathedral, a symbol of London to this day.

The Fire itself was commemorated by the Monument, designed by Wren and Robert Hooke. Built of Portland stone, it is 202 feet high, the exact distance to the start of the fire in Pudding Lane. Surrounded as it is today with drab high-rise office buildings, it is hard to believe that it is the tallest freestanding stone column in the world. Sculpted reliefs around the base depict Charles II, the Duke of York, and various allegorical figures raising London from its ashes, with the Latin inscription "London rises again." At the top, a bronze urn spouting golden flames represents the fire. There are 311 steps to the top, with an enclosed viewing platform.

The Fire also spurred London's westward development. The wealthier of the displaced city dwellers found new advantages in living beyond the city walls, particularly with the court now reestablished at St. James's. The Earl of Southampton laid out London's first square, now called Bloomsbury Square. It set the precedent for the architectural layout so characteristic of much of the city. The latter part of the 17th century saw the building of some of the most famous addresses today, such as Soho Square and St. James's Square. Several well-known streets, such as Bond Street, Frith Street, and Panton Street, are named for developers of the day.

Pepys ended his diary on May 31, 1669. He gave it up

because his eyes pained him when doing close work and reading by candlelight, and he was afraid he was going blind. It was more likely a case of long-sightedness and astigmatism, for his eyes grew no worse. But he gave up the diary with great regret, writing that it was like a form of death, "almost as much as to see myself go into my grave." Thus, the cover was closed on one of the great literary achievements of the era. Though he never intended his diary to be published, Pepys earned his place among the great London writers.

After giving up the diary, Pepys continued to advance in his career. He was appointed Secretary to the Admiralty in 1673, the same year he was elected a Member of Parliament. Though he is most famous for his diary, he was also a brilliant administrator and made a great contribution to the nation through his improvement of the British Navy into a professional and effective service.

At the end of 1669, Pepys's wife died of fever at the age of 29. She was buried in their parish church, St. Olave's, in Hart Street, where Pepys erected an elaborate memorial to her. Pepys had escaped the Great Fire, but his beloved home in Seething Lane was eventually consumed by flame. The navy office and surrounding houses were destroyed by a fire in January 1673. Pepys managed to save his diary and books, but lost all other possessions. Today, a bust of Pepys in Seething Gardens stands on the site of the old navy office.

Pepys moved into a large, new house on Buckingham Street, off the Strand. The old political troubles reared up again and in 1678 he was wrongly accused of spying for the French and imprisoned in the Tower for six weeks. He returned to office in 1679, but a decade later his loyalty to James II, the Catholic brother of Charles II who succeeded to the throne, caused him to resign from public life when James was forced out in favor of William and Mary.

Pepys spent his final years in Clapham, at the home of his long-time friend Will Hewer. He died on May 26, 1703 and was buried at St. Olave's. He left his diary to his university college, and there it remains, housed in the glass-fronted bookshelves he had specially made to hold his library. These are the first known custom-made bookcases in England. Pepys helped to design them and had them built by a naval joiner.

PRINCE HENRY'S ROOM

Pepys is honored in a small exhibition in Prince Henry's Room, on Fleet Street not far from his birthplace. The fine half-timbered building is one of the few wooden structures that survived the Great Fire. It was originally an inn, and in 1610 this upstairs room was converted into a private office for Prince Henry, the eldest son of King James I. Henry's death from typhoid two years later, at the age of 18, was a tragedy for the country, as a gifted and promising future king was lost and his brother, Charles I, came to the throne instead.

The room's finest feature is its splendid Jacobean plaster ceiling, dating from 1610, one of the few left in London. Its ornate decoration bears the feathers of the Prince of Wales', Henry's title, and the letters PH. The west wall retains its original oak panelling, with Jacobean strap work. It is furnished with 17th-century period furniture.

A central wooden table is filled with Pepys's artifacts and, of course, excerpts from the diary. There is a drawing of his navy office, the front page of a newspaper from the week of the Great Fire, and prints of Pepys and his contemporaries. Old photos of the area are also on display.

When Henry died the building reverted to a tavern, and was an apothecary shop during the Great Plague. It was later taken over by Mrs. Salmon's Waxworks. The archway beneath Prince Henry's Room leads to the Inner Temple, an atmospheric enclave for the legal profession, just as it was in Pepys's day.

Across the street is St. Dunstan's-in-the-West church, where the Great Fire stopped. The curious clock tower was erected by 17th-century parishioners grateful for having been spared in the fire. The two primitive figures represent Gog and Magog, the legendary giants of the city. In a niche in the vestry wall is a stone statue of Queen Elizabeth I, the oldest in existence, which once stood over the Ludgate entrance to the city. The rest of the church was rebuilt in the 19th century.

Pepys was here too, and up to his usual tricks when he stopped in to hear a sermon and ended up pestering a girl next to him in the pew. He confided to his diary "… at last I could perceive her to take pins out of her pocket to prick me if I should touch her again"

Both Prince Henry's Room and St. Dunstan's-in-the-West church survived the Blitz during World War II, when over 300 tons of explosives fell on this area. Pepys's birthplace was not so lucky. Salisbury Court lies further east, on the south side of Fleet Street. Now full of concrete modern buildings, all that remains is a blue plaque noting the site.

A passageway leads to St. Bride's, where Pepys was baptized. It is now known as the journalist's church, and many writers have memorials or have been buried here. Wynkyn de Worde set up his printing press next door to the church in 1500, close to his best customers, the lawyers and clergy, establishing Fleet Street as the center of publishing. Until 1695, London was the only city in the country where commercial publishing was legal. Thus, writers were drawn to the capital, and particularly to this area.

When Pepys wanted to bury his brother Tom in the church in 1664, the vaults were so crowded that he had to bribe the gravedigger with a sixpence to "justle (the corpses) together" to make room for him. Wren rebuilt St. Bride's after the Great Fire, capping his creation with a magnificent spire that is said to have been the inspiration for the first tiered wedding cake. It was attractively rebuilt for a third time after bombs destroyed the interior in the Blitz. In the crypt is a fascinating look at the history of the site and of Fleet Street from Roman times to the present.

Farther east, near the Tower of London, are a few remnants of Pepys's life in Seething Lane. St. Olave's church, Hart Street, was also damaged in the Blitz and has been restored. The bust of

Elizabeth was moved to safety during the war and has been returned to its place high up in the sanctuary, where Pepys had it installed after her death so that he could gaze at his wife during the long sermons. His own monument was erected in 1883, in front of the doorway that once led to the gallery and the Navy Office pew. Dickens called the church "St. Ghastly Grim" because of the skulls and crossbones and spikes around the cemetery entrance on Seething Lane.

At the bottom of Seething Lane, the brick tower that Pepys climbed to survey the Great Fire was the only part of All-Hallows-by-the-Tower to withstand the Blitz. Inside the rebuilt church are a few Roman and Saxon relics, however, and the limewood font cover carved by Grinling Gibbons in 1682, in a chapel in the southwest corner.

Though little of Pepys's physical world remains, his spirit endures and his diary continues to fascinate us with the world of Restoration London. In 2002, Claire Tomalin's aptly-titled biography, *Samuel Pepys, The Unequalled Self,* was voted the Whitbread Book of the Year, one of the most prestigious British literary prizes.

CHAPTER FIVE

Georgian and Regency London

By the early 18th century, London had risen from the ashes of the Great Fire. Its population was around 575,000, about the same as that of Paris. By 1750, London had added another 100,000, and one-tenth of the population of England and Wales was living in the capital.

London was expanding in all directions. Newcomers generally settled in the east and south of the city, where industries were concentrated and rents were cheaper. The most significant changes, however, occurred in the west and north, where wealthy citizens eager to escape the pollution, crime, and unsanitary conditions of the crowded inner city moved to grand new housing developments built around leafy squares. These became the finest places to live in London, and remain some of its most pleasant residential areas today.

The first property boom coincided with a new royal dynasty, which came to the throne in 1714. Queen Anne, the last of the

Stuart monarchs, had died without an heir. Although James Stuart, the son of James II who lived in exile in France, had the strongest hereditary claim, as a Catholic he was barred from the throne. Instead, the crown passed to George of Hanover, the Protestant great-grandson of James I, ushering in a new royal line. He was the first of four successive monarchs named George, whose combined reign lasted over a century. Thus, the period from 1714 to 1837 is known as Georgian London.

GEORGIAN LONDON

Born and raised in Germany, George I spoke little English, and knew nothing about the government of the country he had come to rule. Robert Walpole led an inner circle of ministers on the king's behalf, the forerunner of the modern Cabinet, and in effect became the country's first prime minister. His home at 10 Downing Street has remained the official residence of all prime ministers since.

George I's reign was marked by the first Jacobite uprising in 1715, when the supporters of James Stuart tried unsuccessfully to regain the throne. George II succeeded his father in 1727. During his 33-year reign, Britain was often at war with Spain and France over territory in Europe and the American colonies. A more serious threat was the second Jacobite uprising in 1745, led by Charles Edward Stuart—the dashing Bonnie Prince Charlie, grandson of the exiled king. The Jacobites met their final defeat in a bloody massacre at Culloden.

By 1756, Britain was once again at war with France. During this so-called Seven Years' War, Britain gained control of Canada in 1760, along with several West Indian islands. That same year the king died and was succeeded by his grandson, George III.

George III held the throne for the next 60 years. In 1769–70, the explorer Captain James Cook landed on the coast of Australia and claimed it for the Crown. But by the time another decade had passed, Britain had lost her 13 American colonies in the American War of Independence.

In the 18th century, London's building sprees occurred between periods of war, as each conflict alternately consumed huge slices of the city's finances and manpower. Early Georgian developments included Hanover Square, named for the new royal line, Berkeley Square, and Grosvenor Square, which at six acres was the city's largest residential square. It is now dominated by the American embassy.

The development of the West End was spurred by the capitalistic schemes of aristocrats, rather than by any calculated city planning. The Earl of Southampton had set the tone back in the 1660s with the creation of Bloomsbury Square. Wealthy estate owners parceled out plots of land and leased them to speculative builders, who in turn earned profits by renting the houses they built. The square, with its tall, terraced houses of narrow, rectangular rooms and shared central garden, was a new way of using urban space profitably and had much character besides.

This new style of town house was a great success. A "season" developed from October to June, when rural landowners and gentry came to London for business and pleasure. It was considered essential for the upper classes to own or rent a town house in the West End. Developers named their new streets and squares after royalty or nobility to increase their appeal.

Expansion in the West End coincided with worsening conditions in the old City. The early 18th century brought some of the highest death rates since records were first kept. An ever-present pool of infection was created by overseas trade and the mass of migrants. The widespread burning of coal blanketed the city in a cloud of smoke—the infamous London fog. This, coupled with the smells and refuge of the many industrial trades such as tallow-making and dye works, made inner-city living hazardous and unpleasant. While Londoners had traditionally lived above or near their work, those who were better-off began living away from their places of business.

LONDON'S POPULATION BOOM
London's growth was fueled entirely by migration. Most new-

comers came from within England. A massive influx of youths—estimated at 8,000 a year by 1700—came looking for employment in the capital. Many ended up living in poverty.

But there were also immigrants from abroad. Polish and German Jews settled in Whitechapel and Petticoat Lane, Huguenot refugees in Spitalfields. There were between 5,000 and 10,000 blacks in Georgian London, who worked as seamen, servants, or slaves. Foreign seamen from the East India Company's ships, called Lascars, formed another group.

A new social segregation arose in London. People of "quality"—that is, money and status—took up residence in the western parts of town, craftsmen remained in the city, and the poor and the working class occupied the city's eastern areas. The divide between the West End and East End survives to this day.

Addresses became important. While the appeal of many areas, such as Covent Garden and the Strand, rose and fell over time, the great Georgian estates remain among the most desirable places in London today.

The writer James Boswell had lodgings on Bond Street in the late 1760s. His remarks sum up the Georgian sentiments regarding a fashionable address:

> A genteel lodging in a good part of the town is absolutely necessary. Seeking a lodging was like seeking a wife. Sometimes I aimed at one or two guineas a week, like a rich lady of quality. Sometimes at one guinea, like a knight's daughter; and at last fixed on £22 a year, like the daughter of a good gentleman of moderate fortune. (Porter 133–134)

The 18th century also saw the construction of several new churches, following the Church Building Act of 1711. James Gibbs' St. Martin-in-the-Fields, which stands opposite Trafalgar Square, is a London landmark. Its design, incorporating a Greek temple with a soaring spire, was daring in its day, but many of New England's wooden churches are modeled after it.

Another master builder was Nicholas Hawksmoor, the protégé

of Sir Christopher Wren. His churches are some of London's finest, including Christ Church Spitalfields, St. George's Bloomsbury, St. Mary Woolnoth near Bank, St. Anne's Limehouse, St. Alfege in Greenwich, and St. George-in-the-East in Stepney.

CRIME AND CAPITAL PUNISHMENT

One event that was sure to draw crowds was a public execution. Crime was rife in Georgian London, reaching a peak in the mid-18th century. Unemployed soldiers and sailors discharged from foreign wars swelled the ranks of an often-violent criminal underclass. A combination of poverty and opportunity made thieves increasingly bold.

London's central, public gallows were set up at Tyburn in 1571, near where Marble Arch stands today. A stone plaque on the traffic island across from the cinema marks the general spot. The huge wooden structure could eliminate 21 condemned persons at one time.

There were more than 150 offenses, some shockingly petty, for which both men and women could be executed. About 1,200 Londoners were hanged in the 18th century. Those who were spared were usually transported to the colonies.

Public executions were supposed to be a deterrent, but the "hanging matches" or "Tyburn Fairs," as they were known, were treated as public holidays. Huge, rowdy crowds gathered for the execution of a famous criminal. Gingerbread, gin, and oranges were sold, and a grandstand was built for seating. Villains became heroes in their final hour, especially when they faced their fate with style. Highwaymen made for particularly romantic figures.

The three-mile procession from Newgate Prison lasted about two hours. The condemned, dressed in their finest clothes and carrying flowers, were driven on a cart, stopping at taverns along the way and often arriving drunk at the Tyburn Tree. There, with the rope round their necks, they were allowed a speech to the crowd before the executioner lashed his whip and the horse and cart pulled away, leaving the victims dangling from the gallows. Tyburn was dismantled in 1783.

By 1800, there were 18 prisons in London, of which the most infamous was Newgate. Originally a 12th-century jail in the city wall, it was rebuilt after the Great Fire into a true chamber of horror. The huge edifice had a grim facade, hung with chains. Inside, the dark, filthy cells and dungeons were foul-smelling and full of despair. Many prisoners starved or died of jail fever, a strain of typhoid.

Newgate was demolished in 1902, and replaced by the Central Criminal Court, better known as the Old Bailey, after the street on which it stands. Its dome is topped by a gilded statue of Justice holding sword and scales, but minus her usual blindfold. Many famous trials have taken place here, including that of Oscar Wilde.

The earliest literary heroine of Georgian times, Daniel Defoe's Moll Flanders, is no stranger to such scenes. Born in Newgate Prison, she is abandoned by her mother and through poverty falls into a life of crime. She becomes a thief and marries a handsome highwayman, only to find herself back in Newgate and bound for Tyburn.

> ... 'tis impossible to describe the terror of my mind ... when I looked round upon all the horrors of that dismal place. I looked on myself as lost, and that I had nothing to think of but of going out of the world, and that with the utmost infamy: the hellish noise, the roaring, swearing, and clamour, the stench and nastiness, and all the dreadful crowd of afflicting things that I saw there, joined together to make the place seem an emblem of hell itself, and a kind of an entrance into it.

DANIEL DEFOE

Defoe is often called the first true novelist in the English language. Born in London in 1660 and named Daniel Foe, he lived through the Great Plague and Great Fire as a boy. He wrote his first novel, *Robinson Crusoe*, at the age of 60, after a varied career as a merchant, political writer, journalist, and spy.

Defoe was himself no stranger to prison. He was once jailed for debt, and after publication of his satirical pamphlet *The Shortest Way with Dissenters* in 1702, he was fined and thrown into Newgate. He returned to Newgate to visit the highwayman Jack Sheppard, the subject of one of several Tyburn potboilers he wrote to supplement his income.

As a journalist, Defoe used several pen names. He changed his name to Defoe in 1695, which he felt would wield more political influence than his given name. In his lifetime, he wrote over 500 books, pamphlets, and journals on a variety of subjects. He advocated education for women, and a university, police force, and better street-lighting for London, all of which came to pass in Georgian times.

As a religious Nonconformist, Defoe was unable to live in the City and settled in Stoke Newington. A blue plaque marks the house on the corner of Church Street and what is now Defoe Road, where he wrote *Robinson Crusoe*. Published in 1719, it remains a popular tale to this day. *Moll Flanders* appeared in 1722, followed by *A Journal of the Plague Year,* and *Roxana.*

Until Defoe, stories were written as dramas or long poems. He was among the first to create ordinary characters in believable situations His use of clear, direct, and simple prose and first-person narrative was highly effective. In writing perceptively from a heroine's point of view, he was ahead of his time.

Defoe died in 1731 and was buried in Bunhill Fields, the graveyard for Dissenters. His tombstone was stolen in the 1870s, but was discovered in 1940 and is now in the Hackney Museum. A replica stands in Bunhill Fields, next to the graves of the poet and artist William Blake and the writer John Bunyan.

HENRY FIELDING

Vying with Defoe for the title of Father of the English Novel are two other writers, Samuel Richardson, who published *Pamela* in 1740, and Henry Fielding. Like Defoe, Fielding led a versatile life. Born in 1707 near Glastonbury and educated at Eton, he moved to London at the age of 20 and embarked on a career as a playwright. He became manager of the Haymarket Theatre and wrote over 25 dramatic pieces, but his topical satires ridiculing Robert Walpole's government led to the Stage Licensing Act of 1737, and its censorship spelled the end of his career.

Fielding then studied law at Middle Temple. He was called to the bar in 1740, but never found much success as a barrister. He fared better with his novels *Joseph Andrews* and *Jonathan Wild*, the latter based on a real-life criminal executed at Tyburn. His masterpiece, *Tom Jones*, was completed in 1748 and published the following year.

The lengthy and picaresque *Tom Jones* follows the eponymous hero from his lowly origins as a foundling through his adventures and fervent pursuit of his ladylove, Sophia, and finally to his elevation as a squire. Part of the novel is set in London. It was an instant success, selling 10,000 copies in its first year of publication. It is still acclaimed as one of the first and finest English comic novels.

In 1748, Fielding had also been appointed, along with his blind half-brother John, as magistrate of the new Bow Street Magistrates Court in Covent Garden. He moved into a nearby house on Bow Street, Covent Garden, and wrote his last novel, *Amelia*, which was also a success.

Fielding was greatly concerned with the level of crime in the capital. Writing in his role as a magistrate in 1751, in his *Enquiry into the Causes of the late Increase of Robbers*, he pointed to the layout of London, with its immense number of lanes, alleys, courts, and irregular buildings, as one of the main incentives to crime:

... had they been intended for the very Purpose of Conceal-
ment, they could scarce have been better contrived. Upon
such a View, the whole appears as a vast Wood or Forest, in
which a Thief may harbour with as great Security, as wild
Beasts do in the Deserts of Africa or Arabia. (Porter 183)

To combat crime, the Fieldings founded the Bow Street Runners in 1749, a team of constables that were the forerunners of
the Metropolitan Police. Numbering up to a dozen, they were
paid one guinea a week and received a share of the rewards for
successful prosecutions. A citywide police force was finally
established in 1829.

Bow Street Magistrates Court still stands on the corner of
Bow Street and Broad Court, although the adjoining police station was closed in 1989. Fielding fell ill in 1754 and went to
Portugal to recuperate, writing his last book, *Journal of a Voyage
to Lisbon*, on the way. He died there in 1754. Despite his distinguished life in London and his many contributions, there are no
statues or memorials honoring him.

The gin craze of the 1730s and 1740s also had the city in a
vice. About 6,000 dram shops sold the rough liquor for a penny
or two. By the 1740s per capita consumption averaged two
pints a week. Fielding's friend, William Hogarth, graphically
illustrated the misery of "mother's ruin" in his famous painting
Gin Lane, set in the squalor of St. Giles slum. Rising taxes and
prices finally curbed the gin mania by mid-century.

Hogarth was one of the finest painters of his day, but his skill
as an engraver enabled him to publish his works to a wide audience. He used satire and his sharp observation of human character to comment on what he called "modern moral subjects."
After his highly acclaimed portrayal of John Gay's *Beggar's
Opera*, he published a series of moral allegories including *Marriage à la Mode* and *The Rake's Progress*. These were based on literal scenes from London life.

Hogarth's prints were so successful that pirate copies began to
appear. To protect his works, he urged Parliament to pass the

Engravers' Act in 1735. This legislation, often called "Hogarth's Act," became the basis of all later copyright laws.

Charles Lamb, the essayist, later honored Hogarth with the comment "other pictures we look at—his prints we read". The artist's townhouse in Leicester Square is long gone, but his most famous prints are on display at Hogarth's House in Chiswick. This is the simple country house where he spent each summer from 1749 until his death in 1764. It is now located beside a busy main road, but in Hogarth's day it was surrounded by peaceful countryside.

DOCTOR SAMUEL JOHNSON

Georgian London inspired many outstanding writers, poets, painters, and musicians, from those like Hogarth, who were born there, to others such as George Frederick Handel, composer of *The Messiah*, who made London their home. The giant among them, and friend to them all, was the learned writer Dr. Samuel Johnson.

The inscription on a statue of Johnson, which stands outside his parish church, St. Clement Danes, facing his beloved Fleet Street, records the scope of his talents: Critic, Essayist, Philologist, Biographer, Wit, Poet, Moralist, Dramatist, Political Writer, and Talker. The great man himself, had he been asked to pick just one, would have probably chosen the last. He once referred to himself as "a man who loves to fold his legs and have out his talk ..."

Johnson is said to be the second-most quoted author in the English language after Shakespeare. More than 300 of his pithy sayings are listed in the Oxford Dictionary of Quotations. In his day, he was known for scholarly works such as *Lives of the Poets*, his edition of Shakespeare's play, and countless essays. His only novel, *Rasselas*, was written in a week to pay for his mother's funeral. Today he is remembered for producing the one book that no writer since can do without: the dictionary.

Born in Lichfield in 1709, Johnson came to London with his pupil and friend David Garrick, sharing one horse between them, in 1737. Working as a freelance journalist, he struggled financially until he was commissioned by a syndicate of booksellers to compile a definitive English Dictionary in 1749. The advance enabled him to rent the house at Gough Square, the only one of his 17 London residences to survive.

Dr. Johnson's House is now a fine museum dedicated to the man and his contemporaries. Working in the garret, standing at a long table surrounded by six assistants, he compiled the Dictionary in just three years. His was not the first, but previous dictionaries consisted of mere lists of words and synonyms. Johnson's was by far the most comprehensive dictionary of the English language to that date, and included definitions, etymologies, and various significations. A copy of the Dictionary, in two enormous volumes, has pride of place on the table in the parlor. It contains more than 40,000 words and 140,000 quotations.

With his boundless energy, Johnson also started his magazine *The Rambler* in 1750. It was published twice weekly for two years, and Johnson wrote every essay himself, save four. It became the foremost periodical of its day, outselling the *Tatler*, the *Spectator*, and the *Guardian*—whose content at the time covered moral and religious wisdom, a far cry from the worldly focus of these publications today.

The house, built around 1700, has been restored to its original condition. Its painted American pine paneling was brought back on trading ships from the colonies. Among the artifacts and furniture from Johnson's day is an unusual gout stool that served as his dining chair in Ye Olde Cock Tavern, which still stands on Fleet Street.

The gregarious Johnson knew many of the leading figures of the 18th century. His closest friend was the artist Sir Joshua Reynolds, who painted several portraits of him. These can be seen in the house. Together they founded The Club in 1764, a weekly gathering of like minds at the Turk's Head, which stood at 9 Gerrard Street in Soho. Others in his close circle included David Garrick, the greatest actor of the century, and the Irish-born writer

Oliver Goldsmith. When Goldsmith's landlady threatened to have him arrested for not paying the rent, Johnson came to his rescue by taking the manuscript of his novel, *The Vicar of Wakefield*, and selling it for £60.

Johnson also had many women friends, including the classical scholar Elizabeth Carter, the playwright and poet Hannah More, the novelist Charlotte Lennox, and Mrs. Elizabeth Montagu, known as the Queen of the Blue Stockings for her women's salons. Georgian society did not discourage women from writing and intellectual pursuits in the way that the later Victorians did. Yet Johnson never remarried following the death in 1752 of his beloved wife, Tetty.

Undoubtedly the key figure in Johnson's life was James Boswell, the Scotsman who became his biographer. They met in Davies Bookshop in Covent Garden in 1763, which was located at 8 Russell Street, east of the piazza. In recent times, the building housed Boswell's Coffee Shop and is now Cafe Valerie.

Johnson was a physical as well as an intellectual giant, six feet tall with broad, powerful shoulders. A childhood illness had left him blind in one eye. Boswell wrote of their first meeting:

> Mr. Johnson is a man of most dreadful appearance. He is a very big man, is troubled with sore eyes ... is very slovenly in his dress and speaks with a most uncouth voice. Yet his great knowledge and strength of expression command vast respect and render him excellent company. He has great humour and is a worthy man.... I shall mark what I remember of his conversation. (Davies 233)

And so he did. Boswell became Johnson's friend and traveling companion, and made notes of his conversations for the next 20 years. After Johnson died, he used these and other firsthand accounts and letters to write *The Life of Johnson* in 1791. It is considered to be the first modern biography.

Thanks to Boswell, the life and words of this enthusiastic Londoner have been preserved. Johnson was buried at Westminster

Abbey, and is commemorated in an annual service there on December 18. There is also a statue of him in St. Paul's.

Johnson maintained that "there is nothing which has yet been contrived by man, by which so much happiness is produced as by a good tavern" (Tames 107). In early Georgian times, London was estimated to have 447 taverns, as well as 207 inns, 5,875 beer houses and 8,659 brandy shops. Two of Johnson's favorites are popular watering holes today.

Ye Olde Cheshire Cheese on Fleet Street was Johnson's local, just a stone's throw from his house on Gough Square. Its entrance is down a dark passageway, Wine Office Court, and its interior retains its 18th-century atmosphere of small rooms with fireplaces, wooden benches, and bare floorboards. Many 19th-century literati made pilgrimages here, including Charles Dickens, Mark Twain, William Makepeace Thackeray, and Arthur Conan Doyle.

The Anchor, on Bankside, was formerly connected to a brewery run by Johnson's great friends, Henry and Hester Thrale. It is one of London's best Thames-side pubs. Though much of the interior has been modernized, two small side bars, dedicated to Dr. Johnson and the Thrales, have been preserved with their original dark wood paneling, wooden beams, and fireplace, as they were in Johnson's day.

Coffeehouses also became the fashionable places for socializing in Georgian London. The first had opened in Cornhill in 1652. When George I came to the throne, there were around 500 in the city. Individual venues were noted for particular customers, a gathering of minds according to profession or politics. One of their greatest attractions was the variety of newspapers available to read there.

Londoners enjoyed outings to the parks or the numerous pleasure gardens that were built in Georgian times. Fairs were very popular. Mayfair is named after one of the oldest, which took place there. These annual events lasted between two and six weeks, and featured acrobats, sideshows, wild animals, and all manner of entertainment. In *Moll Flanders,* the heroine attends Bartholomew Fair, which ran from medieval times until 1850, when the new Smithfield meat market was built on its site.

LITERARY LONDON

Since Restoration times, Fleet Street was associated with literary London. John Dryden, the first Poet Laureate, lived in Salisbury Court and Fetter Lane. Dr. Johnson had 10 addresses in a row near Fleet Street.

Soho was another enclave of writers and artists. The former hunting fields—its name was a hunting cry: "so, ho!"—had been developed in the late 17th century. Dryden lived there at the end of his life, on Gerrard Street, the same street where The Club would later meet. Joshua Reynolds lived nearby in Great Newport Street. The poet Percy Bysshe Shelley lived briefly at 15 Poland Street in 1811, after he was expelled from Oxford for distributing the pamphlet *The Necessity of Atheism*

The mystical poet and painter William Blake was born in Soho, above his father's hosiery shop in Broadwick Street in 1757. After running a print shop next door to his family home, he moved to nearby Poland Street. During his six years there he wrote *The Marriage of Heaven and Hell,* and other poems. His paintings can be seen in the Tate Britain art gallery. He died in 1827 and was buried in Bunhill Fields.

London's expansion occurred in fits and starts. There was no grand plan, no stately public buildings set off by great vistas or impressive thoroughfares. The city was developed over a wide area by gradually adding one addition to another to another.

A century after Bloomsbury Square was created, building in the area resumed with the creation of Bedford Square, Fitzroy Square, Tavistock Square, and Brunswick and Mecklenburgh Square between 1776 and 1807. All of these would later become the stomping grounds of Virginia Woolf and the Bloomsbury Group in the early 1900s.

Brunswick Square was immortalized in Jane Austen's *Emma,* when Isabella Knightley sang its praises:

> Our part of London is so very superior to most others!—You
> must not confound us with London in general, my dear sir.
> The neighbourhood of Brunswick Square is very different
> from all the rest. We are so very airy! ... (Porter 137)

Sadly, Brunswick Square was destroyed in World War II, and
many of the other Bloomsbury Squares were also badly damaged. Bedford Square is the only complete Georgian square
remaining. Its houses were solidly built of brick, with fanlights
and blocks of white Coade stone decorating the doorways. The
central house on each side is covered in white stucco.

Jane Austen is one of the most popular and best-known
Georgian writers. Though not a Londoner, she was an occasional visitor to the city. She was born in 1775 and eventually
settled in Chawton, Hampshire, where she wrote most of her
major novels, which include *Sense and Sensibility* and *Pride and
Prejudice.* Though set mainly in the countryside, her books contain London scenes.

When in the city, Austen stayed with her brother Henry, who
lived on Henrietta Street in Covent Garden, above the offices of
his banking house. Shopping was the highlight of her expedi-
tions to London, and she records buying a white-flowered cap
and twenty yards of striped poplin at the mercers Layton &
Shear's, located in the same street.

By the 1780s, Oxford Street had surpassed Cheapside as
London's main shopping street. Built over the old Roman road
leading west, it was named for Edward Harley, 2nd Earl of
Oxford. Today, with tatty boutiques and souvenir shops at one
end and leading department stores on the other, this two-mile
stretch is one of the busiest shopping streets in the world.

London became the center of fashion in Georgian times.
Markets gave way to chic shops in the West End. Defoe noted
how, for the first time, tradesmen invested heavily in shop fit-
tings and lavish window displays. From cutlery to jewelry,
London provenance was the mark of prestige for luxury goods.
Josiah Wedgewood opened showrooms for his china in

Grosvenor and St. James squares. Thomas Chippendale opened workshops in Covent Garden. Famous names from Hamley's toy shop to Christie's auction house all opened in the 1760s to 1780s.

In the 1750s and 60s, the buildings were removed from London Bridge and two new bridges were built at Blackfriars and Westminster. They were instrumental in the expansion of London south of the river. In another move to provide easier access for the growing volume of traffic, the City gates were torn down in the 1760s.

In 1801, Britain held its first official census. It showed London and its environs containing 900,000 people, 10 percent of the country's population. By the second census in 1811, it

Mrs. Radcliffe: London's Queen of Terror

No discussion of literary London could be complete without Ann Radcliffe, the queen and mother of the Gothic. She was born in Holborn, London, in 1764; her husband managed The English *Chronicle*, and she wrote to amuse herself in his absence. Her first novel to see real success was *The Romance of the Forest* (1791); its richly evocative prose, peerless gloom, and improbable horrors charmed her female readers. London was desperate for *The Mysteries of Udolpho* (1794) and even more so for Radcliffe's greatest and final work, *The Italian* (1796). She was successful enough to be lampooned by a teenaged Jane Austen, only ten years her junior.

The Gothic novel had "come out" in mid-century with Horace Walpole and others, and by Radcliffe's time it had become a genre for women. It was Radcliffe who mastered the themes we now associate with the Gothic: innocent heroines trapped in vast, dark, unknowable spaces, menaced by unseen foes and ancient horrors, persecuted by patriarchs, uncovering ghastly secrets. Her influence on later writers was vast.

had surpassed the one million mark, making it the largest city in the western world.

London remained the greatest port in the world. Trade tripled between 1720 and 1800. The cargoes of spices, tea, coffee, silks, and ivory from seagoing vessels was outstripped by food, coal, and timber barges supplying necessities to the capital. To counter the congestion at the ports, new docks spread east along the Thames in early 1800s.

Despite the drain of the Napoleonic Wars (1803–1815), London acquired the infrastructure of a modern city in the early 19th century. Police and fire brigades were established, the first gas street lighting was installed in the West End, and streets were paved. The National Gallery, the University of London, and five new hospitals were founded. The city's first public transportation systems took shape with new roads, coach, and omnibus services. The days of commuting from outlying villages (now suburbs) had begun.

In 1820, George IV acceded to the throne. He had effectively ruled as Prince Regent since 1812, when his father's illness rendered him helpless to fulfill his role. A man of style and extravagance, he was the only king from the House of Hanover to make his mark on the city.

George's favorite architect was John Nash. Between 1817 and 1823, he created the elegant Regent Street, which swept up from the prince's residence at Carlton House, through Piccadilly Circus, and north to a new royal park, Regent's Park. Regent Street became highly fashionable, rivaling Bond Street as a source of luxury goods. It also served the purpose of dividing bohemian Soho from wealthy Mayfair.

Lord George Byron, the most notorious of the Romantic poets, symbolized a Mayfair man. Born in nearby Marylebone, he inherited his title from his great uncle. He was living at 8 St. James Street when, after the publication of *Childe Harold* in 1812, he awoke one morning and found himself famous. Later he moved into splendid bachelor apartments at Albany in Piccadilly.

Byron embraced all the gentleman's delights of Mayfair, especially its parties, and was a rakish character on the social scene. He loved London and called it "a damned place to be sure, but the only one in the world (at least in the English world) for fun" (Porter 134).

Despite his literary success, Byron was widely condemned for his dissolute lifestyle. He left London for travels in Europe, and when he died in Greece in 1824, at the age of 36, he was refused burial at Westminster Abbey. He was later given a plaque in Poet's Corner.

North London was home to two other Romantic poets. John Keats was born in London in 1795, the son of a livery-stable manager. He studied medicine at Guy's Hospital and became a member of the Apothecaries Guild, but was persuaded to give up medicine for poetry by his friend, the journalist Leigh Hunt, who introduced him to Shelley and Byron. By the time Keats moved to Hampstead in 1817, he had published two books of poetry. He first lodged at a house in Well Walk, and nursed his brother—who died from consumption the following year.

The poet then moved to a house in Wentworth Place, now called Keats Grove, which had just been built on the edge of the Heath. Inspired by the peacefulness and by his love for the girl next door—Fanny Brawne, to whom he became engaged—he wrote some of his finest works. *Ode to a Nightingale* was written under a plum tree in the garden. In 1820, however, Keats too fell ill with consumption. Seeking a warm climate, he went to Italy—where he died the following year, at age 25.

Keats's House and the Brawne house are now a museum honoring the poet. It has been beautifully restored and features early-19th-century decoration and furniture. Among the mementoes are Keats's love letters to Fanny, her engagement ring, a bust of the poet, and first editions of his poetry.

By the mid-18th century, Hampstead had established itself as a haven for writers and intellectuals, a reputation it enjoys to this day. In its time, Leigh Hunt's home in the Vale of Heath was one of London's most famous literary houses. He moved there in 1816, having spent two years in prison for libel after referring to the Prince Regent as "a fat Adonis of fifty." Shelley, Keats, and Samuel Taylor Coleridge were frequent visitors.

Burgh House contains exhibits on Hampstead's beginnings as a spa village in 1701, and the literary residents of Well Walk, including Keats and D.H. Lawrence. One room is dedicated to the great Georgian painter John Constable, who painted from Hampstead Heath. Spaniards Inn is an 18th-century coaching inn said to have been frequented by the highwayman Dick Turpin. Literary patrons included Byron, Shelley, and Keats.

On the opposite side of Hampstead Heath, the village of Highgate was the last home of Coleridge. Born in 1772, the poet had come to London as a boy to attend Christ Hospital School, where Hunt and the writer Charles Lamb also studied. He lived at 10 King Street in Covent Garden from 1798 to 1801 and worked as a journalist. In 1798, he published the first edition of *Lyrical Ballads* with William Wordsworth, which established a new freedom of form in English poetry. It opened with Coleridge's *Rime of the Ancient Mariner*, one of his most famous works.

Coleridge became addicted to opium, which had been prescribed for his neuralgic and rheumatic pains. In 1823, he moved to The Grove in Highgate, lodging at No. 3 in the home of Dr. James Gillman, who tried to help him cure his addiction. He had a large attic bedroom with a splendid view across the Heath. He was a popular figure in the village and a great conversationalist, and received many distinguished visitors. Coleridge lived at the Grove until his death in 1834. The house was later owned by the author J.B. Priestly, and is one of the few in London to bear two blue plaques.

Georgian London attracted foreign tourists for the first time, who came to marvel at its elegant squares, its bustling river front, its cornucopia of shops, and its frenetic energy. One literary visitor in particular found great success in London. Born in New York, Washington Irving was the son of a British merchant who fought with the rebels during the American

Revolution. He came to London after the war, and in 1820 published his witty observations of the city as *The Sketch Book*. It was highly praised on both sides of the Atlantic, making Irving the first American writer to gain a reputation outside his own country.

By the end of the Georgian era, London had acquired a new landscape, a new social structure, and all the trappings of a great metropolis. The city's foremost champion, Samuel Johnson, spoke for many residents and visitors alike when he observed: "The happiness of London is not to be conceived but by those who have been in it."

CHAPTER SIX

Victorian London

The 19th century was an era of tremendous social change. A decade after London's first official census in 1801, its population had reached one million. By 1901, it was nearly seven million. The Victorian age is named after Britain's longest reigning monarch, Queen Victoria. She came to the throne a month after her 18th birthday in 1837, taking over from the last Hanoverian king, William IV, her uncle. She ruled until her death in 1901.

A year after her coronation Victoria fell in love with her German cousin, Prince Albert of Saxe-Coburg-Gotha, and they married. The moral and financial extravagance of the Georgian years had produced a backlash and Victoria was the perfect ruler to usher in a new era of respectability. Victoria and Albert, with their happy marriage and nine children, set a new example for the nation. Family values, home life, and morality became the new social order. Some people, however, saw the Victorians' strict code of behavior as unnecessarily repressive.

During the Victorian era, Britain's empire spread round the globe. As commerce mushroomed, London's docklands became the warehouse of the world. Great feats of engineering and advances in manufacturing were also achieved.

BRITAIN'S RISING PROFILE

Britain's new international status was celebrated with the Great Exhibition of 1851. The brainchild of Prince Albert, it saw the building of the Crystal Palace in Hyde Park, a showcase for a vast range of exhibits demonstrating the "works of industry of all nations." It was the first world fair. Although the Crystal Palace was dismantled afterwards, the proceeds from the exhibition were used to purchase land for new London museums, including the Science Museum and the Victoria and Albert Museum.

In the 19th century, London finally gained the great cultural institutions that make a world-class city. Its first national collection had gone on show with the opening of the National Gallery in 1824. This was followed by the National Portrait Gallery and Tate Gallery in 1856 and 1897, respectively. Although the British Museum had been founded in 1753, the magnificent neoclassical building that houses its collections today was not completed until 1050.

Thomas Carlyle and others founded the London Library in 1841, but membership was by private subscription. Within a decade, the Public Libraries Act opened the way for circulating libraries to be built, though these didn't really take off until private benefactors such as Andrew Carnegie and Henry Tate spurred their development. Another major change in public education occurred in 1870 when elementary school became compulsory for the first time.

The dawning of the industrial age brought immense changes throughout Britain and especially in its capital city. As more and more people streamed in, London's overcrowded slums grew and pollution increased. Outbreaks of cholera, smallpox, and other diseases killed thousands of the poor. Industrial progress brought economic progress for the middle and upper classes, but miserable conditions for the underclass of low-paid factory workers. The theories of Karl Marx later in the century arose out of this great divide.

In many ways, the Victorians were progressive in terms of urban modernization. London's public transportation network was established, with buses, railways, and the building of the first underground rail line, the fledgling Tube network. The city acquired sewers, street lighting, and the first public toilets (albeit for men only), as well as proper police and fire brigades.

Attempts at addressing London's social ills were less than adequate. Workhouses were established to help the most destitute, but these were little more than new dens of misery. The demolition of slums in the city center only displaced them to outlying areas, particularly the East End. Individuals such as Captain Thomas Coram, who was so disturbed by the number of abandoned babies and children on the streets that he set up the Foundling Hospital for their care, did more to alleviate the suffering than the city or state.

THE LITERARY WORLD OF CHARLES DICKENS

More than any other writer, Charles Dickens conveyed the atmosphere of Victorian London. His keen observations of characters and language, the social backdrops, and the wide discrepancies between rich and poor tell us more than any historian or journalist of the time. His works are intricately linked with London, both through location and experience. His graphic images of workhouses, prisons, slums, dark alleyways, and the ever-present fog have formed some of our strongest impressions of Victorian London.

Dickens wrote the definitive London novel of Victorian times in *Oliver Twist*, with his portrait of its dirty, crime-infested streets, and the desperate, inner-city poor. Other primarily London novels are *Bleak House* and *Little Dorrit*, and his classic story *A Christmas Carol*.

The entire city was his literary stage. In the setting of his vibrant and complex metropolis, his caricatures and labyrinthine plots are believable. London doubled in size during his lifetime, yet in his novels it appears remarkably compact. Like Pepys before him, Dickens traversed the city on foot and knew its many quarters intimately.

Dickens is often seen as a social crusader, because of his vivid and moving descriptions of the squalor of London's poor areas, and his compassion for his characters and their human failings. He wrote from personal experience, having been deeply scarred by his own childhood poverty. He also portrayed the loneliness and anonymity of the city. The fog is a frequently used metaphor in his works, with characters making dramatic escapes by boat and appearing and disappearing suddenly in the gloom.

Dickens struck a chord with his Victorian readers who valued family life and the virtue of women. Like the Queen, he had nine children (another had died in infancy). The triumph of moral qualities and the evils of degeneracy were common themes in his writing.

Dickens wrote with great compassion and intelligence. He regularly attacked social evils, injustice, and hypocrisy in his works. As an accomplished novelist, he succeeded in getting his message across not by preaching, but by exposing through his descriptions. He captured the contradictions of Victorian times, and of London itself. By raising awareness of the miserable conditions of the poor and the absurdity of the law, he became an influential spokesman and one of the great forces for good in his times.

George Orwell wrote that Dickens "seems to have succeeded in attacking everybody and antagonizing nobody" (Gumbel 113).

Dickens was also a great comic writer. His novels were first published in installments in monthly magazines, and he enjoyed a greater popularity in his own lifetime than any English author before him. The number of his novels sold today shows the genius of his characterizations and the delight readers still take in his work. Dickens's novels are as brimming with life and vitality as was Victorian London itself.

Charles Dickens was born in Landport, Hampshire, where his father John was a clerk in the Navy-Pay Office. After a happy early childhood at Chatham on the Kent coast, he moved to London when he was 11. Because of his father's growing financial difficulties, the family of eight crowded into a small house in Bayham Street in Camden Town.

The Serial and the Triple-Decker

The literature of Victorian London is remarkable for its sheer volume. A rage for fiction in the early part of the century had borne legions of self-styled authors. Back-room publishers offered half-profits schemes, funding publication and splitting with authors whatever profits might accrue.

Monthly serials like those of Dickens and Thackeray were affordable and thus universally popular, but they were difficult to write. The next "number" was never guaranteed, and any hint of a plotline had to be reinforced for years. It was Dickens who broke this pattern, with *Dombey and Son* (1846–1848): his publisher bought the whole thing up front. At last, Dickens could plan his story before writing it.

The middle-class market was dominated by the three-volume novel, or "triple-decker." These were often too costly to own, so the circulating libraries rented them by volume. Huge profits resulted, and soon publishers would produce nothing else. Writers such as Trollope and the Brontës had to lard their work with dialogue and description simply to be published. According to one observer, "[W]ith the exception of the works of fifteen or twenty authors, no individual ever now dreams of purchasing a novel for his own reading. The only copies bought are for the circulating libraries." [James Grant, *The Great Metropolis: The Rise of Urban Britain* (1837)] The triple-decker format is responsible for a great deal of unreadable Victorian fiction.

Dickens's first London home was a 25 minute walk north of the river. As a boy, he often walked across the city to visit his godfather at Limehouse. The teeming life of the capital, from rich to poor, caught his imagination. The docks also held a great fascination for him.

Limehouse, the docklands area east of Wapping, was named after medieval limekilns here that were used to make quick-lime for pottery and building mortar. In the 17th century, it became a center for shipbuilding and mariners. Dickens went there regularly to visit his godfather, a sail-maker who lived in Newell Street. The little Grapes pub on Narrow Street became the model for the Six Jolly Fellowship Porters in *Our Mutual Friend*. Dickens described it as "a tavern of dropsical appearance ... long settled down into a state of hale infirmity. In its whole constitution it had not a straight floor, and hardly a straight line; but it has outlasted ... many a sprucer public-house" (Dickens, *Our Mutual Friend* 55). And indeed it has. The Grapes is one of the most characterful pubs in London, retaining its atmospheric interior and crazy wooden veranda "impending" over the river (Tagholm 155).

Limehouse was London's first Chinatown, home to the Asian seamen who came on trading ships from the Far East. It was sensationalized by many Victorian novelists and journalism as teeming with gambling and opium dens. "Down by the docks," Dickens wrote, "the shabby undertaker's shop will bury you for next to nothing after the Malay or Chinaman has stabbed you for nothing at all" (Humphreys 252). The opening scene in *The Mystery of Edwin Drood* takes place in an opium den there.

At the age of 12, Dickens was sent to work at Warren's Blacking Factory alongside the Thames, below the Strand at Hungerford Stairs. He had a monotonous job for 12 hours a day, labeling jars of boot polish. Villiers Street, which slopes down to the Victoria Embankment beside Charing Cross Station, now covers the old site of the Hungerford Market, where the factory was located along the present walkway called The Arches. It manifests in *David Copperfield* as "a crazy, tumbledown old house abutting the river and literally overrun with rats," where the hero works as a laborer.

Dickens's plight worsened when his father was thrown into jail for debt. From the blacking factory, he had to cross Southwark Bridge to visit his family in Marshalsea Prison. The misery of those years never left his mind. He called it "the secret agony of my soul." It enabled him to create the sense and feeling of what it was like to be poor in his readers' minds.

BOROUGH, SOUTHWARK

Borough, in Southwark, has some of the most Dickensian associations in London. He used it many times as a setting in his novels, particularly *Little Dorrit, David Copperfield,* and *The Pickwick Papers.* There are streets here named for Dickens's characters, including Weller Street and David Copperfield Street.

Since medieval times, Borough had been a stagecoach terminus, and travelers would gather at its coaching inns to await the next coach to their destination. The inns were popular watering holes for the locals as well. In the 17th century, the journalist Thomas Dekker described Borough High Street as "a continued alehouse with not a shop to be seen between." In *The Pickwick Papers,* Dickens refers to them as "Great, rambling, queer old places they are, with galleries and passages and stairways, wide enough and antiquated enough to furnish materials for a hundred ghost stories" (Dickens, *Pickwick Papers* 126).

The George Inn is the only one of these galleried inns to survive in London. It is in here that Tip writes a begging letter in *Little Dorritt.* Set in the cobbled George Inn Yard, down an alleyway off Borough High Street, the George Inn dates back to the 16th century, though the building was rebuilt in 1677 after a fire. It originally comprised three galleried branches surrounding the courtyard. The one long building that remains has kept its historic facade. Inside are a series of cozy, connecting rooms and bars in the traditional tavern fashion. There are outdoor tables in the pleasant courtyard and occasional entertainment in summer.

The parallel White Hart Yard recalls the White Hart Inn, torn down in 1889, where Mr. Pickwick meets Sam Weller in the *Pickwick Papers*. A plaque at 3 Borough High Street marks the site of the Queen's Head Inn, owned by John Harvard before he left for America to set up his distinguished university.

Southwark was also notorious for its seven prisons. The worst, Marshalsea, also stood on Borough High Street. This was where Dickens's father was jailed for debt in 1824. Dickens used this squalid setting as the birthplace of Little Dorritt. It was demolished in 1842 and all that remains is one brick wall, which can be seen from St. George's Gardens, off Tabard Street. The Clink Prison, another Southwark prison mentioned in *Barnaby Rudge*, is now a museum.

To be near his family, who lived with their father in the prison, the lonely Dickens found lodgings in a back attic on Lant Street (now gone). The grim atmosphere of the prison and the surrounding area made a lasting impression. St. George's workhouse, which is thought to have stood nearby on Mint Street, may have been the model for the workhouse in *Oliver Twist*.

On the corner of Borough High Street and Long Lane is St. George-the-Martyr church, where Little Dorritt is christened and later married. It was built in the 1730s. A stained glass window behind the altar commemorates a scene from the novel in which she spends a night sleeping in the vestry.

Borough Market, on the opposite side of the street, has operated as a fruit and vegetable market since medieval times. The covered market building under the railway arches, built in 1851, and its surrounding back streets have a splendid Victorian atmosphere. There is a gourmet food market here—Fridays and Saturdays are the best times to visit.

On the west side of London Bridge is a stairway known as "Nancy's Steps." This is where Nancy tells Rose Maylie Oliver Twist's story. In the novel, the meeting takes place on the same side of the bridge as St. Saviour's Church, which was the name of Southwark Cathedral until the early 20th century.

A walk along Tooley Street leads to the dockland wharves of Bermondsey. The area east of Mill Street was called the "capital of cholera" in Victorian times. St. Saviour's Dock, a pirate lair in the 18th century, is where Bill Sikes meets his fate in *Oliver Twist.* Dickens called it Jacob's Island, a place with "every imaginable sign of desolation and neglect ..." (Dickens, *Oliver Twist* 431).

When his father was released from prison, Dickens was able to return to school for three years before starting work as a law clerk at the age of 15. He did not like the job, and it bred in him an irreverence for the legal profession and proceedings that he would carry for the rest of his life.

The Inns of Court, described in detail in *Bleak House,* have been the center of the English legal system since the early 13th century. Aspiring barristers—lawyers who are qualified to argue cases before the High Court—must study at one of the four Inns: Gray's Inn, Lincoln's Inn, Inner Temple, or Middle Temple. Their appeal for visitors is in the atmosphere of the quiet courtyards and surviving old buildings, which are oases of calm in the busy city.

This phrase from Martin Chuzzlewit, "Brilliantly the Temple Fountain sparkled in the sun and laughingly its liquid music played," describes a scene that has hardly changed in hundreds of years (Dickens, *Martin Chuzzlewit* 698).

Dickens worked at Gray's Inn in 1827–28. It received bomb damage in World War II and much of it has been rebuilt, but the original chambers where Dickens worked in building No. 1 survived intact. The 16th-century wooden screen in the Hall has been preserved, and there is some original 17th-century stained glass in the chapel. The garden in the back was first planted in 1606 by Francis Bacon. Gray's Inn features in several of Dickens's stories and it is described by Mr. Pickwick as "curious little nooks in a great place, like London, these old Inns are" (*Pickwick Papers* 294).

Lincoln's Inn escaped damage in the Blitz and remains the prettiest of the Inns of Court. The 15th-century Old Hall, a former lawyers' residence in the Old Buildings Courtyard, is where the case *Jarndyce v. Jarndyce* was set in *Bleak House.* In this novel, Dickens portrays the bureaucracy, expense, and injustice surrounding legal suits, and their innocent victims. Farther along is the 16th-century gatehouse with its diamond-patterned brickwork.

Nearby is the grassy square known as Lincoln's Inn Fields, a place for grazing cattle in London's early days. The house at No. 58 belonged to Dickens's friend John Forster, who later wrote his biography. It was the model for Mr. Tulkinghorn's house in *Bleak House,* where "lawyers lie like maggots in nuts" (Dickens, *Bleak House* 129). The area is also mentioned in *David Copperfield.*

Near Gray's Inn on Chancery Lane, a large redbrick building has replaced the old Furnival's Inn, one of the nine Inns of Chancery that served as lawyers' offices and student quarters. Dickens lived here with his wife Catherine in the first year of their marriage, just after the first installments of *The Pickwick Papers* were published in 1836. Their eldest child was born here. John Westlock, in *Martin Chuzzlewit,* also has chambers here. There is a bust commemorating Dickens inside the courtyard.

The quiet atmosphere of the little square behind the half-timbered Staple Inn, nearby at the top of Gray's Inn Road, was described by Dickens in *The Mystery of Edwin Drood* as "one of those nooks, the turning into which out of the clashing street, imparts to the relieved pedestrian the sensation of having put cotton in his ears, and velvet soles on his boots" (Dickens, *The Mystery of Edwin Drood* 92). It also features in *Bleak House.*

At Lincoln's Inn Fields on Portsmouth Street is the Old Curiosity Shop. It is not certain whether it actually was the inspiration for Dickens's novel, but it is a rare 16th-century building and the oldest shop in London. The overhanging upper floor was typical of buildings before the Great Fire.

Disillusioned with the law, Dickens turned to journalism. He became a freelance court reporter and also covered Parliamentary debates. He was drawn to the theater and considered a career as an actor. During his brief office life, he was known as a great mimic of street characters, something that must later have served him well in his writing. He had even secured an audition at the Lyceum Theatre, but was laid up with a bad cold when the day of the audition arrived. Before he could rearrange it, he found his true calling.

Dickens was first published in *The Monthly Magazine*, located at 166 Fleet Street. He recalled slipping the manuscript for his story "A Dinner at Poplar Walk"—"with fear and trembling into a dark letterbox, in a dark office, up a dark court in Fleet Street" (Tagholm 147). When it was accepted, he never looked back.

The letterbox was on the office's side door in Johnson's Court. This alleyway lies parallel to Wine Office Court and the entrance to Ye Olde Cheshire Cheese, one of Dickens's favorite pubs and Dr. Samuel Johnson's old watering hole. Dickens's chosen spot is said to have been the table to the right of the fireplace in the ground floor room, across from the bar. It is thought to be the model for the Fleet Street pub where Sydney Carton and Charles Darnay dine in *A Tale of Two Cities*.

Like all London writers, Dickens was drawn to Fleet Street. As a boy, he visited Mrs. Salmon's Waxworks in the old timbered inn that once housed Prince Henry's Room, and David Copperfield brings Peggotty here to see the perspiring wax figures. Across the road is St. Dunstan-in-the-West Church, with its ancient clock tower dating from just after the Great Fire. It was the chiming of the bell by Gog and Magog—the figures depicted on either side of the clock—that woke Scrooge in *A Christmas Carol*. Another Christmas story, *The Chimes*, was dedicated to the church.

While still a law reporter Dickens began publishing *Sketches by Boz*—his pen name—in the *Morning Chronicle*. Here he met his future wife, Catherine Hogarth, whose father was the editor of the *Evening Chronicle*. In 1836, they married at St. Luke's Church in Chelsea. The wedding took place two days after the first publication of *The Pickwick Papers*.

St. Luke's, completed in 1834, was one of the first neo-Gothic churches built in London. Its nave, 60 feet in height, is the tallest of any parish church in the city. The tower is 142 feet high. The church's first rector was the father of Charles Kingsley, who wrote *The Water Babies* and other novels. The interior has changed since Dickens's wedding day, having been altered in the late 19th century. If the church is locked, big glass double doors in the foyer provide a look inside.

After a slow start, sales of *The Pickwick Papers* grew to 40,000 copies a month. Pickwick hats, coats, and canes became popular and today have come to be associated with eccentric Englishness. The book's success enabled Dickens to move his family from their small rooms in Furnival's Inn to the early 19th-century terraced house at 48 Doughty Street.

Of all Dickens's London homes, this is the only one that has survived. He lived here from 1837 to 1839. It was here that he finished the last installments of *The Pickwick Papers* and wrote all of *Oliver Twist* and *Nicholas Nickleby*. His two oldest daughters, Mary (Mamie) and Kate, were born here. Kate revisited the house as an old lady, when it became the Dickens House Museum in 1925.

One of the great tragedies of Dickens's life occurred here not long after the family had moved in. Mary Hogarth, his sister-in-law who lived with them, died in his arms from a sudden heart seizure. She was only 17. Dickens felt her loss deeply and wore her ring all his life. The angelic characters of Rose Maylie in *Oliver Twist* and Little Nell in *The Old Curiosity Shop*, who also dies young, are based on Mary.

The museum provides a fascinating look at Dickens's life. Some of the rooms are laid out as they were when he lived there. Others contain a variety of furniture and artifacts—from the quill pen used to write *Edwin Drood*, to his letters, to first editions of his works.

Even the hallways are full of Dickens memorabilia. In the entrance hall is a small window frame from Dickens's room in the attic at Bayham Street, the only relic of his life in Camden Town. Victorian prints by Fred Barnard depicting characters and scenes from his novels line the stairwells. In the hallway outside the Drawing Room is the original Little Wooden Midshipman, a trade sign Dickens spotted in Leadenhall Street, which appeared as that of Sol Gills in *Dombey and Son*.

The house contains several replicas of portraits of Dickens (the originals are in the National Portrait Gallery). The one in the dining room by Daniel Maclise shows the author at the age when he lived here, and was used as the frontispiece for *Nicholas Nickleby*. In another by Samuel Drummond, this one in the Morning Room, Dickens appears quite the dandy: a successful young man with flowing hair, fashionably dressed—a stark contrast to the downtrodden subjects of his writings, or the later portraits of him with a bushy goatee.

The Morning Room has displays on Dickens's family, particularly his wife Catherine. Their marriage was not a happy one, and in 1858—after more than 20 years together—they separated. By then, Dickens had begun his long liaison with the actress Ellen Ternan.

In the Study, where he wrote his famous novels, Dickens's favorite writing desk is displayed in a glass case. The Drawing Room is decorated as it was when he lived there. A collection of prints by William Hogarth that Dickens owned in his later years still hangs on the walls. Unlike most Victorians, Dickens liked the light and had lots of mirrors in his rooms to brighten them up.

Displays in the Mary Hogarth Room reveal Dickens's sideline in dramatics. Dickens revived his interest in theater in the 1840s. He started an amateur theatrical group, which he managed. He was also a very good actor and performed in many of the plays, as did his friend Wilkie Collins, author of *The Moonstone*, regarded by many as the first English detective novel. The troupe toured and performed twice before the Queen.

The dialogue in Dickens's novels is highly theatrical, so his interest in acting is not surprising. Photographs and playbills advertising his performances are on display. Later in his life, Dickens adapted his own novels for reading from the stage. He gave public readings, some 600 or 700 in all, and made four tours, including two to America.

Dickens moved to Marylebone late in 1839. His house at 1 Devonshire Terrace, Regent's Park, is now gone, but there is a bas relief of several of his characters on the site. During his twelve years here he wrote *David Copperfield* and *The Old Curiosity Shop*, among other works. The area's squares were home to his more well-to-do characters, such as Mr. Dombey and Mr. Podsnap.

In 1851, Dickens moved back to Bloomsbury, to Tavistock House on the east side of Tavistock Square. The house was large enough for him to stage his amateur theatrical productions. He lived there until 1860, and wrote *Bleak House* and *A Tale of Two Cities*. A blue plaque on the British Medical Association building commemorates the site where the house once stood.

The Bloomsbury area surrounding Dickens's house on Doughty Street is also rich in fictional associations. Charles Ketterbell, a character in "The Bloomsbury Christening" in *Sketches by Boz*, is commemorated by a plaque at Nos. 13 and 14 Great Russell Street, a rare honor for a fictional character. St. George's Church on Bloomsbury Way, built by Nicholas Hawksmoor, also features in the story.

Two other Bloomsbury houses are associated with Dickens's family: 22 Cleveland Street, where they lived above a greengrocer's shop, and 25 Fitzroy Street, a later residence. Dickens was a strong supporter of charitable institutions, including Captain Coram's Foundling Hospital on Brunswick Square. He raised money for Great Ormond Street Children's Hospital through talks and public readings of *A Christmas Carol*. He describes the hospital in *Our Mutual Friend*.

Unlike many creative personalities, Dickens was a good businessman and was able to hang on to his money. He was the first author to insist on royalties, rather than sell his work for a lump sum, as was the norm at the time. His readings made a lot of money, both for himself and for charity. He printed posters and promoted his events. People queued for hours and rioted over the tickets. In that sense, he was the predecessor for modern performers: the first celebrity author. He also made extra money by allowing his name to be used for commercial endorsements, much as famous people do today.

Dickens spent the last decade of his life at Gad's Hill, the mansion in Kent that he had once admired as a boy and now owned. *Great Expectations* was written here. And it was here that Dickens died in 1870, at the age of 58, while working on his last novel, *The Mystery of Edwin Drood*. He was buried in Westminster Abbey.

DICKENS'S LONDON

There are countless places in London associated with Dickens and his novels. Covent Garden was another spot that intrigued him as a boy. He loved the bustle and energy of the market area. In *The Pickwick Papers*, Job Trotter spends the night here in a vegetable basket. By Victorian times, the area was full of taverns and brothels and dubious characters. In *Oliver Twist*, Bill Sikes brags that he could find 50 child thieves here every night. The Artful Dodger is taken to the Bow Street Magistrate's Court when caught in the act of picking a pocket.

Dickens had offices from 1859 to 1870 for his popular magazine, *All the Year Round*, at 26 Wellington Street, on the corner with Tavistock Street. Nearby, off the Strand on Surrey Street, is the old Roman Bath where Dickens went as a boy, and where David Copperfield had many a cold plunge.

Dickens often ate at Rules Restaurant in Covent Garden, one of London's oldest restaurants, established in 1798. Some of the memorabilia in the Dickens Room was personally donated by the author.

Manette Street runs alongside Foyles Bookshop, from Charing Cross Road into Soho. Originally called Rose Street, it was renamed in 1895 after Dickens's character, Dr. Manette, from *A Tale of Two Cities*. In the novel, the doctor lives "in a quiet street-corner not far from Soho Square," near a gold-beater's workshop, where "... gold [was] to be beaten by some mysterious giant who had a golden arm starting out of the wall of the front hall—as if he had beaten himself precious ..."

(Dickens *A Tale of Two Cities* 97–99). A figure in the wall here depicts a gold-beater's arm. The life-sized Goldbeater's Arm, taken from 2 Manette Street, is the original sign mentioned in the story and is now in the Dickens House Museum. Dickens was a regular at The Lamb, in Lamb's Conduit Street near Holborn. The Victorian decor and wood-paneled rooms of this popular pub have been carefully restored.

By the early 19th century, the areas of Clerkenwell and Smithfield had become squalid slums. Just behind what is today known as Holborn Viaduct was Saffron Hill, a warren for criminals. This was where Fagin and his boys lived. The Artful Dodger taught Oliver Twist the tricks of the trade in nearby Clerkenwell Green.

A former jousting ground and place for public executions, Smithfield became the city's meat market in the 17th century, alongside the popular Bartholomew's Fair, a cloth and cattle fair dating from medieval times. Live cattle were slaughtered here until 1855, when the abattoirs were moved to the suburbs for hygiene reasons. The covered market was erected in 1867 and a bustling wholesale meat trade takes place from around 4:00 to 9:00 AM. Dickens described Victorian Smithfield in *Oliver Twist*: "The ground was covered, nearly ankle-deep with filth and mire; a thick steam perpetually rising from the reeking bodies of the cattle, and mingling with the fog" (*Oliver Twist* 172).

Little remains today of St. Giles, another notorious slum that once lay north of Covent Garden. Dickens described it in "Sunday Under Three Heads" as: "Women with scarcely the articles of apparel which common decency requires, with forms bloated by disease, and faces rendered hideous by habitual drunkenness—men reeling and staggering along—children in rags and filth—whole streets of squalid and miserable appearance whose inhabitants are lounging in the public road, fighting, screaming and swearing ...". St. Gile's was called Tom-all-Alone's in *Bleak House*.

Dickens visited Newgate Prison several times and confessed to a "horrible fascination" for it. It features in several of his novels. In *Oliver Twist*, Fagin ended up in the condemned hold at Newgate, and would have been executed on the public scaffold outside, which had replaced the one at Tyburn. The Central Criminal Court, better known as the Old Bailey, now stands on its site.

In the City, Sam Weller and Mr. Pickwick were "suspended at the George and Vulture" in comfortable quarters after leaving Mrs. Bardell's in Goswell Street. The old inn still stands in the City in George Yard, Lombard Street. London's great London landmark, the Monument, features in *Martin Chuzzlewit*,

Dickens was a regular visitor at Thomas Carlyle's house at 24 Cheyne Row in Chelsea, along with William Makepeace Thackeray, Alfred Lord Tennyson, and other leading lights of the day. The house of the great historian and founder of the London Library is now a museum, restored to its appearance in Carlyle's lifetime. Dickens dedicated *Hard Times* to him.

The Prospect of Whitby, located along the Thames in Wapping, is one of London's oldest riverside pubs, dating from 1520. It was originally called the Devil's Tavern. The giant wooden beams, open fireplaces, stone floors, and pewter countertop are the same as when Dickens drank here. Another atmospheric spot is the Trafalgar Tavern on Park Row in Greenwich. Dickens came here with George Cruickshank, his illustrator for *Oliver Twist*. The tavern was built in 1837 and was instantly popular for its whitebait dinners. In those days, the tiny fish could be caught locally in the Thames. Politicians, lawyers, and the literati would come by boat for celebratory banquets. Dickens used it as the setting for the wedding feast in *Our Mutual Friend*. Whitebait is still served here in season.

In Hampstead, Dickens and Thackeray drank at Jack Straw's Castle. The pub is named for one of the leaders of the Peasants' Revolt of 1381. Dickens also visited another watering hole on Hampstead Heath, Spaniard's Inn, and used its beautiful rose garden as the setting for the tea party in *The Pickwick Papers*.

William Makepeace Thackeray was the other leading London author of Victorian times. He and Dickens had a long-standing relationship. When Dickens was living at Doughty Street, he called on Thackeray, who lived nearby at 13 Coram Street, and interviewed him as a possible illustrator for *The Pickwick Papers.* Hablôt Knight Browne got the job, and Thackeray pursued his own career as a novelist. He later illustrated his own masterpiece, *Vanity Fair.*

The two writers became friendly rivals. Professionally, they had much in common. Thackeray also started out in law and studied at Middle Temple, but never practiced as a barrister. He too turned to journalism, and wrote for many periodicals of the day. In 1842, he began contributing articles and sketches to the famous humor magazine, *Punch.*

In 1850, Thackeray was Dickens's guest at the Star and Garter Inn in Richmond for the celebration of the publication of *David Copperfield.* The Poet Laureate, Alfred Lord Tennyson, author of *The Charge of the Light Brigade,* was also present.

WILLIAM MAKEPEACE THACKERAY

Thackeray came from—and wrote about—a world quite different from that of Dickens's history and writings. He was born in Calcutta, India in 1811. His father was a wealthy English merchant. As a boy, he attended Charterhouse school in London, which features in his novels *Pendennis* and *The Newcomes.* He attended Cambridge University, but left without taking a degree.

When he turned 21, Thackeray inherited a fortune from his late father, but soon lost it through gambling and bad investments. He went to Paris, studied art, and in 1836—the year his first volume, *Flore et Zephyr,* appeared—married Isabella Shawe. In 1837, they returned to London, where the first of their three daughters was born.

In 1846, Thackeray moved to 16 Young Street at Kensington Square. Here he wrote *Vanity Fair,* the novel that brought him fame, followed by *Pendennis,* and *The History of Henry Esmond.* A blue plaque commemorates his residence here.

A favorite tale told about Thackeray was his walk in later

years with a friend in Kensington Square. When they passed his old house, he exclaimed with mock seriousness: "Down on your knees, you rogue, for here *Vanity Fair* was penned, and I will go down with you, for I have a high opinion of that little production myself" (Hutton 303).

Like Dickens's works, *Vanity Fair* was published serially in monthly parts. It follows the interwoven fortunes of two very different women, the gentle, well-born Amelia Sedley, and Becky Sharp, the ambitious, scheming adventuress and daughter of a poor artist. The novel studies the intricate social relationships that characterized England in the early 19th century. Becky Sharp became a literary model for many future heroines.

While Dickens exposed the plight of the poor, Thackeray is known for his humorous and ironic portrayals of the middle and upper classes. His work was true to life, rather than melodramatic. It was written to be read aloud, a common activity in the long family evenings of Victorian times. His narrative, description, and dialogue are considered by many to be greatly entertaining.

Thackeray saw moralizing as an important function of a novelist, and he often explored such themes as hypocrisy, human behavior, and secret emotions. *Vanity Fair* was subtitled *A Novel Without a Hero*, and the author's stated aim was to show "that we are for the most part ... foolish and selfish people ... all eager after vanities."

Several London locations feature in *Vanity Fair*. The novel opens at Miss Pinkerton's academy for young ladies, on Chiswick Mall in Hammersmith. Today, this row of grand houses along the Thames is a delightful place to stroll on a sunny day, with several waterfront pubs for refreshment. Nothing remains of Vauxhall Gardens, where Joseph Sedley attempts to propose to Becky Sharp.

The Osborne and Sedley families live in Russell Square, which in Thackeray's day was a solid, respectable residential area. When Becky and her husband Rawdon Crawley return from Paris, they settle in a very small comfortable house in Curzon Street, May Fair, then—as today—a well-to-do area. The character of Lord Steyne is based on the 3rd Marquess of Hertford, who acquired the exquisite Wallace Collection in Manchester Square, one of London's finest small art galleries.

In 1853, Thackeray moved to 36 Onslow Square, also in Kensington. His two visits to America to deliver his lectures were the inspiration for another novel, *The Virginians*. In 1860, he became the editor of the *Cornhill Magazine*. In 1862, he moved to his last home, 2 Kensington Palace Gardens, a house he designed himself. The house has since been altered, and most of the houses in this street are now embassies.

Thackeray belonged to three gentlemen's clubs: the Athenaeum and the Reform Club, both on Pall Mall, and the Garrick in Covent Garden, the club of the literary set. The fictional adventurer Phileas Fogg set out from the Reform Club for his incredible journey in Jules Verne's *Around the World in Eighty Days*.

Dickens was also a member of the Athenaeum. He and Thackeray had not spoken for several years after a quarrel when they were reconciled here in 1863. Thackeray was talking with another member when Dickens entered the club and walked by without acknowledging them. Thackeray went after Dickens and stopped him as he started up the stairs. After a few words, Thackeray held out his hand and the two shook hands and made up. Returning to his companion, Thackeray remarked, "I'm glad I have done this."

A few months later, on Christmas Eve, Thackeray died at his home, in his sleep, at the age of 52. He was buried in Kensal Green Cemetery.

VICTORIAN NOVELS AND WOMEN AUTHORS

Some of the greatest Victorian novels were written by women. Though they covered important social and moral themes, they were not set predominately in London. It is a sign of the strictures of Victorian society that the most enduring women authors of the 19th century—including Jane Austen, the Brontë sisters, and Mary Ann Evans—all published initially under men's names.

The Bronte sisters were rare visitors to London. Charlotte and Anne came here to meet their publisher, George Smith, for the first time in 1848 at the offices of Smith, Elder & Co. at 32 Cornhill (now the Cornhill Insurance Company). Thackeray, who was also present, was as surprised as the publisher when he met the real Currer and Acton Bell (their pseudonyms). A panel on the bottom right of the door commemorates their meeting. Thackeray hosted a reception for Charlotte at his home in Young Street to celebrate the success of *Jane Eyre*, and she later attended one of his lectures in 1851.

Evans, who wrote under the pen name George Eliot, came to London in her 30s after spending the first part of her life in the Midlands. Her relationship with the writer and editor George Henry Lewes, who was married and unable to obtain a divorce, offended Victorian morality and dampened her literary prestige in her lifetime. Between 1860 and 1863, they lived at 16 Blandford Square in Marylebone. Here she wrote *Silas Marner, The Mill on the Floss*, and *Romola*. They subsequently moved to St. John's Wood, where she wrote her most acclaimed novel, *Middlemarch*, followed by *Daniel Deronda*.

Lewes died in 1878. Twelve years later, at the age of 61, Evans married John Cross, an American banker twenty years her junior, at St. George's Church in Hanover Square. After their honeymoon, they moved into 4 Cheyne Walk in Chelsea. Evans died a few weeks later of a kidney ailment.

Evans was buried in Highgate Cemetery, one of London's great Victorian burial grounds, with magnificent funereal architecture and splendid views. The western cemetery opened in 1839 and became *the* fashionable burial spot in its day; it can only be visited on a guided tour. The eastern cemetery, which opened in 1857 to handle the overload, is more accessible. A wilder place, where the cracked and leaning tombstones are covered with creeping ivy, it is featured in Bram Stoker's *Dracula*.

The most famous monument is the enormous black bust of Karl Marx, who was buried here in 1883.

George Eliot's simple grave lies nearby, its inscription a tribute to all the Victorian writers:

> "Of those immortal dead who still live on in minds made better by their presence." (Hutton 99)

CHAPTER SEVEN

London at the Turn of the Twentieth Century

Victorians certainly understood the days of opulent, imperial, bourgeois England were numbered in the late 19th century. An emboldened, inventive, fully industrial United States, an increasingly imperial Japan, and the ongoing armament of Germany were but a few of the early indicators that Great Britain's role as solitary world superpower would soon fade. Prosperity enjoyed by most of Europe during the Victorian era dwindled as the new century approached. England found the administration of its global empire to be more expensive than its acquisition; preoccupations with morality, the place of women, and capitalism in bourgeois thinking were finally challenged with new attention to the poor, calls for minimum wages and worker's rights, and suffrage for women.

Not surprisingly, the Victorian ability to overlook the urban ills of industrialization eroded with the domestic calm characteristic of Victorian London. Conditions in the City, especially in the East End, had worsened with the swelling population: in the years before the turn of the century almost one-seventh of England's populace lived within London city limits. Attempts to address the problem of poverty were accompanied by public demonstrations for Irish Home Rule and Women's Voting Rights. However illusory for its duration, the tranquility of the Victorian Era faltered in the late-19th century and had vanished by the beginning of the 20th. The end of an age is marked neatly by the turn of a century, the death of a queen, and the embarrassing difficultly of British forces in the Boer War (1899–1901).

Even as the problems of modern urban life were recognized and work got underway to ameliorate living conditions in the East End—and as more and more of the wealthy migrated into the suburbs in the West—the city retained its place as a cultural mecca. In fact, London surpassed all other cities in the late-19th century as the capital of the world. It proved irresistible to members of the *literati.*

OSCAR WILDE

One was Oscar Wilde, author, playwright, critic, and poet of Irish extraction. Son of the Dublin surgeon Sir William Wilde and his wife (the well-known romantic poet Jane Francesca Elgee, who wrote under the name "Speranza"), Wilde showed early talent as a Classicist at Trinity College Dublin and Magdalen College, Oxford. Following a tour of Greece and Italy he settled in London in 1879, and became famous as a witty and controversial aesthete. In 1881, Wilde moved into 44 Tite Street in Chelsea, an area he helped establish as bohemian, with his Oxford friend, the artist Frank Miles.

Wilde's volume *Poems,* published that same year, was dismissed by most readers as shallow and indecent. Yet Wilde's reputation in London had already garnered the attention of the city's A-list. He became identified with the Decadents, British followers of a group with roots in Paris, noted for their interest in finding beauty in the natural world.

On Tite Street, Wilde was known for his playful vituperations with his Chelsea neighbor, the painter James Whistler. Wilde left suddenly, however, when his housemate's, Frank Miles, father fiercely objected to the erotic themes in some of

Wilde's poetry. Miles's father made it clear to the young painter that he would continue living with Wilde at the expense of his inheritance. When Miles told Wilde that he chose the money, Wilde left in outrage, never to speak to his Oxford friend again.

Wilde stayed for a time with his mother and brother, who by this time had taken up residence at 1 Ovington Square, Chelsea. In 1884, Wilde married Constance Lloyd and returned to Tite Street; he and his family would occupy the redbrick house at 34 Tite Street for more than ten years. Here in a primrose-colored study at a desk that once belonged to Thomas Carlyle he penned his most famous works, among them the novel *A Picture of Dorian Gray* (1890) and his celebrated play, *The Importance of Being Earnest* (1894). But Wilde was renowned not so much for his writing as for his command of London society and his place as an art critic. Whistler turned down Wilde's request to decorate his house at 34 Tite Street, saying—characteristic of their many exchanges—"You have been lecturing us about the house beautiful, now's your chance to show us one."

Only a few years into his marriage, Wilde began his first homosexual affair with a young student named Robert Ross, who was 17 years old while Wilde was 32. Ross would become Wilde's lifelong friend and caretaker of his estate after his public shaming and lonely death in 1900, although Wilde would have many more young men for lovers. His habit of bringing blue-collar boys into expensive London hotels drew attention, and where Wilde initially paid many of these young men for their company, he found himself paying even more in blackmail.

Financial troubles forced Wilde to take the post as editor of the magazine *Woman's World,* the offices of which were quite near Newgate Prison and the Central Criminal Court, known to all as Old Bailey. It was here in 1895 that Wilde found himself on trial and imprisoned, his name associated with such iniquity that objections to a plaque commemorating Wilde's tenure on Tite Street were commonplace even in the 1950s.

It seems that by the 1890s all of London knew of Wilde's sexual preference, since he openly met his lover Lord Alfred Douglas, son of the Marquess of Queensbury, at room 346 in the Savoy Hotel in Covent Garden. In 1894, the Marquess appeared in Wilde's Tite Street library drunk with rage, threatening Wilde's ruin if his relationship with Queensbury's son were to continue.

The next year the Marquess showed up where Wilde and Douglas were lunching in the Domino Room at the Café Royal in Mayfair. Wilde invited Queensbury to join them and proceeded to charm the man, but their reconciliation was short-lived. Queensbury began to follow Wilde around London, publicly insulting the author. Wilde felt he could no longer ignore the Marquess when, in April 1895, Wilde found Queensbury's calling card at his club the Albemarle, at 13 Albemarle Street, on which the Marquess wrote his infamously misspelled threat: "To Oscar Wilde, posing Sodomite."

Wilde felt he had no choice but to sue for libel, though the trial led to Wilde's certain ruin. Queensbury's counsel, Edward Carson, focused his defense on proving Wilde's homosexuality, presenting to the court passages from Wilde's works with erotic and homosexual overtones. Wilde treated the questioning with his characteristic wit and humor, though in the end the judge instructed the jury to rule in favor of the Marquess. Queensbury quickly countersued for his legal expenses, and following a conviction of indecency and sodomy, Oscar Wilde was bankrupt. His most prized possessions (Wilde had been a collector of antiques and finery for much of his life) were seized, including his writing desk that once belonged to Thomas Carlyle. While Wilde sat in prison and his wife and children were in hiding, Queensbury's supporters ransacked his home on Tite Street.

Wilde's health failed in Old Bailey, and when he was released two years later, he never convalesced. Forced to move to Paris, he died there in 1900 in utter poverty.

Years before Wilde realized his taste for "the love that dare not speak its name," back in Dublin, Wilde had a girlfriend named Florence Balcombe, snatched away from Oscar by another Dubliner, Bram Stoker, while Wilde was being treated for syphilis and under doctor's orders to remain abstinent for two years. Wilde and the Stokers would later become friends

The Sentencing Statement Against Oscar Wilde

Justice Wills: Oscar Wilde and Alfred Taylor, the crime of which you have been convicted is so bad that one has to put stern restraint upon one's self to prevent one's self from describing, in language which I would rather not use, the sentiments which must rise in the breast of every man of honor who has heard the details of these two horrible trials. That the jury has arrived at a correct verdict in this case I cannot persuade myself to entertain a shadow of a doubt; and I hope, at all events, that those who sometimes imagine that a judge is half-hearted in the cause of decency and morality because he takes care no prejudice shall enter into the case, may see that it is consistent at least with the utmost sense of indignation at the horrible charges brought home to both of you.

It is no use for me to address you. People who can do these things must be dead to all sense of shame, and one cannot hope to produce any effect upon them. It is the worst case I have ever tried. That you, Taylor, kept a kind of male brothel it is impossible to doubt. And that you, Wilde, have been the center of a circle of extensive corruption of the most hideous kind among young men, it is equally impossible to doubt.

I shall, under the circumstances, be expected to pass the severest sentence that the law allows. In my judgment it is totally inadequate for a case such as this. The sentence of the Court is that each of you be imprisoned and kept to hard labor for two years.

while the Stokers, too, lived in Chelsea at 18 St. Leonard Terrace. Florence spent her later years fighting the unauthorized dramatizations of *Dracula* on film after her husband's death in 1912.

Stoker only moonlighted as an author, much of his time being consumed by his position as assistant to the Shakespearean actor Sir Henry Irving, whose draconian management style is said to have inspired the Count. Most of *Dracula* was written while Stoker vacationed in Whitby, but the novel does feature some London scenes. According to Mina's journal, she and Jonathan Harker spot Dracula on upscale Piccadilly, just months after Jonathan escaped from the Count's Transylvanian castle. "My God!" Jonathan exclaims, "It is the man himself!" (Stoker 180–181). After careful detective work, Harker discovers that the Count has purchased a mansion somewhere on Piccadilly.

> At Piccadilly Circus I discharged my cab, and walked westward. Beyond the Junior Constitutional I came across the house described and was satisfied that this was the next of the lairs arranged by Dracula. (Stoker 280)

Historically, the Junior Constitutional was a gentlemens club at 101 Piccadilly, though Stoker later gives Dracula's address as No. 347. Piccadilly, in fact, features many aristocratic mansions, and the Count might have been right at home, though this particular Piccadilly address is fictitious.

SHERLOCK HOLMES AND 221B BAKER STREET

Speaking of fictitious addresses, there is probably none more sought after and difficult to locate in London as 221B Baker Street, home of Conan Doyle's forensic expert, Sherlock Holmes.

Sir Arthur Conan Doyle, like Bram Stoker, was another professional who wrote on the side. His day job as an oculist in his practice at 2 Upper Wimpole Street in Marylebone drew few patients, and to pass the time he penned the Holmes tales. The stories he wrote here were shorter than the two he wrote previously in Southsea, a way of guarding against too much interruption in the writing process should a client arrive. When it became clear that Conan Doyle would be much more successful in writing than in medicine, he gave up his practice and moved to 12 Tennison Road in Norwood, southeast London, where most of Holmes's adventures were written.

Conan Doyle wrote of the sleuth for forty years, earning a considerable fortune and establishing a character so beloved that letters are still received at Holmes' address asking for help. Bored of the character already by 1893—just six years after the publication of Holmes' first caper, *A Study in Scarlet*—Conan Doyle wrote Holmes' demise in the *Strand* magazine story *The Final Problem*. Public backlash was so great that the *Strand*, which owed its tremendous success almost solely to the Holmes tales, suffered 20,000 canceled subscriptions. The former *Strand* offices occupy Southampton Street in Covent Garden, just off Fleet Street.

No. 221 didn't exist in Conan Doyle's time, and it was only in 1930 that Baker Street was extended beyond Crawford Street/Paddington Street. Not for lack of trying, Holmesian scholars have been unable to locate an original model for the famous quarters of Holmes and his chronicler, Dr. John Watson, though one suggested candidate is Camden House at 118 Baker Street, the setting for a 1903 Holmes story entitled *The Empty House* (the story that, incidentally, resurrected Holmes after his death in *The Final Problem*). The address is now a beauty school.

Following the Baker Street extension in 1930, the 221 number fell to the Abbey National Bank and Building Society, which treated Conan Doyle fanatics to a replica of Holmes' famed sitting room during the 1951 Festival of Britain. The room was later moved and may still be seen today at the Sherlock Holmes Pub, 10 Northumberland Street in the Strand. The restaurant is filled with Holmesiania, and the reconstructed sitting room contains the detective's artifacts that fans would expect.

Many Holmes tales take place in and around London, and place-names are frequent in Conan Doyle's work; at the same time, there are enough descriptions of the metropolis to allow those unfamiliar with Conan Doyle's namedropping to grasp a Holmesian London.

> It was a foggy, cloudy morning, and a dun-coloured veil hung over the house-tops, looking like the reflection of the mud-coloured streets beneath. (Doyle 29)

A plaque at St. Bartholomew's Hospital on Giltspur Street marks the location of the meeting place of Sherlock Holmes and his perpetual sidekick, Dr. Watson, and records their first words. Simpson's-in-the-Strand, near the Waterloo Bridge, is mentioned in several stories, and remains an excellent restaurant to this day. Café Royal and The Criterion also earn mentions. The Diogenes Club, where Holmes meets his brother Mycroft in *The Greek Interpreter*, is most likely modeled on the Athenaeum at 107 Pall Mall, a meeting place for the intelligentsia that boasted for its members no lesser personalities than Thackeray and Dickens, Trollope and Kipling, and London's favorite American of the day, Henry James.

HENRY JAMES

Few writers of his time dealt with metropolitan settings like James, whose novels, while often bound up in psychological realism, tend to deal with a solitary traveler in a strange new setting. Having traveled through Britain and the rest of Europe extensively in his early years, he would come to live and die in England, becoming a citizen in 1914. His impressions in 1869, during his first trip without his family at the age of 26, were of a brutish, unfriendly place, "where the natural fate of an obscure stranger was to be trampled to death in Piccadilly and have his carcass thrown into the Thames." He returned to London to live in 1876, lodging for nine years at 3 Bolton Street in Mayfair where he spent his mornings writing such works as *The Europeans* (1878), *Daisy Miller* (1879), *Washington Square* (1881), and *The Portrait of a Lady* (1881).

Many of James's novels are set in London, though James's psychological intentions do tend to obscure the material details of the city. But James can be counted on to pay close attention to people and their activities: in London, James saw the opportunity to observe humanity in a way unavailable in any other place in the world; the sheer populace affords myriad stories, myriad personalities, myriad opportunities for analysis. In his early novel *The American* (1877), the wealthy Christopher Newman ventures to Europe for a wife, and London's sights are presented as a diversion—surely James's experience as a travel writer is behind the text.

> He arrived in London in the midst of what is called "the season," and it seemed to him at first that he might here put himself in the way of being diverted from his heavy-heartedness. He knew no one in all England, but the spectacle of the mighty metropolis roused him somewhat from his apathy. Anything that was enormous usually found favor with Newman, and the multitudinous energies and industries of England stirred within him a dull vivacity of contemplation. It is on record that the weather, at that moment, was of the finest English quality; he took long walks and explored London in every direction; he sat by the hour in Kensington Gardens and beside the adjoining Drive, watching the people and the horses and the carriages; the rosy English beauties, the wonderful English dandies, and the splendid flunkies. He went to the opera and found it better than in Paris; he went to the theatre and found a surprising charm in listening to dialogue the finest points of which came within the range of his comprehension.
>
> He made several excursions into the country, recommended by the waiter at his hotel, with whom, on this and

similar points, he had established confidential relations. He watched the deer in Windsor Forest and admired the Thames from Richmond Hill; he ate white-bait and brown-bread and butter at Greenwich, and strolled in the grassy shadow of the cathedral of Canterbury. He also visited the Tower of London and Madame Tussaud's exhibition. (James, *The American* 350)

In *The Princess Casamassima* (1886), London seems to project itself into and onto the characters in the novel. Miss Henning is hardly separable from the city itself.

She was to her blunt, expanded finger-tips a daughter of London, if the crowded streets and bustling traffic of the great city; she had drawn her health and strength from its dingy courts, and foggy thoroughfares and peopled its parks and squares and crescents with her ambitions; it had entered in to her blood and bone, the sound of her voice and carriage of her head; she understood it with instinct and loved it with passion; she represented its immense vulgarities and curiosities, its brutality and its knowingness, its good-nature and its impudence, and might have figured, in an allegorical procession, as a kind of glorified townswoman, a nymph of the wilderness of Middlesex, a flower of the clustered parishes, the genius of urban civilisation, the muse of cockneyism. (James, *The Princess Casamassima* 59)

Casamassima's protagonist, Hyacinth Robinson, is an anarchist who comes to London in the interest of disrupting social order, but becomes aware of the value of democracy in the city, and resolves to commit suicide. Here, Robinson becomes entangled in London's upper-class miasma.

Everything which in a great city could touch the sentient faculty of a youth on whom nothing was lost ministered to his conviction that there was no possible good fortune in life of too "quiet" an order for him to appreciate—no privilege, no

opportunity, no luxury to which he mightn't do full justice.
It was not so much that he wanted to enjoy as that he wanted
to know; his desire wasn't to be pampered but to be initiated.
Sometimes of a Saturday in the long evenings in June or July
he made his way into Hyde Park at the hour when the throng
of carriages, of riders, of brilliant pedestrians was thickest;
and though lately, on two or three of these occasions, he had
been accompanied by Miss Henning, whose criticism of the
scene was rich and distinct, a tremendous little drama had
taken place on the stage of his inner consciousness. He
wanted to drive in every carriage, to mount on every horse,
to feel on his arm the hand of every pretty woman in the
place. In the midst of this his sense was vivid that he belonged
to the class whom the "bloated" as they passed didn't so much
as rest their eyes on for a quarter of a second. They looked at
Millicent, who was safe to be looked at anywhere and was one
of the handsomest girls in any company, but they only
reminded him of the high human walls, the deep gulfs of tradition, the steep embankment of privilege and dense layers of
stupidity fencing the "likes" of him off from social recognition. (*The Princess Casamassima* 125–126)

James was fully prepared to critique his city of choice, and he
did so in his letters and travel essays. He called Hyde Park
Corner a "[bungled] attempt at a great public place;" he wrote
of "the grimy desert of Trafalgar Square;" and held that the royal
palace was "lamentably ugly." But the surrounds of Mayfair
proved to be the perfect tonic for James's social and intellectual
life: the famed literary lodgings at Albany House off Piccadilly
had attracted men of literature since its conversion into luxury
apartments in 1802, attracting tenants of such stature as Lord
Byron, J. B. Priestly, Aldous Huxley, and Graham Greene. Just
across Piccadilly, the clubs of St. James—including not only the
Athenaeum but also the Reform club, where Phileas Fogg
accepted his famous wager in Verne's *Around the World in Eighty
Days*—were quite literally a refuge for James: after settling at the

Lamb House on the Sussex coast in 1897, he would spend his winters lodging at the Reform.

James wrote from the Lamb House for many years, but became weary of country living. In 1911, he wrote from Sussex that "I can't stand the lonely hibernations here, where for several years I have had too much of it. Miles of pavement and lamplight are good for me." His rooms at the Reform Club allowed him brief returns to the metropolitan life he loved, though the quarters presented pragmatic difficulties for his writing. Since he had suffered from pains in his right wrist since the late 1890's, James was now writing exclusively through dictation to his typist, Theodora Bosanquet. Since Theodora's presence (as a woman) in James's chambers would constitute a serious breech of the Reform Club rules, and since his morning taxi to Theodora's home was a burden, he moved to 21 Carlyle Mansions, on Cheyne Walk, Chelsea, near his typist's home on Lawrence Street. The luxury apartments of Carlyle Mansions on the Thames were later home to T. S. Eliot and James Bond creator Ian Fleming.

Henry James suffered his first stroke just months after moving to Chelsea, in spring 1914. The Great War had awakened such a sense of nationalism in him that by this time he had declared his British citizenship after decades as an American foreign national. He died in Carlyle Mansions in 1916, and services were held in the nearby Chelsea Old Church, part of which was once Sir Thomas More's private chapel. Edmund Gosse, a close friend and librarian of the House of Lords, gave the eulogy. A plaque here honoring James reads "lover and interpreter of the fine amenities of brave decisions and generous loyalties: a member of this parish who renounced a cherished citizenship to give his allegiance to England in the first year of the Great War." A memorial in Poet's Corner in Westminster Abbey aligns him with the likes of Chaucer, Blake, Keats, and T.S. Eliot.

H.G. WELLS

H.G. Wells was born in his family's Atlas House in Bromley, which at the time of Wells's birth was a distant village, but is now a thoroughly London suburb southeast of town. He refers to the area as "Bun Hill" in 1908's *The War in the Air* and as "Bromstead" in *The New Machiavelli* (1911), largely a diatribe on its irresponsible development.

> The whole of Bromstead as I remember it, and as I saw it last—it is a year ago now—is a dull useless boiling-up of human activities, an immense clustering of futilities. It is as unfinished as ever; the builders' roads still run out and end in mid-field in their old fashion; the various enterprises jumble in the same hopeless contradiction, if anything intensified. Pretentious villas jostle slums, and public-house and tin tabernacle glower at one another across the cat-haunted lot that intervenes. Roper's meadows are now quite frankly a slum; back doors and sculleries gape towards the railway, their yards are hung with tattered washing unashamed; and there seem to be more boards by the railway every time I pass, advertising pills and pickles, tonics and condiments, and suchlike solicitudes of a people with no natural health nor appetite left in them.... (Wells 38–39)

The house has been demolished and a department store now sits on this science-fiction pioneer's birthplace, but the raucous Wells has made his mark elsewhere in London. He gravitated toward literature and science while his mother worked as a housekeeper in a Sussex mansion, and moved to London in 1888 at the age of 21 to lodgings on Theobald's Road in Bloomsbury. He left shortly thereafter to live with his aunt and cousin, Isabelle, at 12 Fitzroy Road in Camden Town. He fell in love with Isabelle and planned to marry her, though he lacked the monetary freedom to afford a place of their own. A raise at the Henley House School following his Bachelor's of Science from London University in 1890 meant enough income for rent, and they married in 1891. But Wells's infidelity promised a short marriage, and by 1895 he had married his erstwhile pupil Amy Robbins and moved to Surrey. He built a mansion, Spade House, in 1900 near Folkstone, but sold it in 1909 and moved back to London, taking a residence at 17 Church Row, Hampstead.

A few doors down from Lord Alfred Douglas, Oscar Wilde's lover, Wells found city life here claustrophobic compared to his former pastoral surrounds. But here, at least, he could enjoy London society, and the house was home to a few of the more infamous Bloomsbury group gatherings. During this time, he likely frequented Ford Madox Ford's address above an odiferous poultry shop at 84 Holland Park Avenue in Notting Hill, where Ford edited the successful *English Review*, his publication dedicated to the best new English writing. The first issue saw contributions from Henry James and Leo Tolstoy, and featured Wells's *Tono-Bungay*. Wells owned the house on Church Row until 1910, but having run off with yet another woman, Amber Reeves, shortly after his return to the city, he spent relatively little time here.

Wells returned to London in 1927 to a flat at 47 Chiltern Court, Baker Street, in Marylebone, where he lived for eight years, though he traveled extensively. In 1937 Wells bought a house at 13 Hanover Terrace, Marylebone, designed by John Nash, where he grimly awaited his death, though it would take nine years and a second World War for his time to come in 1946.

Wells stubbornly refused to leave London during the Blitz, even as the house next door was reduced to rubble. It wasn't the first German offensive Wells would survive in London; in a sort of literary consortium, Wells, J.M. Barrie, Thomas Hardy, Arnold Bennett, and George Bernard Shaw all sought refuge from German bombs during the Great War in an apartment at 1 Robert Street in Covent Garden. At a party at Lady Sibyl Colefax's house during World War II, an air raid began, and the cantankerous Wells refused to take cover. It seems Wells refused to let the German bombing ruin his lunch, and insisted that the lights be left on (though allowed blackout screens for the windows as a concession) while the company, who included Somerset Maugham, continued to dine.

Wells died at No. 13, but not before renting the apartment above the garage to George Orwell and his wife—only to evict them months later on the paranoid suspicion that the couple was gossiping about him.

J.M. BARRIE

Born in Scotland, J.M. Barrie came to London in 1885 and never left. While working as a journalist he wrote many plays, books, and novels, and married the actress Mary Ansell in 1894. They moved to 133 Gloucester Road in South Kensington where Barrie wrote the novels *Sentimental Tommy* and *Margaret Ogilvy*. The Barries left Gloucester Road in 1902, and by this time their marriage began to dissolve due to Barrie's homosexuality. Barrie's friendship with Llewellyn Davies' sons, especially Jack, in nearby Kensington, only caused more marital strife, though their divorce wouldn't be finalized until 1909.

Barrie based the hero of his most famous work, *Peter Pan*, on the real-life character of Jack Davies, which he wrote from his summerhouse on Bayswater Road in West London, near Hyde Park, in 1904. He loved the nearby Kensington Gardens, and made it the home of the Darlings in the story. Already a successful writer and lover of children, Barrie donated much of the royalties from the play to the Hospital for Sick Children on Great Ormond Street in Bloomsbury. A wing in the hospital, now known to children who stay there as GOSH, carries the Barrie name, and even has a Peter Pan ward. Barrie also gave royalties from *Peter Pan* to its inspiration, Jack Davies, who earned a halfpenny for each performance. The Peter Pan statue in Kensington Gardens, Hyde Park, was erected in 1912, its construction kept secret and assembled in a studio; Barrie wanted it to seem to children that it had just magically appeared.

At 1 Robert Street in Covent Garden Barrie lived for 26 years following his divorce, from 1911 until his death 1937. It was here one night during the Great War that Wells, Shaw, and others sought refuge from German bombing. With the Great War literally falling on London, and raging in the mud just across the Channel, English literature was changed forever.

CHAPTER EIGHT

London between the Wars

How great were the changes in Great Britain from the reign of Queen Victoria through the end of World War II? Ask George Bernard Shaw, whose long life spanned two armed Germanys and two great conflagrations, a peak of British imperialism and its total dissolution, the mercurial plights of the working classes in enduring struggles for some brand of socialism, the values of the bourgeoisie giving way to suffrage and early sexual revolution, and the advents of electricity and flight. For American context, Shaw was eight years old when Abraham Lincoln was assassinated, and he was eighty-eight when Franklin Delano Roosevelt died. At his death in 1950, he was 94 years old.

GEORGE BERNARD SHAW

Shaw became active in the political struggles centering in London early in his adulthood. Shortly after charitable organizations such as the Salvation Army began to fight against poverty in the East End, a new attention to the poor emerged in the midst of Victorian capitalism, augmented by the writings of Karl Marx, whose *Das Kapital* was published in 1867. Marx was convinced that a worker's uprising was inevitable, and he awaited proletariat revolutions in Europe's most industrialized nations, including Great Britain and Germany. Yet the British interpretation of socialism, due in a large part to the young George Bernard Shaw, saw the advent of a socialist state not by means of a violent revolution, but by a gradual, "evolutionary" process, wherein a group of intellectuals would convince politicians and others of the necessity of the socialist state. To this end, he and others formed the extremely influential socialist coterie, the Fabians, in 1883.

Shaw and his mother (a music teacher) first moved to London from Ireland in 1876, at 13 Netherton Grove off of Brompton Road. The same year he got his first job in letters ghostwriting as a music critic for the publication *The Hornet*. Also that same year, Shaw began a writing streak that produced five novels in five years, though none were published until Shaw earned transatlantic fame.

From 1881 to 1886, Shaw and his mother lived at 37 Fitzroy Street, where he began his fourth novel in four years, *Cashel Byron's Profession*. This novel—and Shaw's other attempts at fiction—wouldn't be published until Shaw earned a reputation in other venues. Aware of his tendency to shy away from others, Shaw joined a debating society in 1880 and forced himself to speak in public. He took boxing lessons to augment his physical confidence, and became a principled vegetarian. He loathed his accommodations on Fitzroy Street—the flat being without a bathroom—but its proximity to the British Museum lent an escape. By the time he became an active socialist in 1882, influenced by the writing of economist Henry George, he was preaching socialism in public and making a name for himself as an orator. A very intelligent person, Shaw was able to read for as long as he could remember, and he read Shakespeare before he was ten.

Shaw spent much of his time at the British Museum, quite near his Fitzroy Street accommodations, which at the time also housed the British Library. Its oak-paneled reading room has been a sanctuary to many writers over the last century, including Karl Marx. It was perhaps in his spirit that Shaw met Marx's daughter Eleanor and others at the Museum as part of a group called the Fabians. In 1883, he met the drama critic William Archer in the reading room, who found work for Shaw as a reviewer for the *Pall Mall Gazette*.

In 1889, the Fabians published their influential tract, *Fabian Essays in Socialism*, which was edited by Shaw. The treatise—which provided a detailed walkthrough of the origin of the group's cause, as well as specific instructions on achieving its end—sought to persuade Liberals and Conservatives alike. From Shaw's chapter, "Transition":

> Confiscation of capital, spoliation of households, annihilation of incentive, everything that the most ignorant and credulous fundholder ever charged against the Socialist, rages openly in London, which begins to ask itself whether it exists and toils only for the typical duke and his celebrated jockey and his famous racehorse. (Shaw III.1.15)

Despite attempts to include their ideas on the platforms of existing parties, the Fabians in 1906 helped to form what would become the Labour Party, and have remained close to that faction ever since.

From 1887 to 1898, Shaw lived at 29 Fitzroy Square—the same five-story Georgian house Virginia Woolf and her younger brother Adrian would occupy ten years later. One night in 1890, Shaw—by his own account—was imbibed by a ballet he had seen at the Alhambra Theatre and decided to try to pirouette around Fitzroy Square, one of the few green spaces in this part of London. A curious policeman, who had been watching Shaw spin and fall around the square for several minutes, decided to give it a try himself. The two were later joined by a milkman and a mailman, and, unsuccessful, the group suffered casualties. The policeman fell in a ditch and got a bloody nose, but the dancing only ended when the milkman broke his leg and had to be taken to the hospital by the other three.

Still unsuccessful as a novelist, he began playwriting in the early 1890s. His first, *Widower's Houses* (1892), saw two performances at the Independent Theatre Club and reviewed poorly. Politically- and morally-charged, it exposed the greed and irresponsibility of slum landlords. His second to be staged in public, *Mrs. Warren's Profession*, written in 1893 but not performed until 1902, was banned for obscenity due to its intimations of incest. Ostensibly Marxist, the play holds that prostitution finds its source in the economic dependency of women. *Arms and the Man* (1894) saw the stage that same year in London and New York; a lighter questioning of military glory, *Arms* finally made Shaw's name as a playwright.

Shaw fell ill again by the end of the 1890s. It was during this time that he began his relationship with the woman who nursed him back to health, Charlotte Payne-Townshend, an Irish millionaire. They married in 1898, and Shaw moved in to Charlotte's home at 10 Adelphi Terrace, where he lived for the better part of 30 years, writing *Man and Superman, Pygmalion, Saint Joan*, and many of his best-known plays. The Shaws moved to Ayot St. Lawrence, Hertfordshire, in 1936 when plans were announced to demolish their Classical colonnaded structure in the Adelphi complex, though the couple purchased another apartment in Whitehall Court to satisfy their need to be close to London's Theatre District.

SHAW'S LONDON TODAY

Shaw enthusiasts will find several locations in London to visit. Trafalgar Square, the site of many public demonstrations over the years, was the location of the infamous "Bloody Sunday" riot on November 13, 1887. Here socialist activists, Shaw included, tried to enter the Square in demonstration, but were stopped by a ring of police. An attempt to break through the two-deep ring of police by activist and short story writer R.B. Cunninghame-Graham resulted in a lost toenail.

Shaw's *Pygmalion* begins with the players taking refuge from a summer rainstorm under the spacious portico of St. Paul's

Church on Bedford Street in Covent Garden. The Church—the first Anglican church built after the Reformation—was designed by Inigo Jones in the 1620s; it was rebuilt when a fire destroyed much of the original in 1795, though the 18th century builders had Jones's plans, and followed them diligently.

The Royal Court Theatre in Sloane Square, Chelsea, has been known since the late-fifties for its presentation of the most bohemian new drama in London. Many of Shaw's plays were first staged here. A bust of Shaw commemorating the over 700 performances of his plays in the early part of the 20th century has been missing since recent renovations were completed.

BRITAIN AND THE GREAT WAR

Perhaps owing to the unique position of the poet as a social barometer, and perhaps otherwise to the draw of theosophy at the end of the 19th century among artists and intellectuals, writers such as H.G. Wells predicted a great change at the end of the Victorian Era, and many saw the possibility of a Great War. When it happened, the fragile set of treaties holding Europe together failed practically overnight. The assassination in the summer of 1914 of the archduke Ferdinand and his wife by Serbian nationalists prompted Austro-Hungarian retaliation, even though the Serbs granted most of Austria-Hungary's demands. The Russians stood with the Serbians, who were greatly outmatched against Austria-Hungary; the Germans, who had previously pledged support to Austria-Hungary in a conflict with Serbia, supported Emperor Franz Josef's mobilization in Serbia. Germany's directives to France and Russia to stay out of any martial affairs in Serbia were expressly ignored.

Britain had every reason to stay out of the impending conflict until a mobilized Germany demanded passage for its troops through Belgium, whom the British were obliged to defend. By the end of August, warring factions included Japan and Italy. The Great War was underway.

The possibility of a quick, glorious end to war (which most people in the countries involved believed would come to pass) was made impossible by the modern artillery developed late in the previous century. Used on a large scale for the first time, chain-fed machine guns could reliably spew 600 rounds at distances of over a thousand yards, forcing foot soldiers into trenches for their survival. Advances in chemistry, including the extraction of nitrogen from the atmosphere to manufacture explosives instead of mining nitrates in the earth, allowed the production of explosives without the burden of import. These developments, in practice, resulted in spectacularly high casualties for spectacularly little ground.

LONDON AND WOMEN'S SUFFRAGE (OR LONDON AS SUFFRAGETTE CITY)

Back in England, the war had tangentially garnered, at last, widespread support for women's suffrage. The debate had been raging for decades, and was in full swing as early as the 1860s, yet repeated setbacks and sidesteps had kept Parliament from granting women the right to vote in Parliamentary elections.

Through the end of the Victorian era, politicians repeatedly backed away from the issue, in no small part due to the Queen's own opposition to franchisement for women. But in 1897, the array of disparate suffrage organizations merged to form the National Union of Women's Suffrage Societies, a crucial step in determining common goals; it acted as an umbrella organization for a number of causes distinct from the question of suffrage per se, such as the white slave trade and the low pay of women workers. The National Union exploited every available democratic venue for change, publishing newspapers and other literature, organizing public meetings, petitioning and writing to politicians. A split occurred in 1903 when Emmeline Pankhurst and others, increasingly frustrated by the failure of constitutional methods to produce any real change from the Liberal Party, formed the Women's Social and Political Union, which by 1912 had become extremely militant. In its more banal incarnations, these suffragettes, as they were called, exacted damage on property: one instance in 1914 had an elderly woman named Mary Wood hack three large gashes with a meat cleaver in John Singer Sargent's recently unveiled portrait of Henry James at the Royal Academy. Believing that real attention would come only from the most sensational acts, the suffragettes engaged in smashing windows, and eventually arson. But when World War I began, the suffragists wholeheartedly—on both peaceful and militant sides of the movement—directed their energies to the war effort in the interest of national unity. This turn, along with the clear example of the benefaction of women in society while most men were fighting on the front, led to overwhelming public support of the suffragists. Women over 30 were granted the right to vote in 1918, and rights on par with men were granted in 1928.

London and the towns of southeastern England came under attack from the air for the first time in 1915, when Germany's huge dirigible airships, the zeppelins, began dropping bombs from altitudes unachievable by the airplanes of the day. One British tactic against the zeppelin raids was the required use of black fabric hung over windows to prevent sighting the city from the air. One man served a summons for showing too much light out his blackout curtains was T.S. Eliot, newlywed and living at 18 Crawford Mansions, Crawford Street in Marylebone.

T.S. ELIOT

Eliot was doing postgraduate work in Marburg, Germany, when World War I broke out, and sensibly fled to England. A diligent scholar, he had earned a PhD from Harvard by the age of 26 and studied at the Sorbonne in Paris, where he wrote *The Love Song of J. Alfred Prufrock* in the summer of 1911. But Eliot's interests were in philosophy, and with a war on, he made his way to Merton College, Oxford, to complete his dissertation on F.H. Bradley. The transfer granted a sojourn in London, and he took an apartment at 28 Bedford Place in Bloomsbury. During his short stay here he met his close friend and fellow American expatriate, Ezra Pound, who exerted an immeasurable literary influence on him. In the end, though, it took not Pound but a girl, Vivienne Haigh-Wood, to steer Eliot from the academy. He married her in 1915, stalled his dissertation, and moved to London.

Eliot taught at Highgate School for a time, and all but giving up a career as a poet, he took a job as a clerk in the Colonial and Foreign department at Lloyd's Bank, at 17 Cornhill in the West End. He soon published *The Love Song of J. Alfred Prufrock*—thanks largely to Ezra Pound, who persuaded Harriet Monroe, editor of the Chicago-based *Poetry*, of Eliot's genius, writing that Eliot "has actually trained himself *and* modernized himself *on his own*." Eliot's sudden success as a poet did not deter him from his day job. A frustrated Ezra Pound wrote to his friend John Quinn in 1920, "It is a crime against literature to let him waste eight hours per diem in that bank." (*The Letters of Ezra Pound,* 40)

Though not a member of the Bloomsbury Group per se, Eliot was among its circle of friends. His second book of poetry, *Poems*, was published in 1919 by Leonard and Virginia Woolf's Hogarth Press. Woolf remembered him on their first encounter as a "strange young man," but she liked his verse enough that the Hogarth press published *The Waste Land* in 1922. The poem was instantly recognized for its brilliance in weaving the literary past with the horror of the post-War modern age.

Eliot stayed on at Lloyd's even through its publication, leaving the bank only in 1925 to work as an editor for the publisher Faber & Gwyer (later Faber & Faber). Instrumental in establishing the company as a publisher of the best new poetry, Eliot worked with the Bloomsbury-based company for forty years at 25 Russell Square.

By Eliot's time, London's financial district, known simply as "the City," was virtually devoid of residential areas, with the railroads allowing commuter traffic to the area. Cornhill, where Eliot worked, was the heart of the banking industry in London, and consequently, the heart of the banking capital of the world. Nearby Fleet Street remained the home of newspapers and

publishing houses, though in the present day most of the newspapers have moved east to the Docklands. The Temple, further
west, is still a home to the legal profession, not far from the
money or the seat of Government. It is this area, the busy City
Eliot witnessed daily while he worked at Lloyd's, that supplies
much of the setting for *The Waste Land*.

> Unreal City,
> Under the brown fog of a winter dawn,
> A crowd flowed under London Bridge, so many, I had not
> thought death had undone so many. (Eliot I:60–63)

Working in the financial district, Eliot saw "a crowd flowing
over London Bridge" daily, as it was a popular commute for
many working in the area (though not for Eliot, who lived
north of the Thames). Funereal tones and vocabulary at every
mention of metropolitan life connect London—ostensibly rep-
resentative of all cities—with Dante's vision of hell in *Inferno*.
There is, indeed, direct allusion to Dante in much of the poem,
famously indicated—along with almost every other work to
which *The Waste Land* alludes—with Eliot's own footnotes.

> And each man fixed his eyes before his feet.
> Flowed up the hill and down King William Street,
> To where Saint Mary Woolnoth kept the hours
> With a dead sound on the final stroke of nine. (Eliot
> I:65–68)

Over the river on London Bridge, King William Street cuts
diagonally straight to Cornhill. Eliot footnotes the sound of St.
Mary Woolnoth's bells to say its odd strike at nine is "a phe-
nomenon I have often noticed" (Eliot 1963, 71). Said to have
been built on the site of an ancient Roman temple, St. Mary
Woolnoth burned and was rebuilt by Sir Christopher Wren
after the Great Fire in 1666, and rebuilt again by Nicholas
Hawksmoor in 1716, accounting for its Georgian style. Sitting

at the intersection of King William and Lombard Streets, it has escaped demolition even as the real estate of London's financial district grew ever more precious.

Eliot recalls Edmund Spenser in "part III, The Fire Sermon," with "Sweet Thames, run softly, till I end my song" (III: 176), and then describes the antithesis of the modern river (i.e., an unpolluted one), one fulfilling Buddha's teaching in "The Fire Sermon" that worldly things must be abandoned:

> The river bears no empty bottles, sandwich papers,
> Silk handkerchiefs, cardboard boxes, cigarette ends
> Or other testimony of summer nights. The nymphs are
> departed. (Eliot III:177–9)

There is a sense throughout the poem that the Thames is dirty and wasted, and this only contributes to a leitmotiv of loss. A few lines later Eliot writes, "By the waters of Leman I sat down and wept ..." (Eliot III:182) invoking at once the destruction of cities through the well-known Psalm "by the waters of Babylon, yea, we wept, when we remembered Zion" (Psalm 137:1), and the Whitechapel throughfare, Leman Street, so known for its prostitutes that by Elizabethan times a leman had come to signify one such woman. The biblical lamentation conveys a strong sense that something very important has passed away, echoed later in the poem with images of a lack of water, of desolate rock. References to a pre-war Germany in the first part of the poem inform the interpretation that, in the wake of the Great War, humanity has lost something of itself that it can never regain.

One of the few positive fragments in the poem appears in "The Fire Sermon," where the speaker remembers a world of music and beauty quite different from *The Waste Land.*

> "This music crept by me upon the waters"
> And along the Strand, up Queen Victoria Street.
> O City city, I can sometimes hear
> Beside a public bar in Lower Thames Street,

The pleasant whining of a mandoline
And a clatter and a chatter within
Where fishermen lounge at noon: where the walls
Of Magnus Martyr hold
Inexplicable splendor of Ionian white and gold.
(Eliot III:257–265)

The Strand and Queen Victoria Street are two of the largest streets running east and west through London, following the Thames; the lines continue the poem's insistence that the streets in the city flow like waterways. There aren't any more bars on Lower Thames Street, though the church of St. Magnus Martyr, among many of London's awesome churches built by Sir Christopher Wren, escaped sale and probable demolition by city officials in 1926 when a concerned public, Eliot included, protested in the streets by singing Christmas hymns. Its brilliant white nave and gold-decked ionic columns can still be seen today on Lower Thames Street.

The Waste Land goes a long way to describe the contemporary scene. We overhear a conversation at an East End bar that tells of a woman anxious for her husband to return from the war, who spent the money he gave her for a new set of teeth on an abortion (Eliot II:139–172). We witness a numbed typist unwilling to thwart the advances of her one-sided lover, comforting herself after his abrupt departure with music on a gramophone (III:222–256)—even passionate, intimate moments between people are vacuous. The Thames-daughters sing of the polluted river, which "sweats / Oil and tar" (III:266–267).

And yet Eliot had originally penned many more lines connecting modern society and London with death and oblivion. Famously edited by Ezra Pound, *The Waste Land's* first draft, entitled "He Do the Police in Different Voices," had lines like "London, the swarming life you kill and breed, / Huddled between the concrete and the sky" (Eliot 31). Most who have read the facsimile of the draft with Pound's redaction, presented in 1971 by Valerie Eliot, Eliot's second wife, agree that the poem was greatly improved through Pound's eye—some even arguing for Pound's coauthorship.

"Part II, A Game of Chess," contains a startling scene between a man and a woman whose relationship is fraught with neurotic drudgery. It is reminiscent of some of the personal instability Eliot underwent during (and after) he wrote the poem. His wife had a history of psychiatric problems, and if she was stable during their short courtship, her mental condition weakened after they were married, and only grew worse with time.

> "My nerves are bad to-night. Yes, bad. Stay with me.
> "Speak to me. Why do you never speak. Speak.
> "What are you thinking of? What thinking? What?
> "I never know what you are thinking. Think."
>
> I think we are in rats' alley
> Where the dead men lost their bones.
>
> "What is that noise?"
>   The wind under the door.
> "What is that noise now? What is the wind doing?"
>   Nothing again nothing. (Eliot III:111–120)

Vivienne Eliot's insomnia, neuralgia, and overall poor health exacerbated her failing mind, and she showed symptoms of what today would probably be diagnosed as an obsessive-compulsive disorder. Her condition took its toll on Eliot, who suffered a breakdown in 1921. He took three month's vacation from Lloyds, retreating first to the coast

> On Margate Sands.
> I can connect
>
> Nothing with nothing. (Eliot IV:300–302)

and then seeking treatment at a sanitarium in Lausanne, Switzerland, recommended by Lady Ottoline Morell. While Eliot had been gathering material for *The Waste Land* for years, the poem was composed here, in Lausanne.

By the time of *The Waste Land*'s publication, T.S. and Vivienne had moved out of their tiny Crawford Street apartment to a more comfortable Marylebone abode, Flat 9 at Clarence Gate Gardens near Regent's Park. They lived at different addresses in Clarence Gate Gardens in the years up to 1932—No. 68 being their last—when Eliot left for an American tour. While he would return to London shortly, he never returned to Vivienne. After Eliot moved out, she often showed up at his office at Faber & Faber, asking to see her husband. His secretary would politely tell Mrs. Eliot that Mr. Eliot was terribly busy, and that he could not be seen at the moment, while Eliot would meanwhile sneak out a back door. After two years she placed an ad in the *Times* reading "Will T.S. Eliot please return to his home 68 Clarence Gate Gardens which he abondoned Sept. 17th 1932." On occasion, she might be seen on the street outside the Faber & Faber offices with a sandwich board that read "I am the wife that T.S. Eliot abandoned." She was committed in 1938 and died in a hospital nine years later.

Eliot moved to modest lodgings in 1933, first to 33 Courtfield Road and then to the now-demolished 9 Grenville Place, both in South Kensington, after he separated from Vivienne. He became active with the Church of England, having converted in 1927, and served as a warden to St. Stephen's on Gloucester Road in South Kensington for 25 years, from 1940 to 1965. The religious nature of his poetry following *The Waste Land* did not suit many of his early admirers, yet he had success in drama, writing many plays through the 1930s including *Murder in the Cathedral*, commissioned by Bishop Bell in 1934. As a joke for friends, he wrote the collection of poems called *Old Possum's Book of Practical Cats*, inspired by the cats he met in the Gloucester Road surrounds of South Kensington.

The reading public finally forgot *The Waste Land* for a time with the publication of *Four Quartets* in 1943, its more secular tones finally palatable *en masse*. He received the Nobel Prize for literature in 1948, in part for his most recent work. At 68, he married his secretary, the young Valerie Fletcher, and enjoyed eight years before dying in London. He is buried in East Coker, though is one of a few naturalized English citizens to have a memorial in Poet's Corner, Westminster Abbey. The lines on the memorial are taken from *Little Gidding*, the fourth and last poem in *Four Quartets*, reading "the communication of the dead is tongued with fire beyond the language of the living."

THE BLOOMSBURY GROUP

Before the war, a group of intellectuals began meeting in house in what was then the highly bohemian neighborhood of Bloomsbury. Beginning around 1905, Thoby Stephen extended his Cambridge University society, the Apostles, inviting Cambridge friends to his sisters' home where, on Thursday nights, at 46 Gordon Square, they discussed literature, art, and politics. Clive Bell, Desmond McCarthy, and Lytton Strachey, in addition to Thoby Stephen's brother Adrian and his sisters, Vanessa and Virginia, comprised the first incarnation of what would come to be called the Bloomsbury Group. Leonard Woolf, Roger Fry, Duncan Grant, and Maynard Keynes were later intimates. Virginia was likely first an observer to the progressive conversation of the Cambridge men, though she and her sister became participants in short order. The Bloomsberries, as they were sometimes called when the group earned recognition enough to be named, considered themselves among London's avant-garde, questioning at length the mores of Victorian society and struggling to locate beauty and truth with an agnostic frame of mind. Specific views of the Bloomsbury Group are ephemeral; they didn't comprise a school per se, unlike other groups of the time, and they never published a manifesto. Visitors to their discussions usually reported on their overall self-righteousness.

At least some of the Bloomsbury Group's fame is due to the

legendary trysts and triangles they formed relationship-wise. Lytton Strachey, a practicing historian, proposed to Virginia Stephen in 1909, though he quickly withdrew the offer. Virginia had reservations about marriage to begin with, and Strachey had been having a homosexual relationship with his cousin, Duncan Grant, a painter and fellow Bloomsbery, for a number of years anyway. Strachey instead convinced his Cambridge friend Leonard Woolf of Virginia's virtues. Woolf fell deeply in love with Virginia, and despite many concerns on Virginia's part, anti-Semitism among them, Leonard and Virginia found themselves together often. When he proposed in 1912, she agreed to marry him. Duncan Grant left Strachey for the talented young economist Maynard Kenyes, though Grant fathered a child with Vanessa Bell, who loved Grant deeply. Clive Bell, Vanessa's husband, came close to having an affair with Virginia Woolf, though there is no evidence of consummation. This is just the short list; for a coterie known for their intelligent discussions, one wonders how frequent were the awkward silences....

Yet the group might have faded into history if it weren't for the talents of Virginia Woolf, who is widely credited with a new approach to the novel, was at the center of the inter-war literary scene, and was a Londoner through and through.

VIRGINIA WOOLF

On July 25, 1882, Virginia (Woolf) Stephen was born at 22 Hyde Park Gate, Kensington, to Sir Leslie and Julia Stephen. With her two older siblings, Vanessa and Thoby, and a younger brother Adrian, the family practiced an annual migration from their five-story house just opposite Hyde Park to a summer home, Talland House, in Cornwall. Their Kensington neighborhood was stiffly upper-middle class, and Virginia grew up with servants and access to a world of books. Young Virginia was determined to be a writer early, beginning her first newspaper, the *Hyde Park Gate News*, in her preteen years, chronicling the events of the family in the city and in the country. Her father Leslie Stephen was an active scholar: much of his time during Virginia's formative years was spent compiling and editing the *Dictionary of National Biography*. Though she never had formal schooling, Virginia's promise earned her a private tutor in 1897.

Her mother's death in 1895, and her father's about ten years later were devastating blows. On their own in their early 20s, the Stephen siblings, Virginia, Vanessa, and Adrian—Thoby was studying at Cambridge—rented the house at 46 Gordon Square, Bloomsbury in 1904, and Virginia dedicated herself to writing.

Following Thoby Stephen's early demise, the huge house on Gordon Square went to Vanessa and her husband Clive, and though Virginia moved with her younger brother Adrian to 29 Fitzroy Square—former home of George Bernard Shaw—the Bloomsbury Group's gatherings went on. Virginia and Adrian soon bought a bigger house at 38 Brunswick Square, where Keynes and Leonard Woolf moved in. The famous address where the Bloomsbury Group began, 46 Gordon Square, is now (like a great deal of Bloomsbury) part of the University of London's campus.

Virginia married Woolf in 1912, and returned to London following their honeymoon on the Continent. Virginia suffered a nervous breakdown soon after, her first since her mother died. She attempted suicide in 1913. The Woolfs moved to Paradise Lane, Richmond, in 1915, where they founded the Hogarth Press in their home, the tedious work of hand-printing intended at least in part as a remedy to Virginia's depressive moods. The Hogarth Press turned down Joyce's *Ulysses*, but published T.S. Eliot's *The Waste Land* after a visit from the "strange young man" in 1922. They also published Virginia's novels, of course, but their hand press would not be practical for commercial publishing, and as the Hogarth Press grew, the Woolfs contracted commercial printers more often. The press was finally assimilated into Random House UK in 1987.

Woolf's novels tend to explore the roles of women and men

against an upper-class backdrop. She is concerned with the psychology of her characters, and her attempt to locate the human experience in fiction, to portray emotional realities—often using a stream-of-consciousness style—is her contribution to the novel.

And they are full of London. Perhaps due to her yearly peregrinations to Cornwall in her youth, Woolf is able to depict the city with the fresh insight of an outsider and the comprehension of a seasoned denizen:

> London, in the first days of spring, has buds that open and flowers that suddenly shake their petals—white, purple, or crimson—in competition with the display in the garden beds, although these city flowers are merely so many doors flung wide in Bond Street and the neighborhood, inviting you to look at a picture, or hear a symphony, or merely crowd and crush yourself among all sorts of vocal, excitable, brightly colored human beings. But, all the same, it is no mean rival to the quieter process of vegetable florescence. Whether or not there is a generous motive at the root, a desire to share and impart, or whether the animation is purely that of insensate fervor and friction, the effect, while it lasts, certainly encourages those who are young, and those who are ignorant, to think the world one great bazaar, with banners fluttering and divans heaped with spoils from every quarter of the globe for their delight. (Woolf, *Night and Day* 386)

Woolf enjoyed a degree of fame in London during the interwar years (though she attracts even more attention in the present from the field of Gender Studies as a foundational figure), and her writing is timely. She had begun working on her second novel, *Night and Day* (1919), as early as 1916, its poignance evident in Mary Datchet's involvement with the women's suffrage movement. Even after 1918, while doubtlessly an *annu mirabilis* for suffragists, Parliamentary voting rights had only been given to women over the age of 30, while men could vote at 21.

Happily for Mary Datchet she returned to the office to find that by some obscure Parliamentary maneuver the vote had once more slipped beyond the attainment of women. Mrs. Seal was in a condition bordering upon frenzy. The duplicity of Ministers, the treachery of mankind, the insult to woman-hood, the setback to civilization, the ruin of her life's work, the feelings of her father's daughter—all these topics were discussed in turn, and the office was littered with newspaper cuttings branded with the blue, if ambiguous, marks of her displeasure. She confessed herself at fault in her estimate of human nature.

"The simple elementary acts of justice," she said, waving her hand towards the window, and indicating the foot-passengers and omnibuses then passing down the far side of Russell Square, "are as far beyond them as they ever were. We can only look upon ourselves, Mary, as pioneers in a wilderness. We can only go on patiently putting the truth before them. It isn't *them*," she continued, taking heart from her sight of the traffic, "it's their leaders. It's those gentlemen sitting in Parliament and drawing four hundred a year of the people's money. If we had to put our case to the people, we should soon have justice done to us. I have always believed in the people, and I do so still. But—" She shook her head and implied that she would give them one more chance, and if they didn't take advantage of that she couldn't answer for the consequences. (*Night and Day* 268)

Woolf makes the case in *Night and Day* and elsewhere that women's rights are not beneficial to women exclusively, but to larger humanity. In the novel, Mary Datchet views a common-enough London street scene, wherein Woolf deftly makes the case that the qualities of ambition and productivity so valued by society can be found precisely in those women working for the right to become ambitious and productive.

Thus thinking, on the particular morning in question, she

made her away across Lincoln's Inn Fields and up Kingsway, and so through Southampton Row until she reached her office in Russell Square. Now and then she would pause and look into the window of some bookseller or flower shop, where, at this early hour, the goods were being arranged, and empty gaps behind the plate glass revealed a state of undress. Mary felt kindly disposed towards the shopkeepers, and hoped that they would trick the midday public into purchasing, for at this hour of the morning she ranged herself entirely on the side of the shopkeepers and bank clerks, and regarded all who slept late and had money to spend as her enemy and natural prey. And directly she had crossed the road at Holborn, her thoughts all came naturally and regularly to roost upon her work, and she forgot that she was, properly speaking, an amateur worker, whose services were unpaid, and could hardly be said to wind the world up for its daily task, since the world, so far, had shown very little desire to take the boons which Mary's society for woman's suffrage had offered it. (*Night and Day* 75–76)

Mary Datchet, a secretary at an organization fighting for women's suffrage, is ostensibly a fictionalization of Woolf herself, who was active in the movement. For the People's Suffrage Federation she, like Datchet, performed secretarial tasks, and she became active in the Women's Co-operative Guild later, holding meetings of the Richmond branch at her home there. The lectures she gave at Cambridge in 1928 became the material for her landmark essay, *A Room of One's Own*, in which Woolf presents the difficulties faced by women who might endeavor to write literature on par with Shakespeare. It is postulated that the success of women in literature depends upon the altogether pragmatic conditions of a private space to write and a certain degree of financial freedom: "it is necessary to have five hundred a year and a room with a lock on the door if you are to write fiction or poetry," said plainly in the essay's conclusion. The absence of these conditions in the history of the sex explains the failure of women, as compared to men, to produce literature. Moreover, she pins the creation of great literature not on the masculine mind, but on the androgynous mind, and looks forward to a day when sex-consciousness has faded; when, quite unlike the polarized time in which she was writing, both sexes might contribute to a canon.

> Coleridge certainly did not mean, when he said that a great mind is androgynous, that it is a mind that has any special sympathy with women; a mind that takes up their cause or devotes itself to their interpretation. Perhaps the androgynous mind is less apt to make these distinctions than the single-sexed mind. He meant, perhaps, that the androgynous mind is resonant and porous; that it transmits emotion without impediment; that it is naturally creative, incandescent and undivided. In fact one goes back to Shakespeare's mind as the type of the androgynous, of the manwomanly mind, though it would be impossible to say what Shakespeare thought of women. And if it be true that it is one of the tokens of the fully developed mind that it does not think specially or separately of sex, how much harder it is to attain that condition now than ever before. Here I came to the books by living writers, and there paused and wondered if this fact were not at the root of something that had long puzzled me. No age can ever have been as stridently sex-conscious as our own; those innumerable books by men about women in the British Museum are a proof of it. The Suffrage campaign was no doubt to blame. It must have roused in men an extraordinary desire for selfassertion; it must have made them lay an emphasis upon their own sex and its characteristics which they would not have troubled to think about had they not been challenged. And when one is challenged, even by a few women in black bonnets, one retaliates, if one has never been challenged before, rather excessively. (Woolf, *A Room of One's Own* 89)

Mrs. Dalloway (1925), like James Joyce's *Ulysses*, takes place in one day's time, and consists of several "walks" through London by the various characters, through Regent's Park, Trafalgar Square, Oxford Street and Piccadilly, and many other recognizable London places, with the hours chimed by Big Ben: "There! Out it boomed. First a warning, musical; then the hour, irrevocable" (4). So precise is Mrs. Dalloway in parts (and so vague in others) that it has inspired Woolf enthusiasts (again like Joyce's Ulysses) to undertake some of the novel's walks themselves. The novel ultimately comments on the world of Clarissa Dalloway, whose universe consists of the wealthy and powerful neighborhoods of Mayfair and Westminster, but which remains small. Other characters in the book occupy the fringes of London: Septimus Warren-Smith, the shell-shocked veteran, throws himself from a Bloomsbury rooftop, off Tottenham Court Road; Peter Walsh, Clarissa's one-time beau, has lodgings in the same area.

Set on a June day in 1923 London, when the city was finally beginning to move past the experience of the World War I, the novel follows, in a parallel to Clarissa Dalloway, the last hours of Septimus Warren-Smith, a young veteran haunted by his wartime experiences. Woolf was a pacifist during the First World War, and she makes Septimus join the fighting for romantic reasons. Following the war, Septimus is guilt-ridden for his youthful ideas of what constituted being a good soldier, and as a symptom of his insanity, he talks out loud to his dead war buddy, Evans. On Broad Walk in Regent's Park among the Elms, most of which succumbed to Dutch elm disease in the 1970s, Septimus sees his dead, grey friend walking towards him. That Septimus eventually commits suicide demonstrates that for some, the war was too terrible to move beyond. Ultimately, it is the sanity of those who *are* able to forget the destruction that took place just a few years earlier that is in question.

In *Orlando: A Biography* (1928), the protagonist meanders through London and time, beginning in the Elizabethan age and ending up 500 years later—to the novel's present—just

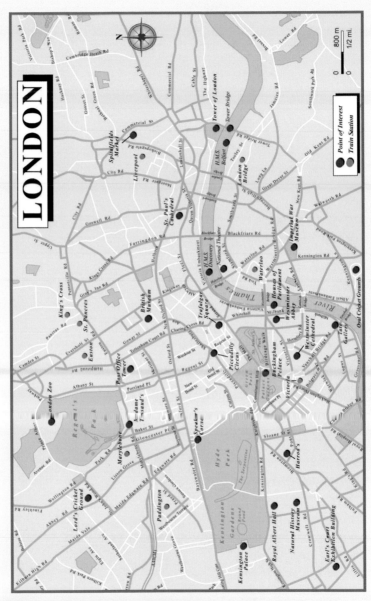

■ Central London, as pictured here, has many points of interest
scattered around the River Thames. Common points of reference
for the city listed from west to east are: Kensington and South
Kensington; Chelsea, Belgravia, and Knightsbridge; Westminster;
Trafalgar Square and Soho; Bloomsbury; Covent Garden; and the City.

■ The Globe Theatre, first constructed in 1599, was made famous by William Shakespeare and his many original productions; the theater closed in 1642 and later was destroyed. Two hundred yards from its original site, Sam Wanamaker began to reconstruct the Globe, and although he died before it was completed, Theo Crosby saw it to its finish in 1997 when it opened for its first season of 17th-century plays.

■ William Shakespeare (1564–1616), was born in Stratford-upon-Avon in Warwickshire, but later lived in Bankside, London. During his life Shakespeare authored 38 plays and 154 sonnets, and his portrait was the first hung in the National Portrait Gallery near Trafalgar Square. He is buried in the chancel of the Church of the Holy Trinity in Stratford.

■ Often pictured on postcards, Westminster Abbey celebrated its 900th anniversary in 1965–66. The building, an architectural masterpiece of the 13–16th centuries, has been the setting for every monarch's Coronation since 1066, except for Edward V and Edward VII. Poet's Corner, located in the South Transept, is the final resting place for many famous writers including Geoffrey Chaucer, Dr. Samuel Johnson, Charles Dickens, and Thomas Hardy.

■ Surrounded by many of London's famed theaters, Piccadilly Circus is one of the busiest traffic circles in the world. Five major roads converge around the "circus" in which a bronze fountain stands, topped by a winged archer. "Piccadilly" originates from the 17th-century frilled collar "piccadil," whose creator, Roger Baker, lived in the area.

■ Cheapside, London is most famous for having been the birthplace of John Milton (1608–1674). Milton was born on Bread Street, and first educated at the nearby St. Paul's School. Another poet, Thomas Hood, was born here in 1799. He became one of England's most famous social-protest poets, influencing similar poets in Germany, Russia, and the United States.

■ Charles Dickens (1812–1870) remains among the greatest of English novelists. His works are generally characterized by attacks on social evils, injustice, and hypocrisy. Born in Landport, Hampshire, Dickens moved to London in 1814. He, his wife Catherine, and their son Charles, moved onto Doughty Street in 1837 where he wrote the *Pickwick Papers* (1837), *Oliver Twist* (1837–1839), and *Nicholas Nickleby* (1838–1839).

■ The original Old Curiosity Shop stood near Charing Cross Road. Like the one pictured here it was made famous by Charles Dickens's novel The Old Curiosity Shop (1840–1841).

■ One of the many symbols of London, London Tower Bridge is confused with the less flashy London Bridge, which was the first bridge over the Thames River. Additional bridges were built to the west, but, by the 19th century the east end of London had become so densely populated that public pressure demanded a bridge to the east. Horace Jones and John Wolfe Barry designed a bridge, powered by steam, which could open to let ships go past. London Tower Bridge was completed in 1894 after 8 years of construction.

■ Sherlock Holmes and his partner Doctor John H. Watson are characters lovingly created by Sir Athur Conan Doyle in the *Strand Magazine* in 1891. According to his stories they lived at 221b Baker Street between 1881–1904. The house was last used as a lodging house in 1936, and to this day the first floor study overlooking Baker Street remains as it was in Victorian times.

■ Virginia Woolf (1882–1941), a novelist, distinguished feminist essayist, critic, and central figure of the Bloomsbury group was born in London, grew up at Hyde Park Gate, and moved to Bloomsbury after her father's death. In 1905 Woolf began to write for the *Times Literary Supplement,* and in 1912 she married the political theorist Leonard Woolf and published her first book, *The Voyage Out* (1915). During the inter-war period Woolf was at the center of literary Society as a member of The Bloomsbury group.

after World War I. Orlando, who was a young man during the court of Queen Elizabeth I, wakes up as a woman mid-way through the book; through this turn Woolf presents the different ways men and women have been treated through time, and places gender firmly under the influence of society. Along the way, Woolf cannot resist introducing her character to London's famous literary personalities. Thus Orlando visits Elenor's Cross at Charing Cross station; watches Johnson and Boswell have tea in Bolt Court, off of Fleet Street; meets Nicholas Greene at Ye Olde Cocke Taverne (190 Fleet Street); and walks Piccadilly Circus with Alexander Pope.

Virginia and Leonard survived zeppelin bombings near Hogarth House during World War I, and moved back to Bloomsbury at 52 Tavistock Square with the Hogarth Press in 1923. She wrote five novels here, but the Woolfs were forced to move when word came in 1939 that the house was to be demolished

Hogarth Press

Founded in 1917 by Virginia and Leonard Woolf, the Hogarth Press began as a small handpress operated out of the Woolf's home, Hogarth House in Richmond, Surrey. Though it began as a hobby for the couple, and as a diversion for Virginia, the press became a commercial enterprise after the successful publication of Virginia's Kew Gardens (1919). When presented with the opportunity to publish Joyce's Ulysses, the press turned it down. Among those author published by Hogarth were, Katherine Mansfield, T.S. Eliot, C. Day Lewis, Robert Graves, E.M. Forster, John Maynard Keynes, and the Woolf's themselves. The press was operated by Leonard and Virginia until Virginia gave up her partnership in the business in 1938. Leonard remained involved with the publishing house until his death in 1969, and then in 1987 the press was bought by Random House UK in 1987.

for new development—specifically, the Tavistock Hotel, which stands on this site today. They sadly moved to Mecklenburgh Square, and their Tavistock home was demolished, not by bulldozers but by German bombs during the Blitz. The Woolfs's stay at the roomier Mecklenberg Square home was short-lived: with windows blown out during the bombing and a land mine dropped into the back yard, Virginia and Leonard finally moved to the country. Virginia's mind worsened during the Blitz, even in the Sussex countryside that had, in the past, remedied her mental instability. Feeling she could not recover from her current affliction, however, and afraid she was a burden to her husband, she drowned herself in the Ouse River in 1941. She is recognized more in the present for her work in literature and feminism than she ever was in her own time.

GEORGE ORWELL

More than any other writer of his time, George Orwell, born Eric Blair, tried to understand the city of London and its people, in a way quite different from Henry James's upper-middle class observations in Mayfair and St. James. Born to British parents in India, he studied at Eton and served a stint with the Burmese police. When the muse struck him in the 1920s he moved to London, staying with friends, the Fierzes, at 1B Oakwood Road, Hampstead. With an idea for a book in mind, Orwell changed into shabby clothes at his house and set off to London's underbelly—largely Limehouse in the East—posing as a tramp, disguising his Eton accent and cavorting with the sailors, the homeless, and the unemployed.

In Paris for a time, Orwell wore the same guise, and moved back to London in 1927. An old friend, the poet Ruth Pitter, found him lodgings at 22 Portobello Road in Notting Hill with a haughty woman named Mrs. Craig. The environs of Notting Hill at the time allowed a mix of working and moneyed classes, and the juxtaposition only firmed Orwell's socialist dream of a classless utopia.

He continued his tramping in the late 1920s, using Pitter's

pottery studio to change into his rags, and always walked the seven miles to Limehouse. He spent nights sleeping with indigents in Trafalgar Square, and on the benches and lawns of the Victoria Embankment by the Thames, kept awake by the noisy trams and neon lights across the river. He had done some writing work for the *Adelphi*, a magazine with offices on Bloomsbury Street, but in 1930 he announced to family and friends that he would pursue a career as a writer. He used the Fierzes' house to type the manuscript of his experiences in August 1931, calling it *Down and Out in Paris and London*. T.S. Eliot rejected the manuscript at Faber & Faber, and though Orwell asked Mabel Fierz to destroy the manuscript (but save the paper clips), she managed to cajole Victor Gollancz to publish the work; it appeared in January 1933. In the event the book flopped, he chose to publish it under one of the aliases he used while tramping—Orwell.

Down and Out reads like something between a documentary, a guidebook, and a morality tale on life on the streets of London. He includes gritty details of homeless life, the nights spent outdoors, the sleeping quarters and the bathrooms in spikes—temporary housing intended for the temporarily homeless. An intimate he met while tramping, Paddy, explains the trick to sleeping on the Victoria Embankment.

> De whole t'ing wid de Embankment is gettin' to sleep early. You got to be on your bench by eight o'clock, because dere ain't too many benches and sometimes dey're all taken. And you got to try to get to sleep at once. 'Tis too cold to sleep much after twelve o'clock, an' de police turns you off at four in de mornin'. It ain't easy to sleep, dough, wid dem bloody trams flyin' past your head all de time, an' dem sky-signs across de river flickin' on an' off in your eyes. De cold's cruel. Dem as sleeps dere generally wraps demselves up in newspaper, but it don't do much good. You'd be bloody lucky if you got t'ree hours' sleep. (Orwell, *Down and Out in Paris and London* 289)

He goes out of his way to explain the London many of his readers might never see.

> When we got into London we had eight hours to kill before the lodging-houses opened. It is curious how one does not notice things. I had been in London innumerable times, and yet till that day I had never noticed one of the worst things about London—the fact that it costs money even to sit down. In Paris, if you had no money and could not find a public bench, you would sit on the pavement. Heaven knows what sitting on the pavement would lead to in London— prison, probably. (*Down and Out* 154)

And he proposes legislation that might ease the conditions for London's poor.

> At present there is all manner of legislation by the L.G.C. about lodging-houses, but it is not done in the interests of the lodgers. The L.G.C. only exert themselves to forbid drinking, gambling, fighting, etc. etc. There is no law to say that the beds in a lodging-house must be comfortable. This would be quite an easy thing to enforce—much easier, for instance, than restrictions upon gambling. The lodging-house keepers should be compelled to provide adequate bed-clothes and better mattresses, and above all to divide their dormitories into cubicles. (*Down and Out* 211)

"Here is the world that awaits you if you are penniless," Orwell writes in closing (213). Though quite different from the satires that would make him famous, *Down and Out* is above all principled, and the beginning of a writing style pregnant with admonition.

Even after he had written his tramping narrative, Orwell continued researching London as lived by the poor and working classes. He worked pushing fish carts from Billingsgate Market on Lower Thames Street to Eastcheap. In 1931, wishing to experience the inside of a jail cell on Christmas, he set out Christmas Eve to get himself arrested, becoming blind-drunk at a bar on Mile End Road, and staggering along the street until the police apprehended him and locked him up. He later based the scene of Winston Smith's imprisonment in *1984* on the night he spent at the Bethnal Green police station, and the building at 458 Bethnal Green Road—now offices—was the inspiration for the Ministry of Love.

Today Hampstead is an impossibly wealthy neighborhood, but in 1934 when Orwell moved to an apartment on the corner of Pond Street and South End Road, he was able to afford the rent with his part-time job at the bookstore downstairs. Orwell only lived here a few months, but not before Booklover's Corner made enough of an impression on him to include it in *Keep the Aspidistra Flying* (1936) as Mr. McKechnie's bookshop. The site now houses The Perfect Pizza, and a bust and plaque set in the building's bricks mark Orwell's onetime presence. *Keep the Aspidistra Flying*, about a would-be poet jealous of the literary success of others, is so thinly veiled it might be read autobiographically, and uses for its setting much of Orwell's Hampstead stomping ground.

In 1935, Orwell moved to 77 Parliament Square, a brick house at the end of the road, writing much of *Keep the Aspidistra Flying* on the second floor. He met his future wife Eileen O'Shaughnessy at a party held in the house; he is honored by a plaque over the front door, though he only lived here until August, moving south to Kentish Town. At 50 Lawford Road, he shared a house with a ballet critic, Rayner Heppenstall, a friend of Dylan Thomas. Orwell may have been a bear of a roommate: when Heppenstall came home late and drunk one evening, Orwell was infuriated, beating him up and locking him in one of the bedrooms. The next day Orwell threw the ballet critic out of the house, though he himself didn't stay at the residence long, accepting an assignment from his publisher to report on the working conditions of Wigan miners—what would become *The Road to Wigan Pier* (1937).

The next several years were spent out of town, for some months in Hertfordshire, marrying Eileen, and then to Spain, fighting against the fascists. Wounded by a sniper, he returned to London in May, renting a garage apartment from H.G. Wells, who soon evicted the Orwells, fearing they were gossiping about him. George and Eileen tried to mend the relationship by inviting Wells to dinner at their next residence, 111 Langford Court at Abbey Road and Langford Place in St. John's Wood, but, for better or worse, Eileen's curry upset Wells's stomach, effectively severing all ties between the two writers.

In 1942, they moved about 500 yards away, to 10a Mortimer Crescent. When, in 1944, a V-1 bomb landed in the street outside their home, the ceiling fell in, burying the only copy of the manuscript of *Animal Farm* in the debris. Obviously, they found it. The house has been demolished.

During the war, Orwell found work producing radio broadcasts for the BBC to India and Southeast Asia. He loathed the BBC's bureaucracy, calling the place "halfway between a girls' school and a lunatic asylum," and was thus inspired to use the BBC as his model for the Ministry of Truth in *1984*, on both the propaganda he was required to broadcast and the notoriously bad food at the BBC canteen. The model for the imposing edifice that houses the Ministry of Truth—and certainly its aim—is the University of London Senate House on Malet Street, Bloomsbury, where the British based their propaganda machine, the Ministry of Information, during World War II.

In America, *1984* appeared in the midst of the Red scare, when McCarthyism was at its worst and rampant anticommunism took hold at the onset of the Cold War. Like *Animal Farm*, *1984* was and has been read explicitly as a tract against Stalinist totalitarianism. But while Orwell was no friend to that regime, the novel—more than another diatribe against Stalinism (which *Animal Farm* surely is)—is an admonition against the practices of Orwell's own government in Britain. Churchill's wartime government didn't look much like democracy when it enacted price controls, trade and travel restrictions, and censored literature and news through the Ministry of Information. In late May 1940 Parliament legislated that all "persons, their services and their property [are] at the disposal of the Crown." The National Service Act, passed in December 1941, deemed that all women under the age of 30 and all men under 50 were subject to government assignment. The election of 1945 removed Churchill's Tory government in a landslide, and its Labour Party replacement promised to establish many government-run programs in a bid to establish socialism, creating the National Heath Service in 1946 and establishing sweeping public welfare systems. Thus Orwell warns of a Great Britain in the year *1984*.

Many sights around London make their way into *1984*. The Senate House on Malet Street became the Ministry of Truth; the Bethnal Green Police Station the Ministry of Love. Trafalgar Square is renamed Victory Square, and the statue commemorating Horatio Nelson's victory at the Battle of Trafalgar in 1805 is replaced by one of Big Brother. In 1944 the Orwells were obliged to move to Islington, taking an apartment at 27b Canonbury Square, since their home in Maida Vale was destroyed by German bombs. Their new flat on the top floor was in bad shape, but all they could afford, having not yet received income from *Animal Farm*. This is Winston Smith's Victory Mansions, where Orwell wrote the bulk of *1984*, though as luxury apartments in the present-day it is hard to imagine that "the hallway smelt of boiled cabbage and old rag mats" (1). The room above Mr. Charrington's shop, Winston and Julia's love nest, has the flat of Orwell's secretary, Sonia Brownell, for its model.

Eileen died suddenly from complications during surgery in 1945, and Orwell married Brownell in 1949, just months before his own sudden death while convalescing from tuberculosis in 1950. He died in a private wing of the University College Hospital, in Bloomsbury, at the age of 46.

GRAHAM GREENE

Frequently lunching with Orwell at the Elysee, 13 Percy Street, Fitzrovia, (where Orwell was forever being asked to leave for not wearing a jacket, to his glee) was Graham Greene, the long-lived London-based writer of more than two dozen novels.

Graham Greene might have stayed in his position as a sub-editor for the *Times* his entire life if he hadn't managed to publish a novel. Having recently arrived in London, Greene took the post in 1927, and wrote most of *The Man Within* (1929) in Room 2 of the *Times* office, 162 Queen Victoria Street. The *Times*, like many of London's newspapers, has since moved east to the Docklands, but the building survives. Following the publication of *The Man Within*, Greene was able to write full time.

Lady Ottoline Morrell was one of the best-known names in London's literary circles in the first half of the 20th century, though she never published a word. As a hostess, she garnered the attendance of such names as Aldous Huxley, D.H. Lawrence, Bertrand Russell, T.S. Eliot, Virginia Woolf, Roger Fry (another beau), and others in the Bloomsbury Group at her gatherings. Greene wasn't the first to caricature Morrell in literature, where she appears as Lady Caroline Bury in *It's a Battlefield* (1934). She lived at 10 Gower Street, Bloomsbury, for more than a decade.

In 1935, Greene moved to 14 Clapham Common North Side, in a row of terraced Georgian houses that were completely destroyed by German bombings during World War II. Greene destroyed the house again in *The End of the Affair* (1951), a novel that features several scenes around the Commons. The address has since been rebuilt into apartments.

Like many authors in Britain during the Second World War, Greene sought work in the war machine and wound up serving as a propagandist for the Ministry of Information. Quartered in the University of London's Senate House, Greene's first assignment in 1941 was to write a story for *Collier's* prompting Americans to join the war on the side of the Allies. (This was one of several tactics to distribute propaganda to the United States by the Ministry of Information. The British seized and cut Germany's trans-Atlantic cable early in the War, thereby becoming the only source for news and information from Europe.) Greene's *The Lieutenant Died Last* resulted, in which the Germans occupy a British hamlet only to be killed one-by-one by a wretched drunk named Old Purves.

In 1937, Greene helped to found the literary magazine *Night and Day*, the offices of which were located at 197 St. Martin's Lane in Covent Garden. Greene wrote film reviews for the publication—he found himself often involved with cinema—though he suffered a £3,500 charge when Shirley Temple sued for libel after a particularly scathing review. The magazine folded soon after because of poor sales.

Greene's fiction features scenes from all over London. In *The Confidential Agent* (1939), the hero, D., shows up in Bloomsbury looking for an address in a "big, leafless Bloomsbury Square"—Russell Square, just across the street from the University of London's Senate House. D.'s No. 35 is a seedy hotel, but in the present day, the address is an office building. Branching off Russell Square is Guilford Street, where in *The Ministry of Fear* (1943) Arthur Rowe resides, and remains, even though a bomb lands in the middle of the road. In the same novel, 87 Chancery Lane, Holborn, is the address for Orthotex, "the Longest Established Private Inquiry Bureau in the Metropolis." Like much of its surroundings, the address now houses legal offices.

In his 1947 short story, *A Little Place Off the Edgware Road*, Greene wrote a scene with a group of Jewish boys trying to pick up girls in Bayswater, a now downtrodden area near Hyde Park. It is one of a few instances of Greene's apparent anti-Semitism: he was once thrown out of a lecture at the Institute for Contemporary Arts (formerly at 17–18 Dover Street) for making anti-Semitic remarks. When *A Little Place Off the Edgware Road* was included in Greene's *Collected Short Stories* (1987), he removed the controversial lines.

Greene moved to 5 St. James's Street, Westminster, in 1947,

into an apartment formerly belonging to Colonel Claude Dansey, an intelligence agent working for the Secret Intelligence Service (SIS), Great Britain's intelligence agency specializing in military espionage. Dansey played an important role in intelligence since the First World War, though his reputation suffered greatly when the Germans captured one of his Section Z operatives at the very beginning of the Second World War and subsequently learned costly details about British intelligence. Dansey used the apartment during the war to train agents in MI9, which specialized in escape and evasion. Thirty years after Greene moved out of the apartment at St. James's, he cast Dansey as Colonel Daintry in *The Human Factor* (1978), and gives him this address.

EVELYN WAUGH

Greene's contemporary, Evelyn Waugh, was born in West Hampstead, at 11 Hillfield Road, in 1903. While Greene and Waugh shared literary renown from the late 1920s through the 1940s, Waugh's career took a downturn after *Brideshead Revisited* (1945), and he was dead by 1966—a relatively short life compared to Greene's 86 years.

In 1916, Waugh moved with his family to 145 North End Road, Hampstead, northwest of the Heath. His father was in publishing, and being inclined toward literature at a young age, he began an early novel while living here, though he burned it when a friend commented that it was "too English." Notoriously, as a boy he enjoyed bullying Cecil Beaton, who would later become a famous photographer, and Waugh's failure to apologize for this even after both men had earned a certain degree of fame was characteristic of his temperament. Following his studies at Hertford College, Oxford, where through friends he met most of London's bright young ladies, he married Evelyn Gardner (who also associated with the group), and in 1928 moved to 17a Canonbury Square, Canonbury. That year also saw the publication of Waugh's first novel, *Decline and Fall,* its hilarity setting the pace for the author's fiction until the denser

Brideshead Revisited appeared in 1945. Waugh's marriage to Evelyn Gardener (dubbed She-Evelyn) disintegrated quickly, and he left Canonbury Square in 1930.

Waugh's divorce affected him deeply, and like Graham Greene, he found solace in the Catholic Church. He was received in 1930, the same year *Vile Bodies* was published. In the novel, Lottie Crump's hotel is a reincarnation of one of Waugh's favorite London restaurants, the Eiffel Tower Hotel, 1 Percy Street, in Fitzrovia, which during the 1920s served as a meeting place for many in the literary set, including Ezra Pound and Aldous Huxley.

Scoop (1938) is a tremendous satire of Fleet Street—when it was still the epicenter of London's newspaper industry—and all the politics that go into making a story in modern journalism. Waugh no doubt drew on his very brief time working for the *Daily Express,* whose building still stands at 120 Fleet Street, recast in the novel as the *Daily Beast.* A series of buyouts beginning in the late seventies have since relocated the newspapers east to the docklands, but efforts are being made in the present day to preserve the unmistakable *Daily Express* building, with its glass facade and signature art deco curves.

Greene and Waugh both have war novels in their bibliographies, Greene's *The End of the Affair* set in London during the Blitz, and Waugh's *Sword of Honour* trilogy, in which he treats the whole war with his satirical, comedic wit. These works hastened the Second World War into literature, the start of a process due in no small way to film, wherein World War II garnered the practically mythic status it has today. And since, during the conflict, appreciable advances in aviation from the First World War brought the fight to England and London in ways far more dreadful than anything dropped from floating zeppelins, it was perhaps inevitable that London would be treated on a mythic scale, too.

CHAPTER NINE

The London
of Gravity's Rainbow

On June 14, 1940, to almost everyone's horror, the Germans marched into Paris; the southern- and western-most parts of France would fall within the month. Considered before the Second World War to be the most powerful military in Europe, the French had been vanquished. Hitler hoped for some time to strike a deal with the last remaining military power in Western Europe, but since Lord Chamberlain had at last given the office of the Prime Minister to the belligerent and unwavering Winston Churchill, Hitler ordered, on July 16, a plan for the invasion of Britain.

LONDON IN WORLD WAR II

It was the English Channel that—as in so many conflicts of centuries past—buffered Britain from the forces of the Continent. The formidable British navy blocked the possibility of an amphibious invasion, and Hitler and his generals rightly concluded that any successful maritime advance toward land would have Germany's utter control of the skies for its prerequisite. Thus Herman Göring, head of the Luftwaffe, envisioned a few swift aerial attacks on key depots of the Royal Air Force, with the aim of destroying British air power. The first bombings took place in July 1940 at coastal locations, and British fighters successfully engaged the Germans over and along the Channel. That summer it became apparent to the Germans that the destruction of Britain's advanced radar systems was a precondition to any success in the air, and by August, the Luftwaffe began targeting radar stations and airfields further inland. In September, RAF bombers took the Germans by surprise when they appeared over Berlin. Hitler was incensed. He now directed bombers away from RAF installments in the southern countryside to London and other cities. The winter of 1940–1941 is known as the Battle of Britain. Part of a major German offensive, the Blitz, saw London, its citizens, and its daily life bombed almost daily.

British antiaircraft guns quickly altered initial German tactics of massive daylight attacks featuring 1,000 planes or more; even before the close of 1940, smaller sorties of a few hundred German planes would cross the Channel, splitting up to make their way for London. By April 1941, daylight attacks were altogether abandoned because of the huge losses taken by the Luftwaffe.

Casualties in London were high, and the damage extensive. Official counts by October 1940 claimed over 27,000 casualties, including over 11,000 deaths. The poor East End proved particularly susceptible to attack, yet no building seemed too sacred to evade German bombs and incendiaries. More than two dozen churches were damaged or destroyed; those hit includes St. Paul's, the high altar of which was destroyed when a bomb pierced the roof, Westminster Abbey, St. Mary Woolnoth, and the Church of St. Magnus Martyr—just among those mentioned in this text. The offices of the *Times* newspaper, the Regent's Park Zoo, and the Tower were hit. The glass was blown out of shop windows on Oxford Street, Regent Street, and Piccadilly. The Great Ormond Street Hospital for sick children, which received benefaction from J.M. Barrie, and Hogarth House, historic home of the satirist and painter William Hogarth, both suffered damage before the New Year.

Assaults in December specifically targeted the City, London's financial district. The damage prompted all businesses in London's center to engage in fire watching, which had T.S. Eliot staying nights at his Faber & Faber offices on duty. London saw a lull in attacks from the end of February through much of March 1941, but in April the nighttime raids began. Among the great loss of lives and structures, Chelsea Old Church, where Henry James's funeral services were held, was completely destroyed. The last great raid of the year was on the night of May 10, the night of a full moon that would come to be known as a "bomber's moon," when German incendiaries set fires in a wide swath of the city. Dr. Samuel Johnson's house at 7 Johnson's Court off Fleet Street, where he lived from 1765 to 1776, was demolished, along with the Central Criminal Court and Old Bailey, landmarks of Oscar Wilde's downfall. The fire brigades won the day, though, preventing the fire from engulfing much more of London than it did.

Although the worst of the Blitz had passed, the tremendous devastation wrought on London since 1940 had presented predictable difficulties in the city. A great mass of homeless—especially families from the East End—camped in green spaces and slept in subways. Perhaps a half million houses were rendered unlivable at least temporarily, with 40,000 destroyed completely. The city enacted programs to shelter over 100,000 people, evacuated children, and built canteens and restaurants providing lost-cost meals. The war was still on, of course (in fact it may be argued that if not for the steadfastness and vigilance of Londoners the war *could have been* over, with Germany occupying the British Isles), food and gasoline rationing was still in effect, and there was much repair work to be done to roads, sewers, and embankments of the Thames.

Yet air raids were virtually nonexistent from 1942 through 1943, giving London time to recover. Hitler was preoccupied with Eastern Europe and the Soviet Union, facing unforeseen setbacks on the front, including the Soviet encirclement of 250,000 German soldiers in Stalingrad at the onset of the

Russian winter in November 1942. Hitler would hear nothing of retreat, and 91,000 men surrendered to the Soviets before he allowed their withdrawal to the Black Sea in January 1943. The battle represented huge physical and psychological blows to Germany. Axis forces were utterly vanquished by Generals George Patton and Bernard Montgomery in North Africa by May; Hitler had only to guess where, of the vast borders of his occupied Europe, the Allies would plan their invasion. In December 1943, Churchill and Roosevelt met with Stalin in Tehran, where both factions agreed to a simultaneous invasion, with Anglo-American forces pushing from the West and the Soviet Union from the East, sometime in 1944. The offensive began in June of that year. That same month, Hitler launched the first of his *vergeltungswaffen*, or vengeance-weapons, at London.

From a post-war perch, we know that Hitler looked to "unmanned planes" as a way of pummeling the British into peace as early as 1942, when it became clear the Britons would not fold under attacks from the Luftwaffe. Developed at Peenemünde on the coast of the Baltic, these first rockets proved very difficult to control: without proper guidance systems it was nearly impossible to adjust for wind and the rocket's changing weight as it burned off fuel. By 1944, the *Vergeltungswaffen 1* (V-1) was ready, and though thousands were launched at London, few hit their target, being easily picked up by radar and shot down by anti-aircraft guns. Moreover, having no way to see the actual point of impact for the rockets, the Germans had no way to adjust their coordinates. The British knew this, and purposely published hits by the "flying bombs" in places they had not landed, causing the bulk of the V-1's to detonate harmlessly, far off from their intended targets. Their launch sites could be seen from the air by Allied planes and destroyed. A far more potent nightmare for the London was the V-2, only a few months behind in development.

The much bigger, more explosive V-2 (or A-4, as it was the fourth project in the series of *Aggregat* rocketry experiments at

Peenemünde) was launched from mobile pads and fired verti-
cally, reaching as high as fifty miles up before heading down to
earth (or, more precisely, London) at speeds faster than sound.
There were still problems with accuracy, though as the war
wound down the frequency of launches increased. As many
1,000 V-2s were launched at London from September 1944
through March 1945. When they hit they were extremely
destructive, able to flatten a city block and smash windows a
half-mile from their point of impact. The V-2's inaccuracy was
counterbalanced by the fact that there was no known defense
against them. They traveled too fast to be detected, and, because
they were supersonic, they could not be heard. This is the
London we enter in Thomas Pynchon's post-war masterwork,
Gravity's Rainbow (1973).

> "What's it like in London, Slothrop? When the rockets come
> down?"
> "What?" After fucking he usually likes to lie around, just
> smoke a cigarette, think about food, "Uh, you don't know it's
> there till it's there. Gee, till after it's there. If it doesn't hit
> you, then you're O.K. till the next one. If you hear the explo-
> sion, you know you must be alive."
> "That's how you know you're alive."
> "Right." (Pynchon 222)

Encyclopedic in scope and detail, *Gravity's Rainbow*—more
than any other work of literature—conveys the *mise en scene* in
London at the close of the Second World War in all its chaos
and uncertainty, its bewildering array of intelligence agencies,
civilian-soldiers, and governments-in-exile, its general paranoia
brought on by the strange and horrific threat of the V-2. The
vast text follows, for the most part, the adventures of an American lieutenant, Tyrone Slothrop, whose frequent trysts with
London girls coincide exactly with the location of the rocket
strikes, a connection that attracts a peculiar cadre of behavioral
scientists and intelligence operatives trying to discover why this

should occur. But the plot isn't the whole story. It is the dense, meaningful way the story is told, and—for our purposes—the way war-torn London is painted in words: a labyrinthine mess of iron and brick, a city of dark motives and desperation amidst the horror of the "robot blitz," of vain efforts to live some semblance of one's own life.

But while the novel *is* historical, setting London with enough Joycean minutiae to fill companions and online indices devoted to the work, the elements of fantasy and the absurd in the novel often stage a coup on Pynchon's hard-fought verisimilitude. It may of course be argued that the intrinsic surrealism of *Gravity's Rainbow* only augments its superrealism; that is, the book, including its phantasm, is a testament to real life as lived by some extraordinary people in the extraordinary world of London 1944–45.

The novel opens in the dream of Pirate Prentice, winter 1944. Pirate's night has been haunted by an impossible evacuation of London, one that fails in the chaos of the city that "denied, threatened, lied to its children" (4). "No, this is not a disentanglement from, but a progressive *knotting into—*" (3). The scene, with its doomed "rush of souls," is evocative of T.S. Eliot's depictions in *The Waste Land,* as is much of *Gravity's Rainbow,* begging a tradition of American authors describing hellish, post-war London.

> It is too late. The evacuation still proceeds, but it's all theatre. There are no lights inside the cars. No light anywhere. Above him lift girders as old as an iron queen, and glass somewhere far above would let the light of day through. But it's night. He's afraid of the way the glass will fall—soon—it will be a spectacle: the fall of a crystal palace. But coming down in total blackout, without one glint of light, only great invisible crashing. (3)

The "fall of a crystal palace" will mean the end of London's world dominance. Constructed in Hyde Park for the Great

Exhibition of 1851, the Crystal Palace was designed with the express purpose of demonstrating Great Britain's global superiority. It was a mammoth structure of glass and iron, containing almost a million square feet. Disassembled and rebuilt in Bromley, south of London, following the exhibition, the Crystal Palace was finally destroyed by fire in 1936. The towers that remained were taken down in 1941 so that they wouldn't be a landmark to German bombers making their way to London proper.

Despite the failure of the evacuation in Pirate's dream, London was able to dispatch many of its inhabitants—especially children—to the countryside during the Blitz. When the Luftwaffe all but gave up on London from 1942–43, many people returned, and it is indicative of the terror caused by the German V-2's that even in these late days of the war, almost as many were evacuated from the city as had been during the Battle of Britain in 1940–41.

Some areas had been vacant since the early evacuations. It is a house in one such area that Roger Mexico and his lover, Jessica Swanlake, adopt for their trysts. "They have found a house in the stay-away zone, under the barrage balloons south of London. The town, evacuated in '40, is still 'regulated'—still on the Ministry's list. Roger and Jessica occupy the place illegally, in a defiance they can never measure unless they're caught" (41). The penalty for this behavior—imposed for fear of looters— was death, and signs around London threatened as much. The barrage balloons, huge blimps tethered to the ground with cables for the purpose of shedding enemy aircraft, were commonplace, and they don't help in locating the town Pynchon had in mind. The balloons worked against the V-1's, too, but did nothing against the vertically-descending V-2.

Pirate, we find, works for a historically accurate (if peculiar) intelligence service called the Special Operations Executive (SOE), chartered by Churchill at the onset of the war. From its headquarters in two flats at 62–64 Baker Street, the SOE engaged in remarkably effective sabotage campaigns on the

Continent, using forged documents to send German trains in the wrong direction and destroying engines by replacing their lubricant with abrasive oils, among other things. They were also committed to contact with a number of underground resistance efforts opposed to German occupation, which explains why Pirate was sent into the Netherlands to rescue Katje Borgesius. Successes early in the war led to an expansion in the SOE, and by 1946, when it was disbanded, there were many addresses between Baker Street and Gloucester Place that were serving as branches of the intelligence agency. The former SOE headquarters on Baker Street is now an office building.

Pynchon tells us that Pirate himself lives in "a maisonette erected last century, not far from the Chelsea Embankment, by Corydon Throsp, an acquaintance of the Rossettis" (5). Corydon Throsp is a fiction, but Rossetti did live in Chelsea, on Cheyne Walk, as did Whistler and other Victorian artists, giving the area a bohemian reputation for some time. It is difficult to

Barrage Balloons

As a means of defending the city, and the country, from low-flying dive-bomb attacks, large blimp-like Balloons were placed around potential targets. The Balloons often measured over 60 feet in length and over 25 feet in diameter. In England, Balloon Command was established in 1938, and by 1940 there were over 1400 balloons scattered around the country, with a third of them placed in and around London. By 1944 that number had grown to over 3000 balloons. The balloons, filled with hydrogen, floated at altitudes of up to 5000 feet and forced low flying aircraft to fly above that altitude and into the range of anti aircraft fire. The balloons also proved effective against the V-1 rocket which flew at an altitude of 2000 feet, approximately 100 or more V-1 rockets were destroyed by the balloons.

surmise where along the Embankment—almost a mile long—Pynchon has in mind for the maisonette, but there are clues enough that Pirate Prentice and most of his co-tenants fit Chelsea's characterization. Pirate, for example, grows bananas on the rooftop. His tremendous harvest provides breakfast for the crew.

> "Now there grows among the rooms, replacing the night's old smoke, alcohol and sweat, the fragile, musaceous odor of Breakfast: flowery, permeating, surprising, more than the color of winter sunlight, taking over not so much through any brute pungency or volume as by the high intricacy to the weaving of its molecules, sharing the conjuror's secret by which—though it is not often Death is told so clearly to fuck off—the living genetic chains prove even labyrinthine enough to preserve some human face down ten or twenty generations... so the same assertion through structure allows this war morning's banana fragrance to meander, repossess, prevail. Is there any reason not to open every window, and let the kind scent blanket all Chelsea? As a spell, against falling objects.... (10)

This early passage sets up Pynchon's ever-present dichotomy: what is northern and metropolitan is bad and associated with death, while what is tropical (bananas) and pastoral is good. Rarely is London defined in terms of pleasantries, and even more whimsical days in the city are described in death and ruin. One of Slothrop's happier memories, before the first V-2 fell on London, maintains a vocabulary of chaos and rubble.

> It was one of those great iron afternoons in London: the yellow sun being teased apart by a thousand chimneys breathing, fawning upward without shame. This smoke is more than the day's breath, more than dark strength—it is an imperial presence that lives and moves. People were crossing the streets and squares, going everywhere. Buses were

smeared with year's pitiless use and no pleasure, into haze-gray, grease-black, red lead and pale aluminum, between scrap heaps that towered as high as blocks of flats, down side-shoving curves into roads clogged with army convoys, other tall buses and canvas lorries, bicycles and cars, everyone here with different destinations and beginnings, all flowing, hitching now and then, over it all the enormous gas ruin of the sun among the smokestacks, the barrage balloons, power lines and chimneys brown as aging interior wood, brown growing deeper, approaching black in an instant—perhaps the true turn of the sunset—that is wine to you, wine and comfort. (26)

Smoke and fog almost always accompany a panorama of London, and a haze would have been quite common in the sky this winter, not just from the numerous chimneys, but from the ubiquitous fires set by the incoming rockets. London's fire brigade managed a commendable control of these blazes, but they only added to the gray air of a city already famous for its "fog." Mrs. Quoad's, where Slothrop is forced to sample the worst of England's candy, is a third floor flat "with the dome of faraway St. Paul's out its kitchen window visible in the smoke of certain afternoons" (115). Other times St. Paul's Cathedral would not be visible at all.

From Pirate's flat in Chelsea, Katje notes the lack of clarity in her view across London; here rain, like smoke, hampers the possibility of comprehending the city all at once. Rain is another threat from the sky, eating away at London, however more slowly than the rockets. Katje's sadomasochism allows her to take the threat with a certain degree of apathy.

Outside, the long rain in silicone and freezing descent smacks, desolate, slowly corrosive against the medieval windows, curtaining like smoke the river's far shore. This city, in all its bomb-pierced miles: this inexhaustibly knotted victim ... skin of glistening roofslates, sooted brick flooded high

about each window dark or lit, each of a million openings
vulnerable to the gloom of this winter day. The rain washes,
drenches, fills the gutters singing, the city receives it, lifting,
in a perpetual shrug.... (93)

This overall gloom only adds to London's austerity, and the
city's inhabitants sense an imminence not, as we might expect,
of the end of a long war, but of death—even as the Allies march
into Berlin. The statistician Roger Mexico surveys, "the city he
visits nowadays is Death's antechamber: where all the paper-
work's done, the contracts signed, the days numbered. Nothing
of the grand, garden, adventurous capital his childhood knew"
(40). Jessica Swanlake dreams in one of the novel's most memorable lines, "something's stalking through the city of smoke—
gathering up slender girls, fair and smooth as dolls, by the
handful" (53), indicating the sublime horror of the city itself.

To the smoke and rubble, the complex of military and
civilian intelligence agencies, the populace frightened and apa-
thetic, Pynchon's London includes another of the peculiarities
of the time: the very real influx of peoples and governments
from all over the world, carrying out the politics of their own
countries in the city. It only further exacerbated an already complex political panorama.

Pirate wonders if Mexico isn't into yet another one of the
thousand dodgy intra-Allied surveillance schemes that have
sprung up about London since the Americans, and a dozen
governments in exile, moved in. In which the German curi-
ously fades into irrelevance. Everyone watching over his
shoulder, Free French plotting revenge on Vichy traitors,
Lublin Communists drawing beads on Varsovian shadow-
ministers, ELAS Greeks stalking royalists, unrepatriable
dreamers of all languages hoping through will, fists, prayer to
bring back kings, republics, pretenders, summer anarchisms
that perished before the first crops were in ... some dying
wretchedly, nameless, under ice-and-snow surfaces of bomb

craters out in the East End not to be found till spring, some
chronically drunk or opiated for getting through the day's
reverses, most somehow losing, losing what souls they had,
less and less able to trust, seized in the game's unending
chatter, its daily self-criticism, its demands for total attention
... and what foreigner is it, exactly, that Pirate has in mind if
it isn't that stateless lascar across his own mirror-glass, that
poorest of exiles.... (34)

On the morning Pirate picks his banana breakfast, he can see
the vapor trail of a rocket being launched across the sea in The
Netherlands, and—with its incredible speed and altitude
making it impossible to be seen or heard—can only await its
impact. After a few moments and no explosion he assumes it
landed in the sea or exploded in midair, but finds out shortly
that the rocket landed in Greenwich—right on the Prime
Meridian, 0° longitude.

Pirate is summoned by his "employer" to the crash site and
heads east over the Vauxhall Bridge to get there. The route is
appropriate enough to get to Greenwich from Chelsea, though
notable because the Vauxhall is flanked by Government offices,
including the present-day headquarters of MI6, located on the
Thames at the southeast foot of the bridge, Vauxhall Bridge
Road. Though the Special Operations Executive originated in a
spin-off from MI6's own "Section D," tensions between the two
intelligence services grew as the war went on, particularly
because the SOE's sabotage sometimes set back MI6's intelligence gathering. Their current headquarters near the Vauxhall
Bridge were built in 1995.

Pirate's first job for SOE, or "The Firm," was—with his
talent to see the fantasies of others—to redirect the attentions of
Lord Blatherard Osmo, whose work for the Foreign Office in
Novi Pazar had been interrupted by an adenoid "at least as big
as St. Paul's, and growing hour by hour" (14). The scene shows
Pynchon's imagination at work:

Before long, tophats are littering the squares of Mayfair, cheap perfume hanging ownerless in the pub lights of the East End as the Adenoid continues on its rampage, not swallowing up its victims at random, no, the fiendish Adenoid has a *master plan*, it's choosing only certain personalities useful to it—there is a new election, a new preterition abroad in England here that throws the Home Office into hysterical and painful episodes of indecision ... no one knows what to do ... a half-hearted attempt is made to evacuate London, black phaetons clatter in massive ant-cortege over truss-work bridges, observer balloons are stationed in the sky, "Got it in Hampstead Heath, just sitting *breathing*...." (15)

The situation finally stabilizes when the Adenoid grows to cover all of St. James, evicting the area's government ministries, when Pirate is sent in to try to communicate with the thing. After two years Osmo is able to continue his work at Novi Pazar, saving the Balkans from war in the 1930s. The flashback serves its purpose of showing Prentice's gift and his usefulness to The Firm, in addition to introducing the sorts of tools, i.e., supernatural abilities, the British Government was willing to exploit in its war effort.

One of the men funded by the war is arguably the most evil character in the novel, Pointsman, a Pavlovian behavioral scientist determined to prove that Slothrop is able to "predict" rocket strikes by sensing some kind of stimulus. Pointsman's interest in the lieutenant is highly personal, as Slothrop has a history as a subject in behavioral psychology, and Pointsman dreads the end of the war because it means the end of his funding.

Pointsman is from Harley Street in Marylebone, though whether he actually grew up there or has simply spent a substantial amount of time in the vicinity is uncertain. Regardless, the street is mentioned several times in the novel as an explanation for his xenophobia and apathy. Perhaps he taught at the elite Queen's College on Harley Street, which has educated daughters of the Churchills and Kennedys, not to mention the writer

Katherine Mansfield; more likely he served in a medical capacity at one of the nearby Marylebone clinics. Whatever his business in what is still an opulent neighborhood, at 28 years of age he decided "to abandon Harley Street for a journey more and more deviant, deliciously on, into a labyrinth of conditioned-reflex work ..." (88). Still, his past accounts for the disparity between himself and Dr. Gwenhidwy, one of the co-owners of The Book, who genuinely cares for his patients suffering in the East End. Thanks to his concern, he can tell that there *is* a pattern to the rocket strikes—they are falling predominantly in the East End, away from the important government centers in Whitehall and St. James, and on the poor in east London. The conditions lead the Welshman to posit his idea of the "City Paranoiac."

In some cities the rich live upon heights, and the poor are found below. In others the rich occupy the shorelines, while the poor must live inland. Now in London, here is a gradient of wretchedness? increasing as the river widens to the sea. I am only asking, why? Is it because of the shipping? Is it in the patterns of land use, especially those relating to the industrial age? Is it a case of an ancient tribal tabu, surviving down all the English generations? No. The true reason is the Threat From The East, you see. And the South: from the mass of Europe, certainly. The people here were *meant to go down first.* We're expendible: those in the West End, and north of the river are not. Oh I don't mean the threat has this or that specific shape. Political, no. If the City Paranoiac dreams, it's not accessible to us. Perhaps the City dreamed of another, enemy city, floating across the sea to invade the estuary ... or waves of darkness ... waves of fire.... Perhaps of being swallowed again, by the immense, the silent Mother Continent? It's none of my business, city dreams.... But what if the City were a growing neoplasm, across the centuries, always changing, to meet exactly the changing shape of its very worst, secret fears? The raggedy pawns, the disgraced bishop and cowardly knight, all we condemned, we irreversibly lost, are left out here, exposed and waiting. It was known, don't deny it—*known*, Pointsman! that the front in Europe someday must develop like this? Move away east, make the rockets necessary, and known how, and where, the rockets would fall short. Ask your friend Mexico? look at the densities on his map? east, east, and south of the river too, where all the bugs live, that's who's getting it *thick*est, my friend. (172–173)

It remains ambiguous whether Gwenhidwy works in the same hospital that shows up repeatedly in the novel, St. Veronica's, the site of a few furtive meetings between owners of The Book, and the place Slothrop is dosed with sodium amytal. Pynchon gives a very specific address for this hospital, in Bonechapel Gate, E1, and because of its location and description the case could be made that Pynchon based St. Veronica's on the historic Royal London Hospital in Whitechapel.

They are approaching now a lengthy brick improvisation, a Victorian paraphrase of what once, long ago, resulted in Gothic cathedrals—but which, in its own time, arose not from any need to climb through the fashioning of suitable confusions toward any apical God, but more in a derangement of aim, a doubt as to the God's actual locus (or, in some, to its very existence), out of a cruel network of sensuous moments that could not be transcended and so bent the intentions of builders not on any zenith, but back to fright, to simple escape, in whatever direction, from what industrial smoke, street excrement, windowless warrens, shrugging leather forests of drive belts, flowing and patient shadow states of rats and flies, were saying about the chances for mercy that year. The grimed brick sprawl is known as the Hospital of St. Veronica of the True Image for Colonic and Respiratory Diseases.... (46)

The Royal London Hospital is just such a brick sprawl, a labyrinth of buildings connected by underground passageways and green spaces. It was badly damaged in the Battle of Britain, and its East Wing was struck by a flying-bomb in August, 1944, when two patients were killed. In the novel, Dr. Kevin Spectro dies when St. Veronica's is struck by a rocket. Its recently renovated Museum and Archives are housed in the basement of St. Phillip's Church on the hospital grounds, off Newark Street, and are open to the public.

Pointsman gets The Book, Pavlov's *Lectures on Conditioned Reflexes,* "sold to him on the sly, in the dark, during a Luftwaffe raid (most existing copies had been destroyed in their warehouse early in the Battle of Britain)" (87). That copies were scarce, forcing Pointsman, Spectro, and the others to pass around their English translation, is plausible. One major book depot called Paternoster Row—right behind St. Paul's Cathedral—was completely demolished during a Luftwaffe raid on the night of December 29–30, 1940. With paper in short supply, few books were published in the early 1940s.

Tyrone Slothrop has probably been in London since the Americans entered the war. His paranoia is well founded, since Pointsman and others at "The White Visitation," a fictional location near the coast housing their organization, PISCES, really have been watching him. Slothrop keeps a map in his cubicle marking his sexual conquests in the city, which he began "last fall." The first V-2 fell in September 1944.

> The stars pasted up on Slothrop's map cover the available spectrum, beginning with silver (labeled "Darlene") sharing a constellation with Gladys, green, and Katharine, gold, and as the eye strays Alice, Dolores, a couple of Sally's—mostly red and blue through here—a cluster near Tower Hill, a violet density about Covent Garden, a nebular streaming on into Mayfair, Soho, and out to Wembley and up to Hampstead Heath—in every direction goes this glossy, multicolored, here and there peeling firmament, Carolines, Marias, Annes, Susans, Elizabeths. (19)

The locations coincide precisely with another map kept at The White Visitation by the young statistician, Roger Mexico, who is plotting rocket strikes. But Slothrop is being followed and manipulated by people echelons above PISCES, and following his narcohypnosis at St. Veronica's hospital, "the cubicle near Grosvenor Square begins to feel more and more like a trap. He spends his time, often whole days, ranging the East End, breathing the rank air of Thameside, seeking places the followers might not follow" (114). During World War II, the American Embassy was housed at 1 Grosvenor Square, Mayfair, in a building now occupied by the Canadian High Commission. Between Eisenhower's headquarters and the nearby embassy, Grosvenor Square took the moniker "Little America" during the war; it is not surprising that Slothrop is experiencing paranoia in what is still an area populated by government offices and officials.

On a Friday evening in September, Slothrop heads toward the Bond Street Underground station—the tube station nearest to Grosvenor Square, on Oxford Street—when he hears the first rocket crack, its sound rolling across London. Slothrop lends the most insight into London in the Blitz.

> He can remember the first Blitz only as a long spell of good luck. Nothing that Luftwaffe dropped came near him. But this last summer they started with those buzzbombs. You'd be walking down the street, in bed just dozing off suddenly here comes this farting sound over the rooftops—if it just keeps on, rising to a peak and passing over why that's just fine, then it's somebody else's worry ... but if the engine cuts off, look out Jackson—its begun its dive, sloshing the fuel aft, away from the engine burner, and you've got 10 seconds to get under something. Well, it wasn't really too bad. After a while you adjusted—found yourself making small bets, a shilling or two with Tantivy Mucker-Maffick at the next desk, about where the next doodle will hit.

But then last September the rockets came. Them fucking rockets. You couldn't adjust to the bastards. No way. For the first time, he was surprised to find that he was really scared. Began drinking heavier, sleeping less, chain-smoking, feeling in some way he'd been taken for a sucker. Christ, it wasn't supposed to keep on like *this*...." (21)

Pynchon's gargantuan text is loaded with details and digressions that add authenticity to *Gravity's Rainbow*. What follows are a few London references that bear more weight than the author's frequent (and impressive) place-namedropping.

Portobello Road
This market street in Notting Hill, west of Hyde Park, is known on the one hand for its designer boutiques, antiques, and fine art, and on the other to support black market commerce and illicit activities, and especially known as a place to buy drugs. In *Gravity's Rainbow*, all the operatives in The Firm carry a Sten— a popular machine gun of the time—except for Pirate Prentice, who uses the heavier Mexican-made Mendoza, even though ammunition for the firearm is scarce: "no one's even *seen* any 7mm Mexican Mauser bullets lately, even in Portobello Road" (107). Clive Mossmoon's lover Sir Marcus Scammony avoids a conversation about Pointsman: "I found the most darling boots in Portobello Road ... They'll look stunning on you. Blood-red cordovan and halfway up your thighs" (615).

Shell Mex House, 80 The Strand
The imposing building on The Strand was owned and operated by Shell until recently. As part of Pynchon's global conspiracy, one rocket is "fired with the help of a transmitter on the roof of the headquarters of Dutch Shell" in The Netherlands,

a rocket whose propulsion system bears an uncanny resemblance to one developed by British Shell at around the same time ... and oh, oh boy, it just occurs to Slothrop now where all the rocket intelligence is being gathered—into the office of Mr. Duncan Sandys, Churchill's own son-in-law, who works out of the Ministry of Supply where but at Shell Mex House, for Christ's sake.... (251)

Slothrop then imagines a raid on Shell Mex House. Sandys actually didn't become the Minister of Supply until 1951, but during the war he worked closely with the rockets as chairman of the War Cabinet Committee, masterminding the eventual cessation of V-2 attacks by bombing rocket bases.

Smithfield Market

Prentice goes to an all-night cinema "around the corner from Gallaho Mews, the intersection with the extra street, the one you can't always see because it comes in at such a strange angle." There he watches a government newsreel featuring the crazed Lucifer Amp, a "former" SOE man "[making] a spectacle of himself" every day in Smithfield market (542). Now called London Central Markets, the complex is on Charterhouse Street in Clerkenwell, north of St. Bartholomew's Hospital. Pynchon may have chosen the location for Amp's display because his animal-like behavior approaches that of the many cattle in the market, butchered here each morning.

Gallaho Mews, incidentally, is a fictional address, site of Twelfth House in the novel. Pynchon is exercising a little word-play here, as a mew or mews can be an alley as well as a secret hideaway. "Gallaho" perhaps comes from Scotland Yard's Inspector Gallaho in Sax Rohmer's 1964 *The Trail of Dr. Fu Manchu.*

Whitehall

Mexico tracks down Pointsman "a roller skate ride away from" here, and, as part of the Counterforce, manages to urinate on Them, the members of the conspiracy, before making his escape via motorcycle. It is hard to imagine any grand plots being hatched anywhere else in the city, since the area of Whitehall houses Parliament, Downing Street, and many other government offices.

King's Road

Mexico speeds away from Whitehall on this thoroughfare. "'I'm fucking *Dick Whittington!* it occurs to him zooming down Kings Road, 'I've come to London! I'm your Lord Mayor....'" (637). Roger would have picked up King's Road in Belgravia and taken it straight into Chelsea, to Prentice's maisonette.

Tate Gallery

There doesn't seem to have ever been a portrait of the legendary chemist and physicist in the Tate Gallery, now called Tate Britain, on Millbank, yet in a tangent through the voice of an enlightened pinball Pynchon asks us to "check out the portrait of Michael Faraday in the Tate Gallery in London, Tantivy-Mucker-Maffick did once, to fill up a womanless and dreary afternoon, and wondered then how eyes of men could grow so lambent, sinister, so educated among the halls of dread and the invisible" (584–585). Pynchon invokes Faraday as one of the few who have "seen the magic serpent and its nakedness, long enough to be changed, to bring back from the writhing lines of force down in that pit an intimacy with power" (584). The first scientist to isolate and describe benzene, the chemical structure of which Pynchon likens to the uroboros, the snake eating its own tail, Faraday also made enormous contributions to electrical theory before becoming senile; his portrait at the National Portrait Gallery, St. Martin's Place, just north of Trafalgar Square, conveys precisely this simultaneous lambency and sinisterity.

St. John's Wood

Scorpia Mossmoon, Pirate Prentice's one true love, resides somewhere in this wealthy neighborhood.

> He is crying of persons, places, and things left behind: for Scorpia Mossmoon, living in St. John's Wood among the

sheet music, new recipes, a small kennel of Weimaraners whose racial purity she will go to extravagant lengths to preserve, and husband Clive who shows up now and then, Scorpia living only a few minutes away by Underground but lost to Pirate now for good, no chance for either of them to turn again.... (544)

The wife of the plastics expert and co-conspirator Clive Mossmoon might be pictured in one of the area's many stately houses.

Pynchon mentions another St. John's Wood address, that of H.P. Blavatsky, who died at her Avenue Road home in 1891. The matriarch of the Theosophical Society fully intended her home to be a mecca to like-minded believers, and it does not escape Pynchon that the anniversary of her death day was shared by another momentous event:

It is peacetime now again, no room for the pigeons in Trafalgar Square on V-E night, everyone at the facility that day mad drunk and hugging and kissing, except for the Blavatskian wing of Psi Section, who were off on White Lotos Day [sic] pilgrimage to 19 Avenue Road, St. John's Wood. (269)

Pointsman's Blavatskian colleagues at The White Visitation were celebrating Madame Blavatsky's death, known as White Lotus Day, apparently more important than marking the end of the Second World War.

CHAPTER TEN

The Millennial City

Quite conspicuously, there emerged in the early 1980s a new sort of fiction coming out of Britain. In a 1983 article, *New York Times* critic Michiko Kakutani first noticed the new books, typically coming from younger authors, written in a style that was a marked departure from the English novel of the 20th century. A new generation of writers was taking shape, writing counter to the realistic narrative of British literary history.

> Superficial similarities can be found—the novels of Martin Amis, Ian McEwan and Julian Barnes, for instance, tend to share a taste for nasty, unpleasant subject matter and cool, sophisticated prose. And yet the novelists actually form a highly disparate group. They come from different classes, different educational backgrounds and, in the case of Salman Rushdie, Kazuo Ishiguro, Buchi Emecheta and Timothy Mo, have different national roots as well. (Kakutuni, "Novelists are News Again")

Through the 1980s, many of the writers Kakutani mentions above wrote novels that would set up British fiction as the new center for the avant-garde, churning out eyebrow-raising, post-modern texts that had been the stuff from across the Atlantic—the stuff of Pynchon, with its pastiche of subtexts and take-it-as-you-will absurdity and apocalypse, and of Gábriel Garcia Márquez, with its matter-of-fact magical realism.

Later, Kakutani would cite a number of reasons for the paradigm shift, the most obvious of which is the regular, generational changing of the guards. In the interest of "defining itself sharply against the achievement of its predecessors," this new generation looked not to the straightforward British narrative, but to American and European sources, "a development perhaps most clearly illustrated by the case of Martin Amis and his father, Kingsley" (Kakutani, "Britain's Writers Embrace the Offbeat"). The younger Amis's acerbic, urban metafictions—novels that wink knowingly at Nabokov, et al—have landed him at the forefront of literary London (and its gossip columns); Amis is the portrait of British literary fame, and like many, a Londoner.

Kakutani suggests that part of the tendency for Amis and his peers to look elsewhere (especially America) for influences owes itself to that same characteristic in Margaret Thatcher's government, which held firm in the United Kingdom from 1979 until Mrs. Thatcher's resignation in 1990. Whether or not Thatcher is responsible for a new willingness to accept ideas from foreign sources, she did provide material for writers who dissented politically with her conservative government. Self-critique is old hat for American writers of the Vietnam era, but the bulk of British narratives had tended to set themselves in other countries, or concern themselves not with the state of political affairs but with conflicts on a personal level: "relations between the sexes, the hypocrisies and pretensions of the class system, the mysteries of self-hood and identity" ("Britain's Writers"). Explained as a symptom of the English artist's political exhaustion in the wake of World War II, Kakutani notes that this new postwar generation suffered none of this. Author Salman Rushdie put it this way:

If you think about World War II—America, Germany, and Italy all produced extraordinary novels about it; England didn't. Perhaps that also has something to do with the fact that the end of the war and the end of the Empire happened at almost exactly the same time. There's a certain amount of living in a green world of the past in England. It keeps behaving as though it were a great power, though it isn't anymore. Alot of the best books to come out of England have been retreats into the past or into other cultures. There have been rather few attempts to come to terms with contemporary England, though perhaps that's beginning to change. ("Novelists are News Again")

A self-fulfilling prophecy, perhaps, Rushdie's great contribution to literature, *The Satanic Verses* (1988), is on the whole a view of Thatcher's England and contemporary London. Of course, Rushdie is not alone among these authors willing to address the London around them. Amis, as early as 1978 in his novel *Success*, brings up his neurotic character Terry's disenfranchisement in modern London.

We live in Bayswater—district of the transients. Nearly everywhere is a hotel now; their porches teem like Foreign Legion garrisons; a fucked-up Arab comes here and is an automatic success. (The local boys are taking over, too. They work the streets, roping off the bits they want. They're winning. I feel that I could join them if I could just wire my nerves up tight.) But I can't. I try to like the way the world is changing, but there seems to be no extra room for me inside. (Amis, *Success* 31–32).

Ian McEwan, too, has turned his pen toward England and its metropolis. McEwan's *The Child in Time* (1987) is set in a London a few years ahead of the book's publication date, and amidst the book's examination of the passage of time there lies a patent critique of an authoritarian, conservative government, here legislating childcare while the main character's daughter has been kidnapped. Indeed, the novel opens with the main character enmeshed in London traffic; the first sentence jabs, "Subsidizing public transport had long been associated in the minds of both government and the majority of its public with the denial of individual liberty" (McEwan 1).

The broad trend for these authors to shift their attentions at once to London—and to treat the city with similar, postmodern narratives—is explainable as a function of demographics. Kakutani draws the comparison between vast and variegated America and the more insular British literary scene.

> While American writers live scattered across the country— isolated at universities and secluded in rural retreats—English writers tend to live in London or within commuting distance, and when they are not at home working, they often see one another at publishing parties, social gatherings, and at such favorite haunts as the London Library. "It's a small country," says [critic] John Gross. "Everything happens in London—it's very concentrated. There's no cafe where everyone congregates, but we all know each other too well." ("Novelists are News Again")

SALMAN RUSHDIE AND *THE SATANIC VERSES*

Among tales of an author's draw to London, Salman Rushdie's is the most sensational. Quoted by journalist Gerald Marzorati, Rushdie said of himself as an aspiring writer, "I wanted to write globe-swallowing, capacious books, ones with that sense of size, novels that expressed history, the public side of things as well as the private, the intimate" (Fiction's Embattled Infidel). Rushdie "chose to settle in London because London was where he could write the fiction he wanted to," Marzorati writes. Raised Muslim and of Indian extraction, Rushdie attended the Rugby School in Warwickshire in 1961, and by 1968 he had earned a Master's degree at King's College, Cambridge. A brief employ in

Pakistani television saw Rushdie back in London by the fall of 1968, where he acted in various productions with the Oval House theatre company, still located at 52–54 Kennington Park Road. In the 1970s, Rushdie found work as a freelance copywriter working largely for the London firm Ogilvy & Maher, until he was able to write full-time with the proceeds from *Midnight's Children,* published in 1981, and winner for Britain's meritorious Booker Prize. In 1983, he began writing *The Satanic Verses,* the 1988 publication of which would spur nothing less than a dozen or more deaths and the near dissolution of diplomatic relations between Iran and the United Kingdom. Yet London allowed him his story.

No doubt the Muslim world's reaction to *The Satanic Verses* seemed to the West as, at best, bizarre, and at worst, extremist. The offensive portions surround the character Mahound, a loosely-veiled avatar of the prophet Mohammed, in a plotline parallel to the main action in modern-day London. Rushdie suggests fallibility in Mahound, both in his human temptations and in his subjective transcription of the words of the archangel Gibreel (Gabriel). Though the Mahound sequences happen in the mind of the ill, schizophrenic Gibreel Farishta, and though they are presented as fiction, Rushdie's book was taken as blasphemy. As is too often the case with books banned and burned, few of those advocating its censorship had actually read the novel. Protests from Muslim groups in India lead the Indian Minister of Home Affairs to use customs laws to prohibit the book from being sold in India on October 5th, and by early February 1989, Ayatollah Khomeini declared a fatwa on the author and his publishers, Viking Penguin. In this, Rushdie was effectively sentenced to death by the Iranian leader, who promised martyrdom, and consequently safe passage to heaven, for anyone killed in the act of killing Rushdie. A bounty was set on the author's head; the book was banned, and—provided a copy was even available—burned in many Muslim countries. Taking Khomeini's fatwa seriously, British intelligence took the author and his wife underground, moving from safe house to safe house as many as 56 times in one month. That Rushdie was under the care of Scotland Yard and Mrs. Thatcher's government is ironic: as an examination of contemporary London, if *The Satanic Verses* is critical of a society it is Thatcherite London, and the city's reception of its many immigrants.

Premised on fantasy, the novel opens with its two heroes, Gibreel Farishta and Saladin Chamcha, aboard a hijacked plane London-bound, which, thanks to disagreement among the Arab terrorists, explodes tens of thousands of feet above England. They survive the fall. The two, brown-skinned "immigrants" make their way to and through the metropolis, and their misadventures in London—set against the enormous text of Islamic and Eastern myth and culture—is Rushdie's vehicle for critique.

Racial prejudices are of paramount concern. *The Satanic Verses* takes pains to describe the Middle Eastern experience in London, and is especially critical of white authority. Chamcha's hard luck begins soon after the pair's landing, when an anonymous call has 57 policemen from towns all along the coast searching for an illegal, "because nobody wanted to miss the fun, the thrill of the chase" (Rushdie 143). When he is found under the care of Rosa Diamond, Saladin Chamcha's paperless protests that he was, in fact, a British citizen solicit laughter and worse from the police:

> Rosa couldn't see, in that laughter-heaving surge of men and dogs, what uniformed arms might be doing to Chamcha's arms, or fists to his stomach, or boots to his shins, nor could she be sure if it was his voice crying out or just the howling of the dogs. (Rushdie 144)

Chamcha's mistreatment by the police and immigration officials is discreet and graphic—they beat him to incontinence in the police van and then force him to eat his own excrement—and his terrible episodes in London after his "Fall" are doubly bruising, as Chamcha has been a lifelong Anglophile. The authorities even seem to expect Saladin Chamcha's sudden metamorphosis into a goat-like devil, complete with horns and hooves. When at last, with the van nearing London, he persuades them to check his record on the computer, the officers abandon Chamcha at a detention center. He escapes, and heads to Ellowen Deeowen, London, where he grows even more beastly.

Opposite Rushdie's grand metaphor of Saladin Chamcha *appearing* to London as a devil is Gibreel Farishta, who has meanwhile become angelic, like his namesake, though by and large he *could never appear* to anyone in London as angelic. In one of his efforts to "redeem" London, he stands on the Victoria Embankment and miraculously enlarges himself:

> It really was incredible. Here appeared a celestial being, all radiance, effulgence and goodness, larger than Big Ben, capable of straddling the Thames colossus-style, and these little ants remained immersed in drive-time radio and quarrels with fellow-motorists. 'I am Gibreel,' he shouted in a voice that shook every building on the riverbank: nobody noticed. Not one person came running out of those quaking edifices to escape the earthquake. Blind, deaf, and asleep. (Rushdie 347)

Farishta's mental illness and other indications from the author that his angelic nature is a delusion notwithstanding, Rushdie's point is clear: this London has, at best, a remarkable indifference to its immigrant population.

Part V of the book is entitled "A City Visible But Unseen," and the title highlights this reluctance to acknowledge the immigrant populace and its experience. Here, Chamcha comes to live under the roof of a family of Bangladeshi immigrants, a wife, Hind, and two daughters, uprooted from their village in Dhaka by the entrepreneurial spirits of husband and father Sufyan, to operate, on the virtues of Hind's cooking, the Shaandaar Cafe. This section along with most of the other action in the book takes place in an area Rushdie has named Brickhall, clearly the Brick Lane neighborhood of London's East End. It is a part of town with a vast and expanding Asian population, where Rushdie lived in the years before he was forced into a life of seclusion by the Ayatollah fatwa. It today maintains a great Bengali population—people, as Marzorati wrote for the New York Times, "whom the city never expected to accommodate" (Fiction's Embattled Infidel). In *The Satanic Verses*, Sufyan's unhappy wife thinks of the neighborhood—the only London she knows—in infernal terms.

> ... they had come into a demon city in which anything could happen, your windows shattered in the middle of the night without any cause, you were knocked over in the street by invisible hands, in the shops you heard such abuse you felt like your ears would drop off but when you turned in the direction of the words you saw only empty air and smiling faces, and everyday you heard about this boy, that girl, beaten up by ghosts. Yes, a land of phantom imps, how to explain; best thing was to stay home, not to go out for so much as to post a letter, stay in, lock the door, say your prayers, and the goblins would (maybe) stay away. (Rushdie 258)

This part of London had been "unseen," too, by Saladin Chamcha, for whom the city has literally become a Hell by virtue of his latest migration. An anglophile from his youth, Chamcha had come to London at his earliest convenience. His talent with voices has earned him a prosperous career in British radio and television, and he has vanquished any trace of "Paki" accent in his speech—evidencing his willful assimilation. Yet on this recent return to the city he has made his home, he sees for the first time none of the romantic refinement of the "Ellowen Deeowen" of his youth, but a shameful, torturous Hell. "The city of London, transformed into Jahannum, Gehenna, Muspellheim" (Rushdie 262).

For Rushdie, it is the act of migration that causes London to become different cities to different people, or even different cities to the same person. As he demonstrates in the novel, the diverse backgrounds people bring to the city account for its ever-changing nature. Rushdie clarified his point in an interview shortly after the publication of *The Satanic Verses*:

> I suppose I was writing about a sense of the city as an artificial, invented space which is constantly metamorphosing. It doesn't have roots, it has foundations. There are things that do not seem to belong together, except that it is part of the metropolitan experience that such things do not belong together and do live side by side—that you can live upstairs from Khomeini. (Chauhan 90)

Thusly, the accounts of Gibreel Farishta's London experience are overcast always by Islamic tradition and Middle Eastern myth. When he first enters the city by train he is haunted by his old lover Rekha Merchant, who chases him around labyrinthine London on her magic carpet—his past and his culture muddling any static view of the city.

> That day Gibreel Farishta fled in every direction around the Underground of the city of London and Rekha Merchant found him wherever he went; she sat beside him on the endless up-escalator at Oxford Circus and in the tightly packed escalators of Tufnell Park she rubbed up against him from behind in a manner that she would have thought quite outrageous during her lifetime. On the outer reaches of the Metropolitan Line she hurled the phantoms of her children from the tops of claw-like trees, and when he came up for air outside the Bank of England she flung herself histrionically from the apex of its neo-classical pediment. And even though he did not have any idea of the true shape of that most protean and chameleon of cities he grew convinced that it kept changing shape as he ran around beneath it, so that the stations on the Underground changed lines and followed one another in apparently random sequence. (Rushdie 207)

Rushdie, Amis, and McEwan have all included in their London narratives a foreboding sense of apocalypse. In *The Satanic Verses* it is realized in the literal sense of the word, with Gibreel in his madness appearing as the angel Azraeel, blowing fire out his trumpet while a race riot breaks out in the streets. In *The Child in Time* the nuclear threat is ever present, and in Martin Amis's *London Fields* unceasing rains have brought on diseases, while even a date is picked—November 5th—for an anonymous doomsday.

MARTIN AMIS AND *LONDON FIELDS*

Amis—like many of his contemporaries—is driven politically to take on the city and its perceived decline in the Tory-ruled 1980s, and *London Fields*, which was published in the 10th year of Margaret Thatcher's government, is a millennial satire of a London ensconced in consumerism and decay.

At once a postmodern murder mystery and an exposition of unseemly London, the narrative in *London Fields* centers on the happenings in a dark, Portobello Road bar in Notting Hill, called the Black Cross. "London is a pub," Amis told Mira Stout for the New York Times. "Not the pub with the jolly butcher and the smiling grannies; it's the pub of eight or nine alcoholics, a handful of hustlers and nutcases and a few token regular people. It's a stew" (Down London's Mean Streets). That Amis is speaking with some degree of hyperbole here does little to counter the idea that Amis is disappointed with modern London: his disgust is evident in interviews, and, moreover, this is precisely the London envisaged in *London Fields*. It is as if Amis is saying, *here is the real London.*

It is a metafictional trick, then, when the book's narrator, Samson Young, begins by insisting that this is a *true story*. In fact, Samson rebukes the idea of his authorship with the claim that he will not write, but merely record the happenings at the Black Cross. "If London's a pub and you want the whole story," asks Samson Young, "then where do you go? You go to a London pub" (Amis, *London Fields* 14). In *London Fields*, the "whole story" is not just a whodunnit murder mystery, but a satiric exposition of London at odds with the accepted (or at least propagated) view of a Thatcherite utopia.

The Black Cross's head honcho is Keith Talent, "a very bad guy," who scrapes out a living as a seller of cheap perfumes on the sidewalks of Oxford Street and Bishopsgate, among other hustles. His dart game draws him to the Black Cross for most of the day every day, and he hopes one day to make it on television—success, in Keith's judgment—though comically not as an actor, but as a player in a televised darts tournament. Amis sets up a class distinction with the character of Guy Clinch whose job is "sitting about in a bijou flatlet in Cheapside, trying

London by the Numbers

Estimated population of London in 2002: 7.36 million.
Total land area of Greater London: 611 sq. miles (1584 sq. km)
Percentage of London's land area devoted to parks and green
  space: 39%
Size of Hyde Park in acres: 615
Average price of a house in London in 2003: £241,818
Average household income per year between 2000 and 2003:
  £38,376
Weight of the spindle and the hub of the London Eye: over 330
  tons
Total length of cable used in the London Eye: 3.7 miles (6 km)
Height of Big Ben: 316 ft. (96m) with 340 steps to the belfry
Length of the Thames: 210 miles (338 km)
Width of the Thames at London Bridge: 870ft. (265m)
First year in which the London Underground was called the Tube:
  1890
Number of Escalators in the London Underground: 408
Maximum depth below mean sea level in the Underground:
  105 ft. (32m)

to keep tabs on the proliferating, the pullulating hydra of Clinch money" (*London Fields* 35). Unhappy Clinch, in an effort to conquer his own fear of the lower classes, ventures one day into the Black Cross.

> ... fear had him go where the shop and flats jostled fascinat-edly over the street like a crown round a bearpit, with slot-game parlors, disastrous beaneries, soup queues, army hostels, with life set out on barrows, on pingpong tables, and decapitated Portakabins—the voodoo and the hunger, the dreadlocks and the dreadnoughts, the Keiths and the Kaths of Portobello Road. Naturally Guy had been there before, in search of a corn-fed chicken or a bag of Nicaraguan coffee. But now he was looking for the thing itself. (*London Fields* 35)

Not long after Guy Clinch makes himself a regular at the Black Cross, the third member of Amis's ménage a trois appears. She is a clairvoyant, death-obsessed temptress named Nicola Six. The bulk of the novel is Nicola's planned-out manipulation of Guy and Keith (and the narrator) to achieve her own death (which she knows is imminent) on her 35th birthday. Downtrodden Keith and well-to-do Guy are the author's stand-ins for the upper and lower classes, and the difference between their lifestyles is exploited throughout *London Fields*.

It appears in the novel that Nicola Six isn't the only one expecting death, soon. Some great, meteorological debacle wherein the Earth is being pulled fractionally closer to the sun, which the novel calls "the Crisis," is thought to culminate on November 5th, when due to a new planetary alignment, London will undergo a total eclipse. The change in the position of Earth in space creates catastrophic weather patterns, bringing with them strange diseases. The governments of the world are tense, and it seems that everyone awaits the launch of a nuclear weapon from one country or another. But still *London Fields* suggests things are bleak enough on a social level; reading a news magazine, Nicola Six thinks apathetically, "Love made the world go round. And the world was slowing up. The world wasn't going round" (*London Fields* 332). There is little room in a seedy bar like the Black Cross for loving relationships. London is so much vice: greed, theft, and violence dominate the cityscape.

As for the departure in style and content from the mass of British literature of the 20th century, Amis blames that, too, on cultural decline.

> The 19th-century British novel was, if you like, a super-power novel. It was 800 pages long, about the whole of society. With decline, the novel has shrunk in confidence, in scope. In its current form, the typical English novel is 225 sanitized pages about the middle classes. You know, "well-made" with a nice color scheme and décor, and matching imagery. I almost try and avoid *form*. What I'm interested in is trying to get more truthful about what it's like to be alive now. (Stout 6)

Though he owned a home in Ladbroke Grove, just north of the area in Notting Hill Gate where most of *London Fields* takes place, Martin Amis did most of the writing in an apartment in Westbourne Park, quite close to the pub scene of Portobello Road. The Black Cross in the novel is modeled on a real Porto-bello Road bar called the Golden Cross, since renamed the Market Bar. It had truly been a den of drugs and drunks for its history, though ironically it became a hip hangout for celebrities in the early 1990s and has cleaned up under new owners.

Amis gives Keith Talent an apartment on the 11th floor of "Windsor House" in the novel, though there are clues that this is based on the nearby Trellick Tower, "the lone tower block at the end of Golborne Road" (60). Trellick and other tower blocks in the city were designed to replace the huge number of homes destroyed in London during the Second World War, though many such buildings became slums. An odd, Modernist building 31 stories high, the crime and degeneracy in the Tower had been so bad for a time that a (false) story circulated claiming that the building's architect had thrown himself from the roof in despair. In the late 1990s the Trellick Tower became a listed building, granting it historical status.

In fact the whole of Portobello Road has cleaned up in the years since *London Fields* was published, though this part of Notting Hill remains a dynamic market center, and peoples from all over the world live and work here.

London continues to attract the attention of storytellers. Ian McEwan's 1998 *Amsterdam* won the Booker Prize that year, a tragic morality tale written in the author's characteristic, minimalist prose. Here, two London friends, one depressed and the other lofty, are thrust out of their own psychologies at the intrusion of bizarre events in their lives. The novel beat out Julian Barnes's *England, England* for the Booker, where a Rupert Murdoch-style visionary buys the Isle of Wight to build a massive theme park with replicas of England's landmarks, including a half-size Big Ben, and a Harrods department store inside the Tower of London. Sir Jack Pitman even brings in the wisdom of a Continental philosopher to explain that tourists will prefer these replicas to the real thing. A satire on the Disneyfication of the world, Barnes's novel bolsters the tradition of imaginative fiction coming from London writers today.

The turn of the millennium saw Salman Rushdie's emigration to New York, a move, he claims, to have been long overdue, adding that the similarities between New York and London as cities of immigrants had make the change particularly easy. Rumors hit the British Press a few years ago that longtime London resident Martin Amis was also thinking of a similar betrayal of the city, though he dismissed any actual plans. It is yet too early to say whether the avant-garde fiction that began to come from London 20 years ago has desiccated, though odds are that this city—which has been so much to so many creative minds—will continue to attract the talents of the world.

London has been described often as a collection of villages as opposed to a unified city, and more often than not, the neighborhoods (neighbourhoods in the UK) blend together and overlap. On the broad scale, some divide the city into the City, Central London, and the East End and the West End. Many travel guides use prominent neighborhood names and tube stops to mark points of interest. For the purposes of this book, it should be expected that some of the sites may be listed under different sections and neighborhoods in other guide books.

STRAND/FLEET STREET

The Strand, the main road linking Westminster and the City of London (or the West End with the City), begins at Trafalgar Square, and curves northeast just south of Covent Garden, roughly 200 meters from the River Thames until at Temple Bar (the boundary of the City of London) it becomes Fleet Street. Many famous monuments have an address on the Strand.

CHARING CROSS STATION

From 1890 to 1891 Rudyard Kipling lived on Villiers Street, right near Charing Cross Station, an experience he wrote about with a mix of chagrin and amusement, speaking of the noise of Charing Cross trains and that of the cars on the Strand.

GORDON'S WINE BAR

47 Villiers Street, London WC2N 6NE • Tel: 020 7930 1408
www.gordonswinebar.com

This gothic-style 14th-century wine cellar is the former home of Rudyard Kipling. To this day it retains its dingy exterior; however, those who know not to trust appearances enjoy wines from around the globe in addition to sherry, port, Madeira, light dishes, and continental cheeses served with French bread. G.K. Chesteron and Hillaire Belloc were customers at this bar, and it has not been altered much since their day. Open Monday–Saturday 11am–11pm. Closed Sundays.

THE ADELPHI

At the north end of Buckingham Street is John Adam Street, the site of the Adelphi, a housing development built between 1768–1774 by the four Adams brothers. All that remains now is 4–6 John Adam Street, 7 Adam Street, and 1–3 Robert Street. Thomas Hardy, Bernard Shaw, H.G. Wells, Thomas Hood, John Galsworthy, and J.M. Barrie lived in the Adelphi at different periods of its existence. From his room at the top of the building Barrie looked for hours at the seven bridges visible across the Thames. He wrote "Charing Cross Bridge is the ugliest of them all, but I never want to see it pulled down. It was across that bridge that the troops trains took our boys to France."

THE SAVOY THEATRE

Savoy Theatre, Strand, London WC2R 0ET
Tel: 0870 166 7372
www.savoy-group.co.uk/Savoy-Theatre/

Located on the Strand, the Savoy Palace, which burned in 1381, was rebuilt by Henry VII as a hospital in 1505. This also burned in 1864, and the land sat abandoned until D'Oyly Carte bought it in 1880 and opened The Savoy Theatre in 1881. The theater became a showcase for the works of Gilbert and Sullivan, which became known as the Savoy Operas. These days it varies in its productions, in 2000 the bill included a musical version of *Thomas Hardy's Tess of the D'urbervilles.*

THE SAVOY HOTEL

Strand, London WC2R 0ET • Tel: 800-63-SAVOY
www.savoy-group.co.uk/savoy/accommodation/default.asp

Opened in 1889 next to The Savoy Theatre, The Savoy Hotel has been, and still is, one of London's most prestigious hotels. The Savoy Hotel's forecourt is the only street in the United Kingdom where vehicles are required to drive on the right. Famous authors who took residence in The Savoy Hotel are: Somerset Maugham, Mark Twain, Noel Coward, Oscar Wilde, Emile Zola, and William Saroyan.

PRINCE HENRY'S ROOM

17 Fleet Street, Holborn, London EC4 • Tel: 020 7936 2710

Samuel Pepys was born near this house, which is one of the few to survive the Great Fire. It features an exhibition of Pepys miscellanea and contemporary artifacts. Open Monday–Friday 11am–2pm. Closed public holidays.

PUNCH MAGAZINE

No. 10 Bouverie Street

Mark Twain and James Thurber were invited by *Punch's* editors to become "members" of the famous *Punch* table, a table in the surface of which, since the middle of the 19th century, all of the magazine's editors and many of its famous contributors have carved their initials. Some of the initials belong to Anthony Powell, Keith Waterhouse, A.A. Milne, John Betjeman, and William Makepeace Thackeray. Charles Dickens was a frequent guest of *Punch*, but was never invited to sign; indeed his work was rejected by the magazine. The table now resides in the magazine's current offices opposite Harrods, whose owner Mohamed Al Fayed bought the magazine in 1996. For more information e-mail: punch.library@harrods.com.

SOMERSET HOUSE

Somerset House, Strand, London WC2R 1LA
Tel: 020 7845 4600
www.somerset-house.org.uk/

Somerset House, named for the London home of Edward Seymour, Duke of Somerset, is a large building situated on the south side of the Strand in central London. It overlooks the River Thames, just east of Waterloo Bridge. The central block of the Neoclassical building (1776–1796) was built by Sir William Chambers; later wings were added to the north and south. After his execution, Somerset house was given to the Crown and used by Princess Elizabeth before she was crowned Queen Elizabeth I in 1558. It was used by various governmental departments, the Royal Society of Literature, and the Courtauld Institute of Art to name a few. In the winter, its courtyard is turned into an open air ice rink complete with lights and music and crisp London air. Open daily 10am–6pm, last admission to collections 5:30pm. For more information e-mail: info@somerset-house.org.uk.

KING'S COLLEGE

King's College London, Strand, London WC2R 2LS
Tel: 020 7836 5454
www.kcl.ac.uk/

King's College London, founded in 1829, is one of the largest colleges in the federal University of London. It began on a site adjacent to Somerset House on the Strand, but has now spread to other campuses. Writers who have studied at King's College include: E.M. Forster, Salman Rushdie, Rupert Brooke, Charles Kingsley, John Ruskin, Leslie Stephen, Sir William Gilbert (of Gilbert and Sullivan), Thomas Hardy, Somerset Maugham, Anita Brookner, Sir Arthur C. Clarke, Helen Cresswell, Maureen Duffy, Radclyffe Hall, Susan Hill, Susan Howatch, Derek Jarman, Hanif Kureishi and Laurence Norfolk. For more information e-mail: ceu@kcl.ac.uk.

COVENT GARDEN/LUDGATE HILL

Located just west of the City, and filling the space between the City and Westminster is the area referred to as Covent Garden and Ludgate Hill.

COVENT GARDEN

www.covent-garden.co.uk

Originally the garden belonged to Westminster Abbey. By the 16th century the monks of the abbey were using the garden as an orchard, selling surplus produce, out of which the market evolved. Many novelists, playwrights, and poets have lived in and around Covent Garden, such as William Blake, François-Marie Arouet de Voltaire, Thomas de Quincey, Beatrix Potter, Samuel Pepys, George Orwell, and Charles Dickens—dramatic enactments of Dickens's life and works take place there in the summer. During their time the famous Bloomsbury Group—including Virginia Woolf, Clive Bell, John Maynard Keynes, Lytton Strachey, and Benjamin Disraeli—walked the streets of Covent Garden.

BOW STREET MAGISTRATE'S COURT

28 Bow Street, London WC2E 7AS • Tel: 020 7853 9241

Formerly a police station where Oscar Wilde spent two weeks awaiting trial at the Old Bailey. This is also where the Artful Dodger from Charles Dickens's Oliver Twist was brought.

THEATRE ROYAL DRURY LANE

Catherine Street, London WC2B 5JF • Tel: 020 7494 5000

There has been a theater at this location since 1663 when Samuel Pepys came to see the theater's first play, and the present building (the fourth), dates from 1811. All three of its predecessors were destroyed by fire.

RULES RESTAURANT

35 Maiden Lane, Covent Garden, London WC2E 7LB
Tel: 020 7836 5314

Known as London's oldest restaurant, the Rules Restaurant opened in 1798 and was a personal favorite of Charles Dickens, William Thackery, John Galzworthy, and H.G. Wells. Today the establishment serves traditional British food and has a Charles Dickens Room, decorated with many authentic Dickens artifacts. Open daily 12pm–12am.

VICTOR GOLLANCZ PUBLISHERS

14 Henrietta Street, London WC2

In 1927 Victor Gollancz opened a publishing house, which published works by George Orwell, Dorothy L. Sayers, Daphne du Maurier, Elizabeth Bowen, and Kingsley Amis. Gollancz founded the Left Book Club in the 1930s to protest the rise of fascism in Europe. His daughter, Livia, ran the company until its sale in 1989 to US publisher Houghton Mifflin, who in turn sold to Cassell in 1992, which was later bought by the Orion group.

ST PAUL'S CHURCH

Bedford Street, London WC2E 9ED • Tel: 020 7836 5221
www.actorschurch.org

Underneath its protruding roof is the spot at which Professor Higgins meets Eliza Doolittle in George Bernard Shaw's Pygmalion. Open Monday–Friday 8:30am–5:30pm, Sunday 9am–1pm. Closed Saturdays. For more information e-mail: info@actorschurch.org.

THE SAVAGE CLUB

1 Whitehall Place, London SW1A 2HD • Tel: 020 7930 8118
www.savageclub.com

Initialized in 1857, the Savage Club became the leading Bohemian Gentleman's Club in London. The club was named after the poet Richard Savage, and its members have included George and

Weedon Grossmith, Edgar Wallace, Somerset Maugham, and Dylan Thomas. For more information e-mail: info@savageclub.com.

THE GARRICK CLUB

15 Garrick Street, London WC2E 9AY

The Garrick Club moved to its present home on Garrick Street in 1864. One of the grandest, most imposing, yet dirtiest buildings in London, the exclusive club's members wear salmon and cucumber ties. Founded so that "actors and men of education and refinement might meet on equal terms," the club claimed Charles Dickens, P.G. Wodehouse, Arthur Wing Pinero, J.M. Barrie, and A.A. Milne as members.

THE THEATRE MUSEUM:
NATIONAL MUSEUM OF THE PERFORMING ARTS

Russell Street, Covent Garden, London WC2E 7PR
Tel: 020 7943 4700
www.theatremuseum.org/

In 1911 Gabrielle Enthoven campaigned for a "National Museum of Theatre Arts". At last, in 1924 the Victoria and Albert Museum eventually accepted her gift of about 100,000 playbills, programmes, playtexts, and prints of the London stage. The collection was joined in 1971 by Harry R. Beard's collection of 20,000 theatrical and operatic prints, texts, and programmes. In 1974 the Theatre Museum was formed by combining the collections with the holdings of the British Theatre Museum Association and Richard Buckle's Friends of the Museum of Performing Arts, branching out from solely paper by adding costumes and scenic cloths. The collection is constantly updated through gift, purchase, and bequest including the archives of the English Stage Company at the Royal Court and of the D'Oyly Carte Company (relating to Gilbert and Sullivan operas), the design collections of the Arts Council and British Council, the Antony Hippisley Coxe Circus Collection and the British Model Theatre and Puppet Guild Collection. In 1987 the Theatre Museum moved its growing collection which includes over a million theatre programmes and playbills—the earliest dating from 1704—to its new home in Covent Garden and to its second branch in Kensington Olympia, which houses the special archives—including the English Shakespeare Company Archive. Open Tuesday–Sunday 10am–6pm, last admission 5:30pm. Closed Bank Holidays.

SOHO

First established in the 17th century, Soho quickly became one of London's most populated districts. Large numbers of immigrants settled here, giving the area a rich history and a vibrant atmosphere leading many famous writers and artists to inspiration. The failure of the German revolutions in 1848 brought both Karl Marx and Freidrich Engels to Soho, and Marx is known for having settled in The German Hotel, just off Leicester Square.

SOHO SQUARE

Laid out in the 1680s Soho Square is the home of the offices of Bloomsbury Publishing which was founded in 1986 and headed by Liz Calder, who also co-founded the Groucho Club. A former model in Brazil, Calder published the early work of Salman Rushdie, Anita Brookner, and Julian Barnes. Bloomsbury Publishing is also the publisher of J.K. Rowling's series on Harry Potter. The square is where Thomas De Quincey, author of *Confessions of an English Opium Eater*, rested on the steps of a house with his favorite 15-year-old prostitute who, as he believed of all prostitutes, exhibited humanity, disinterested generosity, courage, and fidelity.

WESTMINSTER REFERENCE LIBRARY

35 St. Martin's Street, London WC2H 7HP
Tel: 020 7641 4632

In 1710 Sir Isaac Newton moved to Soho and lived on the corner of St. Martin's Street, where he entertained such notable guests as William Congreve and Jonathan Swift. Later Dr. Charles Burney lived in that house, where his daughter, Fanny Burney wrote her epistolary novel *Evelina* (1778). This house is now home to the Westminster Reference Library in which business, UK Official Publications, European Union and Arts subject collections are housed. Open Monday–Friday 10am–8pm, Saturday 10am–5pm. Closed Sundays. For more information e-mail: referencelibrarywc2@westminster.gov.uk.

ST PATRICK'S CHURCH

12 Soho Square, London

Built in 1891, St Patrick's Church stands on the site of the assembly rooms of a failed actress of the 1760s, Theresa Cornelys. The rooms were eventually closed down for being a "disorderly house," but authors such as Laurence Sterne and Fanny Burney were among those to visit her lavish masques and "entertainments."

HOUSE OF ST BARNABAS

1 Greek Street, London W1 • Tel. 020 7437 1894

Now a hostel for women, it was first built in 1846 for London's destitute and homeless. It is believed to be the house that Charles Dickens had in mind for Dr. Manette in *A Tale of Two Cities*, hence Manette Street. Open for short guided tours Wednesdays 2:30–4:15pm, Thursdays 11am–12:30pm.

GAY HUSSAR

2 Greek Street, London W1V 6NB • Tel: 020 7437 0973

A Hungarian restaurant much loved by H.G. Wells biographer, Michael Foot, and publisher André Deutsch.

PILLARS OF HERCULES

7 Greek Street, London W1D 4DJ • Tel: 020 7437 1179

This pub is almost certainly the Hercules Pillars featured in Charles Dickens's *A Tale of Two Cities*. Poet and opium addict Francis

Thompson was also a customer here. Open Monday–Saturday 11am–11pm, Sunday 12–10:30pm.

THE COACH AND HORSES

29 Greek Street, Soho, London W1V 5LL
Tel: 020 7437 5920

An unspoilt, wood-lined pub is now something of a shrine to the writer, Jeffrey Bernard, whose *Spectator* columns, many of them written at the pub, were famously described by Jonathan Meades as "a suicide note in weekly instalments" [*sic*]. Open Monday–Saturday 11am–11pm, Sunday 12–10:30pm.

KETTNER'S RESTAURANT

29 Romilly Street, Soho, London W1D 5HP
Tel: 020 7734 6112

Founded in 1868, *Kettner's Book of the Table* was once a culinary bible of sorts, and Oscar Wilde described the restaurant as his favorite in London. It was here, in October of 1892, that Wilde dined with a group that included Lord Alfred Douglas, with whom he was having a relationship and whose father, the Marquis of Queensberry, Wilde attempted to sue of libel in 1895. Open daily 12pm–12am.

GROUCHO CLUB

45 Dean Street, Soho, London W1V 5AP
Tel: 020 7439 4685

A number of book folk, including publisher Liz Calder, Carmen Callil, and Ed Victor founded this club in 1984. They took its name from Groucho Marx, who famously quipped that he'd never join a club that would have him as a member. The Groucho Club is where media London meets, including Martin Amis and Salman Rushdie. Open Monday–Friday 8am–1am, Saturday 5pm–1am.

THE FRENCH HOUSE

49 Dean Street, Soho, London W1D 5BE
Tel: 020 7437 2477

Formerly the York Minster, this pub generally flies a French flag outside and is arguably the most famous pub in Soho. Known for serving only half-pints to make it seem more sophisticated and French, it drew customers such as Wyndham Lewis, Brendan Behan, Dylan Thomas, Aleister Crowley, Auberon Waugh, and Anthony Burgess. It is here that in February 1960 poet Sylvia Plath signed a contract with Heinemann for the publication of *The Colossus.*

PICCADILLY/MAYFAIR/ST JAMES'S

Known as one of the smartest and most distinguished areas of London, Piccadilly, St James's, and Mayfair are filled with bookshops, clubs, and elegant residential streets.

WATERSTONE'S

203-206 Piccadilly, London W1J 9LE • Tel: 020 7851 2400
www.waterstones.co.uk

The largest bookstore in Europe with six floors of stock, a gift shop, an art gallery, and coffee and juice bars, this shop occupies the former Simpsons Clothes store that was the inspiration for the 1970s sitcom *Are You Being Served?*. Waterstone's bought it in 1998 and on September 14, 1999 the bookstore opened with a party attended by Doris Lessing, A.S. Byatt and her sister Margaret Drabble, Beryl Bainbridge, and Salman Rushdie.

ST JAMES'S CHURCH

197 Piccadilly, London W1 • Tel: 020 7734 4511

Built by Christopher Wren in 1684, the church looks more American than English, matching styles of churchs in New England.

William Blake was baptized here, and in 1918 Robert Graves married his first wife Nancy with Max Beerbohm and Wilfred Owen in the congregation. Open daily 8am–7pm.

ALBANY COURT

Built in 1802–1803 this distinguished address gave bachelor apartments to Byron, Aldous Huxley, Graham Greene, J.B. Priestly, Evelyn Waugh, Sir Harold Nicolson, and Terrence Rattigan.

HATCHARD'S BOOKSHOP

187 Piccadilly, London W1J 9LE • Tel: 020 7439 9921
www.hatchards.co.uk

Frequented by many of Albany's distinguished residents, it is known still as "the top people's bookshop." Hatchard's is the oldest surviving bookshop in London, founded in 1797, and Rudyard Kipling, Lord Byron, Oscar Wilde, Bernard Shaw, and Somerset Maugham all shopped here, and today it is still possible to bump into authors or politicians at any time. Open Monday–Saturday 9:30am–7pm, Sunday 12–6pm. For more information e-mail: books@hatchards.co.uk.

LONDON LIBRARY

14 St James's Square, London SW1Y 4LG
Tel: 020 7930 7705
www.londonlibrary.co.uk

Founded in 1841 the library stands at the northwest corner of St James's Square, as it has since 1845 after briefly occupying the first floor of the Travellers Club at 49 Pall Mall. The library owes its foundation to Thomas Carlyle who was dissatisfied with the library of the British Museum. Charles Dickens was among the founding members and T.S. Eliot was one of the library's presidents. Virginia Woolf, George Eliot, Evelyn Waugh, and H.G. Wells enjoyed the view from the large front windows. Open Monday, Friday, and Saturday 9:30am–5:30pm; Tuesday–Thursday 9:30am–7:30pm. Closed Sundays.

HEYWOOD HILL BOOKSHOP

10 Curzon Street, Mayfair, London W1J 5HH
Tel: 020 7629 0647
www.gheywoodhill.com

A small bookshop, Heywood Hill has been providing personal service to the upper classes since 1936. Nancy Mitford worked here during the warm, and customers included the Sitwells, Muriel Spark, Gore Vidal, and A.S. Byatt.
Open Monday–Friday 9am–5:30pm, Saturday 9am–12:30pm. Closed Saturdays before Bank Holidays.

BROWNS HOTEL

Albemarle Street, Mayfair, London W1S 4BP
Tel: 020 7518 4108

Founded in 1837 by James Brown, valet to Lord Byron, it was here that Rudyard Kipling and Caroline Balestier stayed after their marriage in 1892. Nearly a century later, Stephen King stayed and wrote most of Misery by hand at Kipling's desk before he was informed that Kipling had died at that desk. S.J. Perelman of the New Yorker also stayed at Browns Hotel.

CAFE ROYAL

68 Regent Street, London W1R 6EL • Tel: 020 7437 9090

Here Oscar Wilde had lunch every day at precisely 1pm. Here, too, John Berger who had won the 1972 Booker Prize denounced Booker's "colonialist" treatment of West Indian sugar workers and gave half his prize money to the Black Panthers.

WESTMINSTER

Most well known for being home to Westminster Abbey, Westminster joins the outer edges of London, such as Chelsea and Kensington, with central London.

WESTMINSTER ABBEY

Parliament Square, London SW1P 3PA • Tel: 020 7654 4900
www.westminster-abbey.org/

Authors with the distinction of being buried here include Geoffrey
Chaucer, Edmund Spenser, John Dryden, Dr. Samuel Johnson,
and Charles Dickens. There are memorials to many others in Poet's
Corner, including John Milton, William Wordsworth, John Keats,
Percy Bysshe Shelley, William Blake, T.S. Eliot, Jane Austen, and
the Brontës. Open to tourists Monday–Friday 9:30am–3:45pm,
and until 7pm on Wednesdays; Saturday 9:30am–1:45pm. Wor-
shippers only on Sundays. For more information e-mail:
info@westminster-abbey.org.

WESTMINSTER SCHOOL

Little Dean's Yard, Westminster, London SW1P 3PF
Tel: 020 7963 1000
www.westminster.org.uk/index.asp

One of the top schools in the country, Westminster School is at the
end of Great College Street. Ben Jonson, John Dryden, and A.A.
Milne were educated here.

BUCKINGHAM PALACE

Buckingham Palace Road, London SW1A 1AA
Tel: 020 7321 2233
www.royal.gov.uk/output/page555.asp

The official London Royal Palace, Buckingham Palace was built in
the 18th century by the first Duke of Buckingham. It was not the
royal residence until the reign of Queen Victoria, who found it to
be too small. She had Marble Arch moved and added a fourth
wing. The forecourt, where the changing of the guard takes place,
was constructed in 1911 as part of the Victoria Memorial scheme.
Call for times open to the public.

BRITISH AIRWAYS LONDON EYE

Jubilee Gardens, London SE1 • Tel: 087 0500 0600
www.ba-londoneye.com

At 443 feet tall, this observation wheel was erected in 2000 as part of London's millennium celebrations. With thirty-two capsules, each holding up to 25 people, a full circle takes 30 minutes, and on a clear day the Eye gives a unique 25-mile view which sweeps over the capital in all directions and onto the countryside and the hills beyond. For example, to the north you can see the British Museum, Charing Cross, and Covent Garden; to the south, Westminster Abbey; to the east London Bridge, Tower Bridge, the Millenium Bridge, St Paul's, and the Tate Modern; and to the west, Harrods, Buckingham Palace, and Piccadilly Circus. Open July–August daily 9:30am–10pm; September Monday–Thursday 9:30am–8pm, Friday–Sunday 9:30am–9pm; October–December daily 9:30am–8pm; Bank holidays 9:30am–9pm.

THE REFORM CLUB

King Street 1870-1, London

Founded in 1836 by Edward "Bear" Ellice, membership to the Reform Club was open to those of liberal minds, regardless of their political persuasion. The club's members have included William Thackeray, Henry James, Hillaire Belloc, and H.G. Wells.

THE ATHENAEUM

107 Pall Mall, London SW1Y 5ER

Established in 1823 by John Wilson Croker, Sir Thomas Lawrence, and others, the Athenaeum's reputation for intellectuality, gravity, and deep respectability made Rudyard Kipling describe it as a "cathedral between services." Lord Macaulay, Anthony Trollope, and Matthew Arnold enjoyed working there. Charles Dickens and William Thackeray were also members.

● PLACES OF INTEREST

SHERLOCK HOLMES PUB

10-11 Northumberland Street, Westminster, London
WC2N 5DA • Tel: 020 7930 2644
www.sherlock-holmes.dk

Visitors frustrated at the discovery that 221B Baker Street is not a
house at all will want to visit this restaurant, home to a recreation
of Sherlock Holmes's study as described in Conan Doyle's stories.
Open Monday–Friday 11am–11pm, Saturday 12–11pm, Sunday
12–10:30pm.

CHARING CROSS ROAD/FITZROVIA

TRAFALGAR SQUARE

Located in central London, Trafalgar Square commemorates the
Battle of Trafalgar (1805), a British naval victory of the
Napoleonic Wars. The present architecture of the square is due
to Sir Charles Barry and was completed in 1845. The square,
famous for its pigeons, consists of a large central area surrounded
on three sides by roadways, and on the fourth, stairs lead north
to the National Gallery. To the southwest, the square adjoins The
Mall via Admiralty Arch, to the south is Whitehall, to the east is
the Strand, to the north is Charing Cross Road, and on the west
side is Canada House. Nelson's Column, topped by a statue of
Lord Nelson, the admiral who commanded the British Fleet at
Trafalgar, rises from the center of the square, surrounded by
fountains and four bronze lions, sculpted by Sir Edwin Landseer.
At the corners of the square are four plinths, the two northern
were intended to be used for equestrian statues, they are wider
than the two southern plinths. Three of the plinths hold statues:
George IV (northeast, 1840s), Henry Havelock (southeast,
1861, by William Behnes), and Sir Charles James Napier (southwest, 1855). Charles Dickens complained about the square's
"abortive ugliness," and George Orwell once spent the night in
the square during one of his "tramps."

NATIONAL PORTRAIT GALLERY

National Portrait Gallery, St Martin's Place, London WC2H OHE
Tel: 020 7306 0055
www.npg.org.uk/

Philip Henry Stanhope, Thomas Babington Macaulay, and Thomas Carlyle's busts sit above the entrance of the Gallery as the founders of the National Portait Gallery. Stanhope wanted it to be "a gallery of original portraits, such portraits to consist as far as possible of those persons who are most honourably commemorated in British history as warriors or as statesmen, or in arts, in literature or in science." It was established on December 2, 1856 with Lord Ellesmere, former Trustee of the nearby National Gallery, offering the so-called Chandos portrait of Shakespeare as the first picture in the Gallery's collection. From Byron to Bowie, London's National Portrait Gallery turns 500 years of British history into a compelling story of flesh-and-blood people. Other writers' portraits include John Keats, Mary Shelley, Percy Bysshe Shelley, Lord Byron, and Virginia Woolf. Open daily 10am–6pm, Thursday–Friday until 9pm.

BEEFSTEAK CLUB

9 Irving Street, St. James, London WC2H 7AH
Tel: 020 7930 5722

Founded in Covent Garden in 1735, the original club had only 24 members who dined on beefsteaks, followed by toasted cheese, and washed down by port, porter, punch, or a whisky toddy. Members have included Rudyard Kipling, Sir Harold Nicolson, Osbert Lancaster, and John Betjeman.

THE IVY

1 West Street, London WC2 • Tel: 020 7836 4751

In this restaurant Ray Bradbury celebrated his 70th birthday, Arthur Miller his 80th birthday, and Random House publishers held a reception for A.S. Byatt when she became a Dame of the British Empire in 1999. Open daily for lunch and dinner.

THE FITZROY TAVERN

16 Charlotte Street, Bloomsbury, London W1T 2NA
Tel: 020.7580.3714

Designed in 1897 by W.M. Brutton, The Fitzroy Tavern is known for being the landmark that gave its name to its surrounding district, Fitzrovia, between 1920-1950 when the pub became the residence of Bohemia. During World War II the pub was the bastion of the Queen of Bohemia, Nina Hamnett. After the war it lay next to the Broadcasting House and the BBC and was frequented by broadcasters such as George Orwell. Open Monday–Saturday 11am–11pm, Sunday 12–10:30pm.

SOUTH BANK/SOUTHWARK

South of the City and Westminster stands the south bank section of London within which one can find the National Film Theatre, the Royal National Theatre, Southwark Cathedral, and The Globe.

MILLENIUM BRIDGE

www.arup.com/MillenniumBridge

This 325 meter steel bridge links the City of London at St Paul's Cathedral with the Tate Modern Gallery at Bankside. It is the first pedestrian crossing over the River Thames in central London for more than a century.

TATE MODERN GALLERY

Bankside, London SE1 9TG • Tel: 020 7887 8000
www.tate.org.uk/modern/default.htm

The Tate Modern Gallery houses international modern art and is linked to St Paul's Cathedral by the Millenium Bridge. Open Sunday–Thursday 10am–6pm, Friday–Saturday 10am–10pm. Closed December 24–26.

SHAKESPEARE'S GLOBE

21 New Globe Walk, Bankside, London SE1 9DT
Tel: 020 7902 1400
www.shakespeares-globe.org

The faithful replica of the Globe Theatre as it appeared in Shakespeare's day holds performances designed to provide the authentic experience of Elizabethan theatre. A tour of the building is available mornings before the show. Show dates and times are available online. Open for tours: October–April daily 10am–5pm (except 24th and 25th December); May–September Monday 9am–5pm, Tuesday–Saturday 9am–12:30pm, Sunday 9am–11:30am.

THE GEORGE INN

77 Borough High Street, Southwark, London SE1 1NH
Tel: 020 7407 2056
www.pubs.com/georse1.htm

Rebuilt in 1676 after a Southwark fire, The George Inn was one of Shakespeare's local pubs. Today it is London's only surviving galleried coaching inn. Open Monday–Saturday 11am–11pm, Sunday 12pm–12:30am.

SOUTHWARK CATHEDRAL

Southwark, London SE1 • Tel: 020 7367 6700
www.southwark.anglican.org/cathedral

Parts of this cathedral date from 1520. Within one can find memorials to John Bunyan and John Gower, a poet and friend of Chaucer. Past the Harvard Chapel is a Shakespeare Memorial, erected in 1911, next to which is a memorial to the actor and director, Sam Wanamaker, whose vision rebuilt the Globe Theatre. Open Monday–Saturday 10am–6pm, Sunday 11am–5pm. Closed Christmas Day and Good Friday. For more information e-mail: cathedral@dswark.org.uk.

ANCHOR BANKSIDE

34 Park Street, Southwark, London SE1 9EF
Tel: 020 7407 1577

Another of Shakespeare's locals, the Anchor survived the Great Fire of 1666, and Samuel Pepys, in fact, watched the city burn from here. It, too, had to be rebuilt after the Southwark fire in 1676. It retains some of its old character, despite modernization. Open Monday–Saturday 11am–11pm, Sunday 12–10:30pm.

THE CITY

Called The City, London's financial district is located on the original square mile that the Romans called Londinium.

TOWER BRIDGE

SE1 • Tel: 020 7940 3985
www.towerbridge.org.uk

Tower Bridge is often taken to be London Bridge, the first but less noticeable bridge over the Thames River. Designed by Horace Jones and John Wolfe Barry the bridge was powered by steam so it could open to let ships go through. Tower Bridge was completed in 1894. Open April–October daily 10am–6:30pm, November–March daily 9:30am–6pm. Closed Jan 1, December 24–26.

BANK OF ENGLAND

Threadneedle Street, London EC2R 8AH
Tel: 020 7601 4444
www.bankofengland.co.uk

Located in "Bank," the Bank of England is the central bank of the United Kingdom. Founded in 1694 and nationalized in 1946 the bank gained operiational independence in 1997. Sometimes known as the "Old Lady" of Threadneedle Street, Kenneth Grahame and P.G. Wodehouse once worked here; Grahame joined the bank in

1879 as a "gentleman clerk" and became its youngest Secretary in 1898 before he authored *The Wind in the Willows* (1908). For more information e-mail: enquiries@bankofengland.co.uk.

MUSEUM OF LONDON

London Wall, London EC2Y 5HN • Tel:020 7600 3699
www.museumoflondon.org.uk/

Established in 1975 by the merging of the London Museum and the Guildhall Museum, the museum is a non-departmental public body, funded jointly by the Department for Culture, Media and Sport, and the Corporation of London. From within its donut-shaped frame the residential towers of the Barbican rise. It was here, at the London Festival of Literature in 1999, that Walter Mosley, Bill Clinton's favorite writer, gave a reading. Open Monday–Saturday 10am–5:50pm, Sunday 12–5:50pm. For more information e-mail: info@museumoflondon.org.uk.

CHURCH OF ST BARTHOLOMEW-THE-GREAT

West Smithfield Street, Cloth Fair, London EC1A 7JQ
Tel: 020 7606 5171
www.greatstbarts.com/

London's oldest church and the sole surviving part of an Augus-tinian priory founded in 1123, the church survived the Great Fire of 1666, the bombs dropped in Zeppelin raids in World War I, and the Blitz in World War II. John Betjeman agreed with its reputa-tion today, writing that its architecture, traditional formal worship, music, and preaching brought back a true feeling of Medieval London, and for this reason he chose to live nearby for some time. John Milton found refuge here when his head was wanted by Charles II because of his anti-royal writings in 1660, and in the Lady Chapel, Benjamin Franklin worked as an apprentice. In addition, parts of *Four Weddings and a Funeral* as well as Tom Stop-pard's *Shakespeare in Love* were filmed here. Open Monday–Friday 8:30am–5pm, Saturday 10:30am–1:30pm, Sunday 2–6pm. For more information e-mail: admin@greatstbarts.com.

BUNHILL FIELDS BURIAL GROUND

City Road, London EC1 • Tel: 0207 8472 3584

These fields were once a part of the manor of Finsbury and the plot was used as a burial ground during the Great Plague of the 17th century. Bunhill comes from "Bone Hill," and the area is associated with burials from Saxon times. Bunhill Fields burial ground was the first freehold property owned by the Quakers, who bought it in 1661 and used it until 1855. William Blake is buried here with his wife Catherine Sophia, although no one knows the exact position of their graves, adding intrigue to reverence. Writers Daniel Defoe, Samuel Wesley, and John Bunyan are also buried here. Open October–March, Monday–Friday 7:30am–4pm, Saturday–Sunday and Bank Holidays 9:30am–4pm; April–September Monday–Friday 7:30am–7pm, Saturday–Sunday and Bank Holidays 9:30am–4pm.

DR. JOHNSON'S HOUSE

17 Gough Square, Holborn, London EC4A 3DE
Tel: 020 7353 3745

Johnson lived here from 1748 to 1759, and he compiled his dictionary within its walls. Open May–September daily 11am–5:30pm; October–April daily 11am–5pm. Closed Sundays.

YE OLDE CHESHIRE CHEESE

Wine Office Court, 145 Fleet Street, London EC4A 2BU
Tel: 020 7353 6170
www.yeoldecheshirecheese.com

Located quite near Dr. Johnson's house in Gough Square, other famous patrons include Saumel Johnson, Thomas Boswell, Charles Dickens, Alfred Tennyson, Oscar Wilde, Mark Twain, and William Makepeace Thackery. Open Monday–Saturday 11:30am–11pm, Sunday, 12pm–3pm.

THE OLD BAILEY/NEWGATE PRISON

Central Criminal Court, The City of London EC4M 7EH
Tel: 020 7248 3277
www.oldbaileyonline.org/history/the-old-bailey

While the building on this location dates back to 1907, Old Bailey street and Newgate street have long been associated with crime and punishment. Newgate prison was built on this location in 1188 and then demolished and reconstructed between 1770 and 1778. The original Old Bailey courthouse was built in 1539. The prison was used as both a debtor's prison and as a place to hold prisoners awaiting execution. In 1783 the gallows were moved from Tyburn to Newgate and public executions were held every week. The prison appears in several Dickens novels including *Barnaby Rudge, Great Expectations,* and *Oliver Twist.* Old Bailey is an active courthouse and the courtrooms are free and open to the public. Open Monday–Friday 10:30am–1pm, 2pm–4:30pm.

ST PAUL'S CATHEDRAL

Ludgate Hill, Holborn, London EC4 • Tel: 020 7236 4128
www.stpauls.co.uk

A Cathedral dedicated to St Paul has overlooked the City of London since 604 AD. The current Cathedral the fourth to occupy this site—was designed by the court architect Sir Christopher Wren and built between 1675 and 1710 after its predecessor was destroyed in the Great Fire of London. John Donne was the dean of St Paul's Cathedral from 1621–1631 and he is buried in the south choir aisle. William Blake's "Holy Thursday" poems from *Songs of Innocence and Experience* are set in the cathedral, and John Milton, Samuel Pepys and Gilbert Keith Chesterton were among those who attended St Paul 's school. Other important writers lived and worked in the surrounding area, particularly Charles Dickens. Open Monday–Saturday 8:30am–4pm. Closed for sightseeing on Sundays. For more information e-mail: chapter@stpaulscathedral.org.uk.

BLOOMSBURY

Bloomsbury takes its name from "Blemund's bury." Blemund was William de Blemund, a 13th-century landowner, and "bury" means a manor house. Therefore Bloomsbury really means "Blemund's house." Every house in Bloomsbury is a reminder of Virginia Woolf.

LONDON UNIVERSITY'S SENATE HOUSE

Malet Street, Bloomsbury, London

Designed by Charles Holden and built in the 1930s, this building was home to many writers during the second World War when it was occupied by the Ministry of Information whose staff including Evelyn Waugh, George Orwell, Dorothy L. Sayers, and was employed to help boost the nation's morale. It is the basis of Orwell's "Ministry of Truth" in his novel *1984*.

DICKENS HOUSE MUSEUM

48 Doughty Street, Clerkenwell, London WC1N 2LX
Tel: 020 7405 2127

Dickens and his small but growing family lived here from 1837 to 1839, and as the only surviving residence of the author, the house became a museum in 1925. Open Monday 10am–5pm, Tuesday 10am–7pm, Wednesday–Saturday 10am–5pm, Sunday 11am–5pm.

GREAT ORMOND STREET HOSPITAL FOR CHILDREN

Great Ormond Street, London WC1N 3JH
Tel: 020 7405 9200
www.ich.ucl.ac.uk/

Founded by Dr. Charles West, the hospital first opened its doors on February 14, 1852 as the first children's hospital in the English speaking world. Charles Dickens supported this hospital, raising money for it at talks and public readings of his works, especially *A Christmas Carol*. There is a description of the hospital in *A Mutual Friend*. All royalties from J.M. Barrie's *Peter Pan* go to support the hospital as well.

BRITISH MUSEUM READING ROOM

Great Russell Street, Bloomsbury, London WC1B 3DG
Tel: 020 7323 8299

In 1997, the functions of the Reading Room in the British Museum moved into the new building for the British Library, in St. Pancras, and in 2000, the old Reading Room was restored and opened to all Museum visitors. Here toiled the likes of Karl Marx, George Bernard Shaw, Thomas Hardy, George Eliot, George Gissing, Browning, Kipling, Oscar Wilde, and Virginia Woolf. Open Monday–Saturday 10am–5pm, with extended hours on the first Thursday of every month, Sunday 12–6pm. Closed December 24–26, January 1, Good Friday, May 8.

OLDE MITRE TAVERN

1 Ely Court, Clerkenwell, London EC1N 65J
Tel: 020.7405.4751

The original tavern was built in 1547 for the servants of the palace of the Bishops of Ely, Cambridgeshire. Both palace and pub were demolished in 1772; however, the pub was soon re-built. A stone mitre from the palace gatehouse is built into a wall, just visible under the tumbling ivy, and the preserved trunk of a cherry tree, which marked the boundary of the diocese, is in the corner of the front bar. It is said Elizabeth I danced the maypole around the tree and the playwrights William Shakespeare and Ben Jonson were once patrons of the tavern. Open Monday–Fridays 11am–11pm. Closed on weekends.

THE DEVIL'S TAVERN

57 Wapping Wall, London E1W 3SH • Tel: 020 7481 1095

Dating from 1520, The Devil's Tavern got a reputation in the 17th century as a meeting place for smugglers and villains. After the 18th-century fire it was renamed after the Prospect of Whitby, a three-mast collier built in 1777 which was often moored outside the inn and became a landmark in its own right. To this day it retains its 18th-century arrangement of small rooms with fireplaces, tables, and benches. Known regulars include Samuel Pepys, Dr. Samuel Johnson, Mark Twain, and Charles Dickens. Open Monday–Friday 11:30am–3pm, 5:30pm–11pm; Saturday 11:30am–11pm; Sunday 12pm–10:30pm.

MARYLEBONE

Marylebone is known mostly for its ties with Conan Doyle's stories of Sherlock Holmes. It is now home to the Sherlock Holmes Museum, located at the falsely numbered 221b Baker Street.

SHERLOCK HOLMES MUSEUM

221b Baker Street, London NW1 • Tel: 020 7935 8866

Located at 239 Baker Street, the named No. 221b Baker Street houses the Sherlock Holmes Museum. Opened in 1990, this tourist attraction looks like a film set in which the offices of Sherlock Holmes and Dr. Watson have been recreated based on Conan Doyle's stories. Open daily 930am–6pm. Closed Christmas Day.

MARYLEBONE PARISH CHURCH

Marylebone Road, London NW1 • Tel: 020 7935 7315

The site of the 15th Marylebone Parish Church, in which Byron was baptized in 1788, is marked by a small Memorial Garden of Rest. St Marylebone Parish Chuch is nearby where Robert Browning and Elizabeth Barrett were married in secret in September 1846. It contains a chapel called the Browning Chapel in which a stained glass window commemorates their wedding and various items of Browning memorabilia and old editions of their work are housed. Open Monday–Friday and Sunday 12:30–1:30pm.

REGENT'S PARK/PRIMROSE HILL

LONDON ZOO

Regent's Park, London NW1 4RY • Tel: 020 7722 3333
www.londonzoo.co.uk

The first scientific zoological gardens in the modern world, London Zoo was founded in 1828 in the northeast part of Regent's Park, and opened to the public in 1828 as a way of funding its scientific work. Edward Lear purposefully lived at No. 61 Albany Street so he could easily walk to London Zoo where he liked to work. William Makepeace Thackeray was also a visitor, as was Stevie Smith. Open March 8–October 24 10am–5:30pm, October 25–31 10am–430pm, November 1–December 26 10am–4pm. Closed Christmas Day.

PRIMROSE HILL BOOKS

134 Regent's Park Road, London NW1 8XL
Tel: 020 7586 2022
www.primrosehillbooks.co.uk

Located in an artistic area, this upmarket bookstore is frequented by Alan Bennett, Tobias Hill, Ian McEwan, and Claire Tomlin. Open Monday–Friday 9:30am–6pm, Saturday 10am–6pm, Sunday 12pm–6pm.

KENSINGTON/CHELSEA/ KNIGHTSBRIDGE

Kensington, South Kensington, Chelsea, and Knightsbridge collectively known as the Royal Borough, were the homes to many writers. Several writers' homes were given Blue Plaques to commemorate their owners' importance. Some of those celebrated are: G.K. Chesterton, Thomas Carlyle, A.A. Milne, Mark Twain, Oscar Wilde, Kenneth Grahame, James Joyce, and William Makepeace Thackery.

SLOANE SQUARE STATION

Peter Llewelyn Davies, one of the five brothers J.M. Barrie took under his wing after their parents died and upon whom he based *Peter Pan*, loathed his nickname of the lost boy. He came to think of *Peter Pan* as "that terrible masterpiece," and threw himself under an oncoming train at Sloane Square Station.

ST LUKE'S CHURCH

Penn Road, London N79RE • Tel: 020 7607 1504

Built out of Bath stone between 1820 and 1824 it was here that Charles Dickens married Catherine Hogarth in 1836. It was a quiet affair as his 20-year-old bride was under age.

WINNIE-THE-POOH'S HOUSE

13 Mallord Street, London SW3

It is here that Milne's son Christopher Robin, was born in 1920. The teddy bear that became Pooh was a present from Harrods, and the other characters were other stuffed animals that Christopher Robin played with.

THOMAS CARLYLE'S HOUSE

24 Cheyne Row, Chelsea, London SW3 5HL
Tel: 020 7352 7087

The only London residence of the "Sage of Chelsea," Carlyle lived here from 1834 until his death in 1881. Open April–October Wednesday–Friday 2pm–5pm, weekends and Bank Holiday Mondays 11am–5pm. Closed Good Friday.

CHELSEA PHYSIC GARDEN

A mere two minutes' walk from the house of Thomas Carlyle, it is certain he was a frequent visitor to this 4-acre garden for its tranquillity. The garden was founded in 1673 by the Society of Apothecaries to grow plants for medical study. One early curator,

Philip Miller, sent cotton seeds to Georgia in the United States to establish that staple crop in the new colony.

KENSINGTON GARDENS

Originally the grounds of Kensington Palace, these gardens did not become a public park until 1841. The 40-acre artificial lake was created by damming the West Borne, a stream that no longer exists, and it was here that Harriet Shelley, first wife of Percy Bysshe Shelley drowned herself in December 1816. Henry James and T.S. Eliot enjoyed walking in the gardens and watching children sailing boats on the Round Pond.

HYDE PARK

Kensington Palace Gardens, Kensington, London W8 4PX
Tel: 087 0751 5170 • www.hrp.org.uk

The nucleus of Kensington Gardens, Hyde Park covers approximately 350 acres, and provides facilities for many different leisure activities and sports, as well as being the focal point for public events of all sizes. Henry VIII acquired Hyde Park from the monks of Westminster Abbey in 1536. James I permitted limited access during his reign, but Charles I opened the park to the general public in 1637. Open March–October 10am–6pm, November–February 10am–5pm. Closed December 24–26 and January 1.

PETER PAN STATUE

Commissioned by J.M. Barrie, this statue was erected in secrecy on the night of April 30, 1912 so that early risers would think it had appeared by magic. Barrie lived near Kensington Gardens and it was here that he met the Llewellyn Davies boys. When their father died he became a surrogate father to them, and after their mother died, their legal guardian. Barrie's relationship with the boys became the inspiration for his book, Peter Pan.

ST MARY ABBOTS CHURCH

Vicarage Gate, London W8 4HN • Tel: 020 7937 8885
http://stmaryabbotschurch.org/

The present building, designed by 19th-century architect Sir
George Gilbert Scott in Victorian Gothic style, was completed in
1872 with the tallest spire in London. Beatrix Potter worshipped
here; G.K. Chesterton was married here in 1901, and Ezra Pound
in 1914. Pound had been living near the church for years; he loved
the area except for the ringing of the church's bells.

VICTORIA AND ALBERT MUSEUM

Cromwell Road, South Kensington, London SW7 2RL
Tel: 020 7942 2000
www.vam.ac.uk

Located across the road from the Natural History museum and the
National Science museum, the Victoria and Albert Museum
houses a varied collection of applied and fine art. John Forster, a
noted biographer, critic, essayist, and historian, collected a vast
library of mainly books and pamphlets, which he bequeathed
to his wife and then to the then South Kensington Museum. The
collection contains many 19th-century novels, which were given
to him as review or presentation copies. Some of the authors con-
tained in the collection are: Thomas Carlyle, Robert Browning,
Samuel Taylor Coleridge, Daniel Defoe, Jonathan Swift, John
Keats, Alfred Tennyson, Wilkie Collins, and of course, works by
his good friend, Charles Dickens. Open Tuesday and Thursday
10am–5:45pm, Wednesday 10am–10pm, the last Friday of each
month 10am–10pm.

TATE BRITAIN

Millbank, London SW1P 4RG • Tel: 020 7887 8000
www.tate.org.uk/

The Tate Britain is best known for its collection of British art from
1500–present day. It also features the art of one of the most celebrated British artists, Joseph Mallord William Turner. William

Blake, most known for his poetry, has his illustrations displayed in the collection of British Art 1500–1900. Open daily 10am–5:50pm. Closed December 24-26.

HARRODS

87-135 Brompton Road, Knightsbridge, London SW1X 7XL
Tel: 020 7730 1234 • www.harrods.com

In 1849 Charles Henry Harrod, a wholesale grocer and tea merchant, took over a small Knightsbridge shop. By 1889 the store became a public limited company, and from 1902 through the 1930s Harrods was London's biggest store with 91 departments and a staff larger than 2,000. Known for its service and the motto of "Everything for Everybody Everywhere," it remains one of London's largest attractions, particularly at Christmas time when Harrods has its annual Toy Fair where A.A. Milne purchased the original Winnie the Pooh bear for his son, Christopher.

ISLINGTON

Islington is located on the outskirts of London's West End.

SADLER'S WELLS THEATRE

Named after Thomas Sadler, this is one of London's oldest theaters, having been in existence since 1683. Wordsworth was among the theatre's famous visitors, and Charles Dickens was also associated with the theater.

WIMBLEDON

Located on the outskirts of London, the name is associated most commonly with the tennis tournaments at Wimbledon.

WIMBLEDON COMMON

Protected by the Wimbledon and Putney Commons Act of 1871, Wimbledon Common is looked after by a Board of Conservators. It has its own mounted police force, the Wimbledon Common Rangers. William Makepeace Thackeray and Leigh Hunt often enjoyed the 1,100 acres.

BLACKHEATH/GREENWICH

Quieter than the center of London, Blackheath and Greenwich have a suburban charm that battles with its reputation for chaos.

ALL SAINT'S CHURCH

Duke Humphrey Road, Blackheath, London SE3 0TY
Tel: 020 852 4280

Its famous 19th-century spire rises over the Heath, which had a dark reputation until residential development in the 18th century. Charles Dickens's parents lived in Blackheath for a while, and Salem House, where David Copperfield received his first education was in Blackheath as well. For more information e-mail: vicar_blackheath@hotmail.com.

TRAFALGAR TAVERN

6 Park Row, Greenwich, London SE10 9NW
Tel: 020 8305 3091 or 020 8305 3092
www.trafalgartavern.co.uk/

Built on the site of the Old George Inn in 1837, The Trafalgar Tavern quickly became a popular destination for the famous figures of Victorian London, including William Makepeace Thackeray, Wilkie Collins, and Charles Dickens, who used the site for a wedding breakfast in Our Mutual Friend. For more information e-mail: Gemma Brown at gemma@instinctevents.com. Open Monday–Saturday 11am–11pm, Sunday 12–10:30pm.

HAMPSTEAD

Located to the north of central London, Hampstead is known for being a sophisticated area where the literary and the famous travel.

KEATS HOUSE

Keats Grove, Hampstead, London NW3 2RR
Tel: 020 7435 2062

Though he only lived here for a few years, John Keats wrote many of his most inspired poems here, next door to his fiancée Fanny Brawne. Now a museum, it features many period artifacts and access to the garden. Open daily 12–5pm.

CHRONOLOGY

3 CE   Romans invade Britain.

c. 50   Londinium founded, though there is clear evidence that the area had been settled for millennia.

c. 700   The area becomes an important trading center among the warring Saxon kingdoms.

1065   Anglo-Saxon king Edward the Confessor builds a church on the site of an old monastery, called *west minster* (monastery).

1066   William the Conqueror claims the British throne. Builds a Norman keep, forming the oldest part of the Tower of London.

1337   Hundred Years' War begins.

1348–1359   The "Black Death" takes about one-eighth of the city's population.

1400   Geoffrey Chaucer dies in London.

1455   Houses of Lancaster and York begin their decades-long struggle for the English throne, later called The Wars of the Roses.

1476   William Caxton establishes a printing press in Westminster.

1500   Wynkyn de Worde, an employee of Caxton, moves a press to Fleet Street following Caxton's death.

1558   Elizabeth I assumes the throne.

Apr 1564   William Shakespeare born.

1587   The Rose Theatre built across the Thames in Southwark.

1595   The Swan Theatre founded in Bankside.

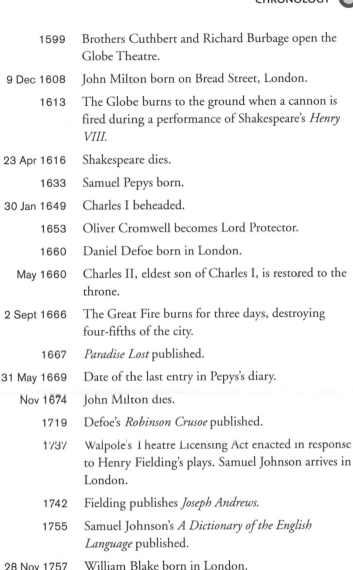

1599	Brothers Cuthbert and Richard Burbage open the Globe Theatre.
9 Dec 1608	John Milton born on Bread Street, London.
1613	The Globe burns to the ground when a cannon is fired during a performance of Shakespeare's *Henry VIII*.
23 Apr 1616	Shakespeare dies.
1633	Samuel Pepys born.
30 Jan 1649	Charles I beheaded.
1653	Oliver Cromwell becomes Lord Protector.
1660	Daniel Defoe born in London.
May 1660	Charles II, eldest son of Charles I, is restored to the throne.
2 Sept 1666	The Great Fire burns for three days, destroying four-fifths of the city.
1667	*Paradise Lost* published.
31 May 1669	Date of the last entry in Pepys's diary.
Nov 1674	John Milton dies.
1719	Defoe's *Robinson Crusoe* published.
1737	Walpole's Theatre Licensing Act enacted in response to Henry Fielding's plays. Samuel Johnson arrives in London.
1742	Fielding publishes *Joseph Andrews*.
1755	Samuel Johnson's *A Dictionary of the English Language* published.
28 Nov 1757	William Blake born in London.
1765	Johnson's edition of Shakespeare published.
13 Dec 1784	Samuel Johnson dies.
22 Jan 1788	George Byron born at 16 Holles Street, Cavendish Square, London.
1788	Jane Austen visits London with parents.

1790   Blake's *Marriage of Heaven and Hell* published.

1795   John Keats born.

1797   Samuel Taylor Coleridge begins composition of *The Rime of the Ancient Mariner.*

1812   Lord Byron's *Childe Harold's Pilgrimage* published. Charles Dickens born.

1819   Keats writes *Odes.* Queen Victoria born May 24.

1825   Samuel Pepys's diary published.

1833   Charles Dickens's first story published.

1834   Thomas Carlyle moves to London. Coleridge dies in Highgate.

28 Jun 1838   Queen Victoria coronated.

1845   London Library opens.

1847   William Makepeace Thackeray's *Vanity Fair* published serially.

1851   Crystal Palace assembled in Hyde Park for the Great Exhibition.

1856   George Bernard Shaw born.

1861   Mary Ann Evans (George Eliot) writes *Silas Marner.*

1867   Marx publishes *Das Kapital.*

1869   Henry James visits London with his family.

14 Jun 1870   Charles Dickens buried in Westminster Abbey.

1877   James's *The American* published.

1879   Oscar Wilde settles in London.

3 Dec 1880   George Eliot moves to 4 Cheyne Walk, Chelsea. She dies weeks later.

1882   Virginia Woolf (Stephen) born.

1884   H.G. Wells attends London University.

1885   J.M. Barrie arrives in London.

1887   *A Study in Scarlet,* Sir Arthur Conan Doyle's first Sherlock Holmes story, is published.

1888	T.S. Eliot born in Missouri.
1895	Oscar Wilde imprisoned in Old Bailey. Wells publishes his first novel, *The Time Machine.*
1897	Bram Stoker's *Dracula* published.
22 Jan 1901	Queen Victoria dies.
1903	Evelyn Waugh born.
1904	Barrie writes *Peter Pan*
20 Apr 1912	Bram Stoker dies in London.
28 Jun 1914	Archduke Ferdinand and his wife are assassinated in Sarajevo.
4 Aug 1914	Britain declares war on Germany.
1914	Henry James becomes a British citizen.
1915	T.S. Eliot moves to London.
31 May 1915	The first zeppelins bomb London.
1916	James dies in Carlyle Mansions, Cheyne Walk, London.
11 Nov 1918	Armistice document signed, ending World War I.
1922	T.S. Eliot's *The Waste Land* published.
1925	Virginia Woolf publishes *Mrs. Dalloway.*
1926	G.B. Shaw awarded Nobel Prize for Literature. Graham Greene moves to London, working as a copy editor for *The Times.*
1928	Women win voting rights equal to men.
1931	The Statute of Westminster recognizes dominions within the British Empire as independent countries.
1933	Orwell's *Down and Out in Paris and London* published.
1938	Evelyn Waugh's *Scoop* published.
1 Sept 1939	Hitler orders the invasion of Poland.
3 Sept 1939	Britain and France declare war on Germany.
1940	Greene's *The Power and the Glory* published.

May 1940	Winston Churchill emerges as Prime Minister following the resignation of Neville Chamberlain.
Sept 1940	German bombers target London.
28 Mar 1941	Virginia Woolf commits suicide.
1943	Eliot's *Four Quartets* published.
1945	Orwell's *Animal Farm* published.
8 May 1945	World War II officially ends.
1947	Salman Rushdie born in India.
Dec 1948	Orwell completes *1984*.
1950	G.B. Shaw dies.
1965	T.S. Eliot dies.
1973	Martin Amis publishes his first novel, *The Rachel Papers*.
1979	Margaret Thatcher becomes Britain's first female Prime Minister.
1988	Salman Rushdie's *The Satanic Verses* published.
1991	Graham Greene dies.

BIBLIOGRAPHY

Amis, Martin. *London Fields.* New York: Vintage, 1991.

Amis, Martin. *Success.* New York: Harmony, 1989.

Baron, Xavier, ed. *London, 1066–1914.* Vol. III, *Literary Sources & Documents.* Mountfield, East Sussex: Helm Information, 1997.

Boswell, James. *The Life of Johnson.* New York: Penguin Books, 1979.Cunningham, Ian. *A Reader's Guide to Writers' London.* London: Prion, 2001.

Chauhan, Pradyumna S., ed. *Salman Rushdie Interviews: A Sourcebook of His Ideas.* Westport: Greenwood Publishing Group, Inc., 2001.

Defoe, Daniel. *Moll Flanders.* New York: Modern Library, 2002.

Dickens, Charles. *Bleak House.* New York: Signet Classics, 2003.

———. *David Copperfield.* Jeremy Tambling, ed. New York: Penguin Books, 1997.

———. *Martin Chuzzlewit.* New York: Oxford University Press, 1998.

———. *The Mystery of Edwin Drood.* New York: Penguin Books, 2002.

———. *Oliver Twist.* New York: Tor Books, 1998.

———. *Our Mutual Friend.* Adrian Poole, ed. New York: Penguin Classics, 1998.

———. *The Pickwick Papers.* Naples: Trident Press International, 2000.

———. *Sketches by Boz.* Dennis Walder and George Cruikshank, ed. New York: Penguin Classics, 1996.

———. *A Tale of Two Cities.* Richard Maxwell, ed. New York: Penguin Classics, 2003.

Doyle, Sir Arthur Conan. *A Study in Scarlet.* London: Penguin Books, 1981.

Eliot, T. S. *Collected Poems, 1909–1962.* New York: Harcourt Brace & Company, 1963.

———. *The Waste Land: A Facsimile and Transcript of the Original Drafts, Including the Annotations of Ezra Pound.* Edited by Valerie Eliot. New York: Harcourt Brace Jovanovich, Inc., 1971.

Fowler, Douglas. *A Reader's Guide to Gravity's Rainbow.* Ann Arbor, Michigan: Ardis Publishers, 1980.

Gumbel, Andrew. *Cadogan London.* Great Britain: Cadogan Books Plc., 1995, 1998.

Humphries, Rob. *The Rough Guide, London,* 3rd ed. London: The Rough Guides, 1999.

Hutton, Laurence. *Literary Landmarks of London.* London: T. Fisher Unwin, 1888.

James, Henry. *The American.* Boston: Houghton Mifflin Company, 1962.

———. *The Princess Casamassima.* New York: Harper & Row, 1964.

Kakutani, Michiko. "Novelists are News Again; London Letter." From *The New York Times,* 1983 [cited October 21, 2004]. Available from http://pqasb.pqarchiver.com/nytimes/.

———. "Britian's Writers Embrace the Offbeat." From *The New York Times,* July 5, 1990.

McEwan, Ian. *The Child in Time.* Lancaster: Anchor, 1999.

O'Neill, Gilda. *My East End.* Great Britain: Viking, 1999.

Orwell, George. *Down and Out in Paris and London.* San Diego: Harcourt Brace Jovanovich, 1933.

———. *1984.* Centennial Edition ed. New York: Harcourt Brace, 2003.

Picard, Liza. *Elizabeth's London.* Great Britain: Weidenfeld & Nicolson, 2003.

Porter, Roy. *London: A Social History.* London: Penguin, 1996.

Pound, Ezra. *The Selected Letters of Ezra Pound to John Quinn, 1915–1924*. Durham: Duke University Press, 1991.

Pritchard, R.E. *Dickens's England, Life in Victorian Times*. Great Britain: Sutton Publishing, Ltd., 2002.

Pynchon, Thomas. *Gravity's Rainbow*. New York: Penguin Books, 1973.

Rushdie, Salman. *The Satanic Verses*. New York: Picador, 2000.

Shakespeare, William. *Hamlet (Arden Shakespeare)*. Jenkins, Harold, ed. London: Arden, 1982.

———. *Henry VI (Arden Shakespeare)*. Brooks, Arden, ed. London: Methuen, 1957.

———. *Macbeth (Arden Shakespeare)*. Muir, Kenneth, ed. London: Arden, 1997.

———. *Romeo and Juliet (Arden Shakespeare)*. Gibbons, Brian, ed. London: Arden, 1980.

Shaw, George Bernard and H.G. Wilshire Various authors. *Fabian Essays in Socialism* Library of Economics and Liberty, 1891 [cited February 18 2004]. Available from http://www.econlib.org/library/YPDBooks/Shaw/shwFS7.html.

Stoker, Bram. *Dracula*. New York: Bantam Books, 1981.

Stout, Mira. *Martin Amis: Down London's Mean Streets*. From *The New York Times*. Book Review, 1998 [cited October 21, 2004]. Available from http://www.nytimes.com/books/98/02/01/home/amis-stout.html?oref=login.

Tagholm, Roger. *Walking Literary London*. London: New Holland Publishers (UK), Ltd., 2001.

Tames, Richard. *A Traveller's History of London*. Great Britain: Windrush Press, 1992.

Thompson, John. *Orwell's London*. London: Fourth Estate, 1984.

Tomalin, Claire. *Samuel Pepys: The Unequalled Self*. London: Penguin Books, 2002.

Weisenburger, Stephen. *A Gravity's Rainbow Companion: Sources and*

Contexts for Pynchon's Novel. Athens, Georgia: University of Georgia Press, 1988.

Wells, H.G. *The New Machiavelli, and, the Food of the Gods.* London: The Literary Press Ltd., 1910.

Woolf, Virginia. *Mrs. Dalloway.* San Diego: Harcourt, 1925.

———. *Night and Day.* London: Hogarth Press, 19 71. Reprint, 9th impression.

———. *A Room of One's Own ; Three Guineas.* London: Penguin Books, 1993.

FURTHER READING

Barnes, Julian. *Letters from London*. New York: Vintage Books, 1995.

Baron, Xavier, ed. *London, 1066–1914*. Vol. III, Literary Sources & Documents. Mountfield, East Sussex: Helm Information, 1997.

Cunningham, Ian. *A Reader's Guide to Writers' London*. London: Prion, 2001.

Fowler, Douglas. *A Reader's Guide to Gravity's Rainbow*. Ann Arbor, Michigan: Ardis Publishers, 1980.

Glinert, Ed. *A Literary Guide to London*. London: Penguin Books, 2000.

Thompson, John. *Orwell's London*. London: Fourth Estate, 1984.

Weisenburger, Stephen. *A Gravity's Rainbow Companion: Sources and Contexts for Pynchon's Novel*. Athens, Georgia: University of Georgia Press, 1988.

WEBSITES

http://www.zardoz.net/orwell/index.html
Using John Thompson's Orwell's London as a reference, Andrew W. MacDonald visited a number of Orwellian locales. His trip is documented with photos and maps on this web site.

http://www.hyperarts.com/pynchon/gravity/index.html
One of a number of exhaustive guides to Pynchon's Gravity's Rainbow, this "Searchable Web-Guide," from curator Tim Ware, features an index both broader motifs and the most trivial details in Gravity's Rainbow.

http://orlando.jp.org/VWSGB

The homepage for the Virginia Woolf Society of Great Britain has a number of reference sources for visitors to the city, including a compilation of Virginia Woolf homes and haunts, accompanied by dates and photographs, and a walking tour of Mrs. Dalloway, both by Stuart N. Clarke.

http://www.urban75.org/photos/london/panorama.html

For those wanting a glimpse of London sites in the present day, this portion of the e-zine Urban 75 has dozens of 360° photographs of London landmarks from the Tower Bridge to Dr. Johnson's house.

INDEX

Adelphi, (housing development), 176
Adelphi, (magazine), 131
Admiral's Men, The, 17
Aggregat rocketry, 143–144
Albany Court, 186
Albert Museum, 6
Alcuin, 10
Al Fayed, Mohamed, 177
Alfred the Great, 10
Alleyn, Edward, 17
All Saint's Church, 206
All The Year Round, (magazine), 84
Amelia, (Fielding), 57
American, The, (James), 100–101
American War of Independence, 51
Amis, Kingsley, 162
Amis, Martin, 161–163, 170, 174
  on cultural decline, 173
Amsterdam, (McEwan,), 174
Anchor, (pub), 2, 25, 62, 194–195
Anglo-Saxon, 8
  on monasteries, 9
Animal Farm, (Orwell), 134–135
Archer, William, 110
Areopagitica, (Milton), 34
Arms and the Man, (play), Shaw, 111
Around the World in Eighty Days,
  (Verne), 89, 102–103
Arthurian legends, 11–12
Athenaeum, 89, 99, 102, 190
Austen, Jane, 2, 6, 63–64, 89–90

Baker Street, G, 97–98
Bank of England, 195
Bankside Power Station, 4
Bard, 26
Bard's Plays, 4

Barnaby Rudge, (Dickens), 77
Barnes, Julian, 161, 174
Barrage Balloons, 147
Barrie, J. M., 105, 107, 141, 176
  his early days, 106
Bartholomew Fair, (Jonson), 25–26
Battlefield, It's a, (Greene), 136
Bear Gardens, 25
Bede, 9–10
Bedford Square, 63
Beefeaters, 3
Beefsteak Club, 192
Beggar's Opera, (Gay), 58
Bell, Clive, 121
Belloc, Hillaire, 176
Bennett, Arnold, 105
Beowulf, (unknown), 9
Betjeman, John, 177
Big Ben, 5, 171
Blackheath, 207
Blake, William, 36, 63, 109, 196
Bleak House, (Dickens), 72, 78–79,
  83, 85
Bloody Sunday, (riot), 111
Bloomsbury, 199
Bloomsbury Group, The, 115, 123,
  136, 179
  and relationships in, 121–122
Bloomsbury Square, 45, 52, 63
Boer War, 93
Book of Martyrs, (Foxe), 12
Booker Prize, 165, 174
Bosanquet, Theodora, 103
Boswell, James, 53
  and influence on S. Johnson, 61
Bow Street Magistrates Court, 58, 179
Bow Street Runners, 58

Boyle, Robert, 39
Brideshead Revisited, (Waugh),
    138–139
Britain
    the Great War, 112–113
British Broadcasting Company, (BBC),
    5, 134
British Museum, 6
British Museum Reading Room, 199
Bronte Anne, 89–90
Bronte, Charlotte, 89–90
Browns Hotel, 187
Brunswick Square, 63–64
Buckingham Palace, 5, 189
Bunhill Fields Burial Ground, 196
Bunyan, John, 56
Burbage, Cuthbert, 17
Burbage, James, 26
    on building first playhouse, 16–17
Burbage, Richard, 17
Burgh House, 68
Burney, Fanny, 183
Byron, Lord George, 66, 102
    his death, 67

Cabot, John, 20
Cafe Royal, 187
Canterbury, 8
Canterbury Tales, The, (Chaucer),
    11–12
Carlyle, Thomas, 71, 86, 94
Carte, D'Oyly, 176
Carter, Elizabeth, 61
Cashel Byron's Profession, (Shaw), 109
Cassell, 180
Catherine of Aragon, 36
Caxton, William, 12, 36
Central London, A
Chamberlain, Lord, 140
Chambers, William, 178
Changing of the Guard, 5
Charge of the Light Brigade, The,
    (Tennyson), 87
Charing Cross, 35

Charing Cross Bridge, 176
Charing Cross Station, 175
Chaucer, Geoffrey, 21, 103
    his careers, 11
Cheapside London, D
Chelsea, 7
Chelsea Physic Garden, 203–204
Chesteron, G. K., 176
Childe Harold, (Byron), 66
Child in Time, A, (McEwan's),
    163–164
    nuclear threat in, 170
Chimes The, (Dickens), 80
Chippendale, Thomas, 65
Christie's (auction house), 65
Christmas Carol, A, (Dickens), 72, 80
Church Building Act of 1711, 53
Churchill, Winston, 134–135, 140
    and meeting with Stalin, 143
Church of St. Bartholomew-The-
    Great, 195
City, The, 194
Civil War, 32–34
Clink Prison, 77
Club, The, 60
Coach and Horses, The, (pub), 184
Cockney, (accent), 2
Coleridge, Samuel T., 68
Collected Short Stories, (Greene), 137
Collins, Wilkie, 82
Comedy of Errors, (Shakespeare), 16, 27
Confidential Agent, The, (Greene), 137
Constable, John, 68
Cook, James, 51
Cornhill Magazine, 89
Covent Garden, 5, 40, 175
    poets who lived near, 179
Coward, Noel, 177
Cromwell, Oliver, 31, 33–35
Crown Jewels, The, 3
Crystal Palace, 71, 145–146
Curtain, The, 17

Daily Express, 139

Daisy Miller, (James), 99–100
Daniel Deronda (Eliot), 90
Dante, 116
Dark Ages, 8
Das Kapital, (Marx), 108
David Cooperfield, (Dickens), 75–76, 79, 83
Decline and Fall, (Waugh), 138–139
Defoe, Daniel, 55–56, 64
Dekker, Thomas, 18, 24, 76
Devil's Tavern, 199–200
Dickens, Charles, 2, 4, 7, 70, 99, E, 177, 179, 183
  his death, 84
  dialogue in his novels, 82
  his early years, 74–75, 77–78
  as good businessman, 83
  his London, 84–87
  his move to Marylebone, 83
  as social crusader, 73
  and turning to journalism, 79–80
  on Victorian times, 72
Dickens House Museum, 81–82, 85, 199
Dictionary of National Biography, (Stephen), 122–123
Dinner at Poplar Walk, (Dickens), 80
Doctor Johnson's House, 196
Dombey and Son, (Dickens), 74, 81–82
Domesday Book, (William the Conqueror), 9–10
Douglas, Lord Alfred, 95, 105
Down and Out in Paris and London, (Orwell), 131–132
Doyle, Arthur Conan, 97–98
Dracula, (Stoker), 90, 97
Drake, Sir Francis, 20
Dr. Faustus, (Marlowe), 17
Dryden, John, 63

East End, (London), 7
Edward the Confessor, 3
Elgee, Jane Francesca, (Speranza), 93
Eliot, George, (Mary Ann Evans), 90

  her gravestone, 91
Eliot, T.S., 103, 129, 145
  his breakdown, 119–120
  his interest in philosophy, 114
  the Nobel Prize, 121
  and WWII, 142
Eliot, Vivienne, (wife of T.S. Eliot), 119–120
Elizabethan Period, 19, 23–24
Emecheta, Buchi, 161
Emma, (Austen), 63
Empty House, The, (Doyle), 98
End of the Affair, The, (Greene), 136, 139
England, (Barnes), 174
English Channel, 140
English Renaissance, 16
English Review, (publication), 105
Engravers' Act, (1735), 58–59
Enquiry into the Causes of the Late Increase of Robbers, (Fielding), 57–58
Europeans, The, (James), 99–100
Evelina, (Burney), 183
Evelyn, John, 37, 44

Fabian Essays in Socialism, 110
Fabians, 109–110
Fastolf, Sir John, 21
Fielding, Henry
  his versatile life, 57–58
Final Problem, The, (Doyle), 98
"Fire Sermon, The," (T.S. Eliot), 117–118
Fitzroy Square, 63
Fitzroy Tavern, 192–193
Fleet Street, 63, 80, 175
Fleming, Ian, 103
Flore et Zephyr, (Thackeray), 87
Ford, Madox, 105
Forster, E. M., 129
Four Quartets, (Eliot), 121
Foxe, John, 12

French House, The, 185
Fry, Roger, 121, 136

Galsworthy, John, 176
Garrick Club, 89, 181
Garrick, David, 60–61
Gay Hussar, (restaruant), 184
Gay, John, 58
George, Henry, 109
George Inn, (pub), 2, 76, 194
Georgian London, 51, 68–69
    coffee houses in, 62
    fashion in, 64
    on public executions, 54–55
    and taverns, 62
Gin Lane, (painting), Hogarth, 58
Globe Theatre, B, 4, 17, 24–25
    the fire, 19
    rebuilding of, 22
Golden Hinde, (ship), 20
Goldsmith, Oliver, 60–61
Gordon's Wine Bar, 175–176
Goring, Herman, 140–141
Grahame, Kenneth, 195
Grant, Duncan, 121
Graves, Robert, 129
Gravity's Rainbow, (Pynchon), 140–160
    London references in, 157–160
    plot in, 144–145
Great Expectations, (Dickens), 84
Great Fire of 1666, 3, 22–23, 29,
    43–44, 50, 116, 179
    monument to, 4
Great Ormond Street Hospital for
    Children, 198
Great Plague, (1665), 41–42
Great War, 107, 112–113
Greek Interpreter, The, (Doyle), 99
Greene, Graham, 102
    his anti-Semitism, 137
    his early years, 136
Greenwich, 7, 206
Greenwich Mean Time, 7
Groucho Club, 184

Guardian, (magazine), 60
Gunpowder Plot, 30
Gwyn, Nell, 39–40

Haigh-Wood, Vivienne, 114–115
Hamlet, (Shakespeare), 17
Hampstead, 7, 207
Hampstead Heath, 68
Hampton Court, 7
Handel, George F., 59
Hard Times, (Dickens), 86
Hardy, Thomas, 105, 176
Harley, Edward, 64
Harrods, 206
Hatchard's Bookshop, 186
Hawksmoor, Nicholas, 53–54, 116
Hayward Gallery, 4
Henry VI, (Shakespeare), 21
Henry VIII, 7, 15, 36
Henry VIII, (Shakespeare), 19
Henslowe, Philip, 17
Hewer, Will, 46
Heywood Bookshop, 187
History of Henry Esmond, (Thackeray),
    87
Hitler, 140–143
Hogarth, Mary, 81
Hogarth Press, 123
    and founded, 129
Hogarth, William, 58, 82, 141
Hood, Thomas, 176
Hooke, Robert, 45
Hornet, The, (publication), 109
Houghton Mifflin Publishers, 180
House of Commons, 5
House of Lords, 5
House of St. Barnabas, 183
Houses of Parliament, 5
How a Gallant Should Behave Himself
    in a Playhouse, (Dekker), 18
Human Factor, The, (Greene), 138
Hunt, Leigh, 67–68
Huxley, Aldous, 102, 139

Hyde Park, 5–6, 171, 204
Hyde Park Gate News, 122

Importance of Being Earnest, (Wilde), 94
Industrial Age, 71–72
Inferno, (Dante), 116
Inigo Jones Theatre, 28
Irving Henry, 97
Irving, Washington, 68–69
Ishiguro, Kazuo, 161
Islington, 205
Italian, The, (Radcliffe), 65
Itinerant poets, 10
Ivy, The, 191

James, Henry, 105, 130
    his death, 103
    on London, 102
    his observing humanity, 100
    and settings of his novels, 99
Jane Eyre, (C. Bonte), 90
Johnson, Samuel, 2, 7, 69, 142
    and compiling a Dictionary, 60
    his death, 61–62
    on London, 1
    his many talents, 59
    the women in his life, 61
Jonathan Wild, (Fielding), 57
Jones, Inigo, 27, 112
    his buildings, 28
Jonson, Ben, 16, 25
Joseph Andrews, (Fielding), 57
Journal of the Plague Year, A, (Defoe), 56
Journal of a Voyage to Lisbon, (Fielding), 58
Joyce, James, 123
Junior Constitutional, 97

Kakutani, Michiko, 161–162
    on American and British literary scene, 164
Keats House, 207

Keats, John, 67–68, 103
Keep the Aspidistra Flying, (Orwell), 133
Kensington Garden, 6, 203
Kensington Palace, 6
Kettner's Restaurant, 184
Keynes, Maynard, 121, 129
Khomeini, Ayatollah, 165
King Charles I, 31, 33, 41
    his execution, 34–35
King Charles II, 39, 45
King Edward, 9
King George I, 51
King George II, 51
King George III, 51
King George IV, 66
King James I, 18, 29, 41
King Lear, (Shakespeare), 27
King's College
    and writers who studied at, 178
Kingsley, Charles, 81
Kings Men, 18
King's Road, 159
Kipling, 99, 175

Labour Party, 110, 135
Lamb, Charles, 59
Lawrence, D.H., 68
Left Book Club, 180
Leicester Square, 5
Le Morte d'Arthur, (*The Death of Arthur*), Malory, 12
Lennox, Charlotte, 61
Lewes, George Henry, 90
Lewis, C. Day, 129
Lieutenant Died Last, The, (Greene), 137
Life of Johnson, The, (Boswell), 61
Limehouse, 75
Lincoln's Inn, 78–79
Little Dorrit, (Dickens), 72, 76
"Little Gidding," (T.S. Eliot), 121
Little Place Off the Edgware Road, A (Greene), 137

Lives of the Poets, (Johnson), 59
Londinium
  and first settlement, 2
London
  as collection of villages, 175
  and early existence, 8
  ethnic mix in, 1–2
  expansion of, 63
  experiences of, 1
  the financial district, 115
  in 1558, 15
  first census, 65–66, 70
  French influence in, 9–10
  Georgian London, 51–52
  the gin craze, 58
  as great port, 66
  on population, 14, 50, 53, 65–66
  statistics of, 171
  the theatre, 16
  on women's suffrage, 113–114
  and wool trade, 9
  in WWII, 140
London Bridge, F, 3–4, 20–21, 171
London Eye, 4, 171, 189
London Fields, (M. Amis), 174
  and doomsday, 170, 172
  theme of, 170–173
London Library, 71, 186
London Tower Bridge, F
London University's Senate House,
  198
London Zoo, 201
Lord Chamberlain's Men, 17
Love Song of J. Alfred Prufrock, (Eliot),
  114–115
Ludgate Hill, 179
Lyrical Ballads,
  (Wordsworth/Coleridge), 68

Macbeth, (Shakespeare), 17
Malory, Thomas, 12
Man and Superman, (play), Shaw, 111
Mansfield, Katherine, 129
Man Within, The, (Greene), 136

Margaret Ogilvy, (Barrie), 106
Marlowe, Christopher, 16–17
Marquez, Gabriel Garcia, 161–162
Marriage a la Mode, (Horgath), 58
Marriage of Heaven and Hell, The,
  (Blake), 63
Marshalsea Prison, 77
Martin Chuzzlewit, (Dickens), 86
Marx, Karl, 72, 91, 108–109
Marylebone, 201
Marylebone Parish Church, 201
Marzorati, Gerald, 164, 168
Maugham, Somerset, 177
Mayfair, 185
Mayflower, (ship), 30
McCarthy, Desmond, 121
McEwan, Ian, 161, 163–164, 170,
  174
Mecklenburgh Square, 63
Members of Parliament, (MPs), 5
Messiah, The, (Handel), 59
Middlemarch, (Eliot), 90
Midnight's Children, (Rushdie), 165
Mill on the Floss, The, (Eliot), 90
Millennium Bridge, 4, 193
Milne,, A. a., 177
Milton, John, 29, 32–33
  his death, 36
  on freedom of press, 34
Ministry of Fear, The, (Greene), 137
Mockney, (accent), 2
Moll Flanders, (Defoe), 56, 62–63
Montagu, Edward, 33–34, 36, 38, 40
Montagu, Elizabeth, 61
Montgomery, Bernard, 143
Monthly Magazine, The, 80
Monument, 45
Moonstone, The, (Collins), 82
More, Hannah, 61
Morrell, Ottoline, 136
Mo, Timothy, 161
Mrs. Dalloway, (Woolf), 128
Mrs. Warren's Profession, (play), Shaw,
  111

Murder in the Cathedral, (Eliot), 120
Museum of London, 195
Mysteries of Udolpho, (Radcliffe), 65
Mystery of Edwin Drood, The,
    (Dickens), 75, 79, 84

Napoleonic Wars, 66
Nash, John, 66
National Film Theatre, 4
National Gallery, 5, 71
National Heath Service, (1946), 135
National Portrait Gallery, 5, 71, 82,
    191–192
National Service Act (1941), 135
National Union of Women's Suffrage
    Societies, 113
Necessity of Atheism, The, (pamphlet),
    Shelley, 63
Nelson, Admiral, 5
Newcomes, The, (Thackeray), 87
Newgate Prison, 54–55, 85–86, 197
New Machiavelli, The, (Wells), 104
News from Hell, (Dekker), 18
New York Times, 161
Nicholas Nickleby, (Dickens), 81–82
Night and Day, (Woolf), 124–126
Night and Day, (magazine), 137
1984, (Orwell), 133, 134
    sights of London in, 135

Ode to a Nightingale, (Keats), 67
Old Bailey, 197
Old Curiosity Shop, The, (Dickens), E,
    81, 83
Olde Mitre Tavern, 199
Old English works, 10
Old Possum's Book of Practical Cats,
    (Eliot), 120
Oliver Twist, (Dickens), 72, 77–78,
    84, 179
Orion Group, 180
Orlando: A Biography, (Woolf),
    128–129
    protagonist in, 128–129

Orwell, George, 73
    the BBC, 134
    his death, 135
    on London, 130
Othello, (Shakespeare), 17
Our Mutual Friend, (Dickens), 83, 86
Oxford Street, 6

Pall Mall Gazette, 110
Pamela, (Richardson), 57
Paradise Lost, (Milton), 36
Patton, George, 143
Pendennis, (Thackeray), 87
Penn, Sir William, 44
Pepys, Samuel, 33–35, 177, 179
    as administrator, 46
    his death, 46
    his diary, 29, 37, 45–47
    on fashion, 41
    the Great Fire, 43–44
    and honored, 47
    his imprisonment, 46
    his marriage, 36
    the plague, 41–42
    on work and ambition, 38
    and writing the diary in shorthand,
    37–38
Peter Pan, (Barrie), 106
Peter Pan Statue, 203
Piccadilly Circus, D, 6
Pickwick Papers, The, (Dickens),
    76–77, 79–80, 84
Picture of Dorian Gray, (Wilde), 94
Pillars of Hercules, (pub), 184
Pirate Prentice, (character in *Gravity's*
    Rainbow), 145–147, 159–160
    on the rocket, 151
Pitter, Ruth, 130
Poems, (Eliot), 115
Poems, (Wilde), 93
Poet's Corner, 103, 121
Portobello Road, 157, 174
Portrait of a Lady, (James), 99–100
'Posh', (accent), 2

Pound, Ezra, 114–115, 118–119, 139
Powell, Anthony, 177
Pride and Prejudice, (Austen), 64
Priestly, J.B., 102
Primrose Hill Books, 202
Prince Albert of Saxe-Coburg-Gotha,
   70–71
Prince Henry's Room, 47–48, 177
Princess Casamassima, The, (James)
   protagonist in, 101–102
Princess Diana, 6
Pubs, 2
Punch, (magazine), 87, 177
Puritans, 16, 30, 33
   on closing London's theaters, 19
Pychon, Thomas, 144, 161–162
Pygmalion, (play), Shaw, 111–112

Queen Anne, 50–51
Queen Elizabeth, 29–30, 47–49
Queen Victoria, 108
   set new example, 70

Radcliffe, Ann, 65
Rake's Progress, (Hogarth), 58
Rambler, The, (magazine), 60
Random House UK, 123
Rasselas, (Johnson), 59
Reform Club, 89, 102–103, 190
Regent Street, 6
Restaurants, 2
Richard III, 27
Richard VI, (Shakespeare), 17
Richardson, Samuel, 57
Rime of the Ancient Mariner,
   (Coleridge), 68
Road to Wigan Pier, The (Orwell), 133
Robinson Crusoe, (Defoe), 56
Rohmer, Sax, 158
Romance of the Forest, The, (Radcliffe),
   65
Romeo and Juliet, (Shakespeare), 23, 25
Romola, (Eliot), 90

Room of One's Own, A, (essay), Woolf,
   126–127
Roosevelt, F.D.
   his death, 108
   and meeting with Stalin, 143
Rose Theatre, The, 17, 24–25
Roxana, (Defoe), 56
Royal Borough, 202
Royal Court Theatre, 112
Royal Festival Hall, 4
Royal London Hospital, 154–155
Royal Observatory, 7
Royal Society of London, 39
Rules Restaurant, 180
Rushdie, Salman, 161, 170
   and contemporary England,
      162–163
   the death threat against him,
      165–166
   his emigration to New York, 174
   on London, 168–169
   his schooling, 164

Sadler's Wells Theatre, 206
Saint Joan, (play), Shaw, 111
Samuel Pepys, The Unequalled Self,
   (Tomalin), 49
Saroyan, William, 17
Satanic Verses, The, (Rushdie), 163,
   168–169
   apocalypse in, 170
   banning of, 165
   on London, 168
   and Muslim's reaction to, 165
   racial prejudices in, 166–167
Savage Club, 180–181
Savoy Hotel, 177
Savoy Operas, 176
Savoy Theatre, 176
Scoop, (Waugh)
   and satire of Fleet Street, 139
Sense and Sensibility, (Austen), 64
Sentimental Tommy, (Barrie), 106

Seven Deadly Sins of London, The, (Dekker), 18
Seven Years' War, 51
Seymour, Edward, 178
Shakespeare's Globe, 193–194
Shakespeare, William, B, 3–4, 17
    on coming to London, 16
    his writings, 19
Shaw, George Bernard, 105, 176
    his death, 108
    as socialist, 109
Shelley, Percy Bysshe, 63, 68
Shell Mex House, 157–158
Shelton, Thomas, 37
Sherlock Holmes, G, 6–7, 97
Sherlock Holmes Museum, 200
Sherlock Holmes Pub, 190
Shortest Way with Dissenters, The, (Defoe), 56
Silas Marner, (Eliot), 90
Sir Gawain and the Green Knight, (anonymous), 11–12
Sketch Book, The, (Irving), 69
Sketches by Boz, (Dickens), 80, 83
Sloane Square Station, 203
Smithfield Market, 158
Soho, 63, 182
Somerset House, 178
South Bank Center, 4
Southwark, 7, 21–22, 76–77
Southwark Bridge, 4
Southwark Cathedral, 194
Spectator, (magazine), 60
Square Mile, 2–3
Stage Licensing Act of 1737, 57
Stalin, 143
Stationers' Company, 34
Stephen, Leslie, 122–123
Stephen, Toby, 121, 123
St. Dunstan's-in-the-West, 47–48
St. James's Church, 186
St. James Park, 39
St. John's Wood, 159–160
St. Luke's Church, 203

St. Margaret's Church, 36
St. Martin-in-the-Fields, 43
St. Mary Abbots Church, 204
St. Michael Paternoster Royal, 11
Stoker, Bram, 90, 96–97
St. Paul's Cathedral, 3–4, 8, 197
    destroyed by fire, 44
St. Paul's Church, 180
Strachey, Lytton, 121–122
Strand, (main road), 175
Strand (magazine), 98
Stuart Dynasty, 29
Study in Scarlet, A, (Doyle), 98
Success, (Amis), 163
Sword of Honour, (Waugh), 139

Tale of Two Cities, (Dickens), 80, 83–85, 184
Tambourlaine the Great, (Marlowe), 17
Tate Britain, 4, 63, 204–205
Tate Gallery, 4, 71, 159, 192
Tate Modern, 4, 192
Tatler, (magazine), 60
Tavistock Square, 63
Temple Bar, 175
Temple and the Inns of Court, 4
Tennyson, A. L., 87
Thackeray, William M., 86, 99, 177
    and clubs he belonged to, 89
    his death, 89
    his life, 87–88
Thames, (river), 2–4, 20, 171, 175
Thatcher, Margaret, 162
Theatre, The, (playhouse), 16–17
Theatre Museum, The, 181–182
Theatre Royal Drury Lane, 179
Thomas Carlyle's House, 202
Thomas Hardy's Tess of the D'urbervilles, 176
Thurber, James, 177
Times, (Britain), 136, 141
Titled Peers, 5
Titus Andronicus, (Shakespeare), 17

Tolstoy, Leo, 105
Tomalin, Claire, 49
Tom Jones, (Fielding), 57
Tono-Bungay, (Wells), 105
Tower Bridge, 3, 194
Tower of London, 3
Trafalgar Square, 5, 35, 175, 190
Trafalgar Tavern, 206–207
Trail of Dr. Fu Manchu, The,
    (Rohmer), 158
Trellick, Tower, 173–174
Triple-Decker novel, 74
Trollope, 99
Tube, The, (London Underground), 6,
    72, 171
Tudor Dynasty, 12–14
Twain, Mark, 177
Twelfth Night, (Shakespeare), 27
Tyburn Fairs, 54

Ulysses, (Joyce), 123, 128

Vanity Fair, (Thackeray), 87, 89
    London locations in, 88
Vergeltungswaffen-1, (V-1), 143
V-2, 143–144, 146
Verne, Jules, 89, 102–103
Vicar of Wakefield, The, (Johnson), 61
Victor Gollancz Publishers, 180
Victoria Embankment, 4
Victoria and Albert Museum, 6, 205
Victorian Age, 70, 112
    end of, 92–93
Viking Penguin, (publisher), 165
Vile Bodies, (Waugh), 139
Virginians, The, (Thackeray), 89

Wanamaker, Sam, 22
War in the Air, (Wells), 104
Washington Square, (James), 99–100
Waste Land, The, (Eliot), 115–118,
    123, 145
Water Babies, The, (Kingsley), 81

Waterhouse, Keith, 177
Waterstone's, 185
Waugh, Evelyn, 2
    his early years, 138
Wedgewood, Josiah, 64
Wells, H.G., 112, 176
    his death, 106
    his early days, 104–105
West End Theatre District, 5
Westminster Abbey, C, 3, 5, 9, 179,
    188
    and war, 141
Westminster Reference Library, 183
Westminster School, 188
Whistler, James, 93–94
Whitbread Book of the Year, 49
Whitehall, 158–159
White Tower, 9
Widower's Houses, (play), Shaw, 111
Wilde, Oscar, 2, 55, 105, 142, 177,
    179
    his death, 95
    his homosexuality, 94
    his imprisonment, 96
    his marriage, 94
    and suing for libel, 95
William the Conqueror, 3, 9
Wimbledon, 206
Wimbledon Common, 207
Winchester Palace, 25–26
Wind in the Willows, The, (Grahame),
    195
Winnie-the-Pooh's-House, 203
Woman's World, (magazine), 94
Women's Social and Political Union,
    113–114
Wonderful Year, The, (pamphlet),
    Dekker, 18
Woolf, Leonard, 121–122, 129
Woolf, Virginia, H, 63, 110, 122, 198
    her characters, 123–124
    her death, 130
    her early years, 122

and roles of women and men,
123–124
and writing about London, 124
Worde, Wynkyn de, 12
Wordsworth, William, 68
World War I, 114, 139
World War II, 108, 139–140

Wren, Sir Christopher, 3, 7, 39,
44–45, 48, 53–54, 116

Ye Olde Cheshire Cheese, (pub), 2,
62, 197
Ye Olde Cock Tavern, 40, 60

Zola, Emile, 177

PICTURE **CREDITS**

CONTRIBUTORS

HAROLD BLOOM is Sterling Professor of the Humanities at Yale University. He is the author of over 20 books, including *Shelley's Mythmaking* (1959), *The Visionary Company* (1961), *Blake's Apocalypse* (1963), *Yeats* (1970), *A Map of Misreading* (1975), *Kabbalah and Criticism* (1975), *Agon: Toward a Theory of Revisionism* (1982), *The American Religion* (1992), *The Western Canon* (1994), and *Omens of Millennium: The Gnosis of Angels, Dreams, and Resurrection* (1996). *The Anxiety of Influence* (1973) sets forth Professor Bloom's provocative theory of the literary relationships between the great writers and their predecessors. His most recent books include *Shakespeare: The Invention of the Human* (1998), a 1998 National Book Award finalist, *How to Read and Why* (2000), *Genius: A Mosaic of One Hundred Exemplary Creative Minds* (2002), and *Hamlet: Poem Unlimited* (2003). In 1999, Professor Bloom received the prestigious American Academy of Arts and Letters Gold Medal for Criticism, and in 2002 he received the Catalonia International Prize.

DONNA DAILEY is a journalist and author. She earned a B.A. from the University of Northern Colorado and later moved to London, England, where she first worked at a magazine located next door to the Charles Dickens House. She has written more than twenty travel guides and books about London, Paris, Ireland, and other cities and countries worldwide.

JOHN TOMEDI earned his B.S. in English from the Pennsylvania State University. He is a freelance writer and researcher living in Howard, Pennsylvania. He has also written the book *Kurt Vonnegut* for the GREAT WRITERS series (2004).